W9-CAI-836

More praise for *Love & Betrayal*

"An important book for people who want to heal and grow from the pain of old or recent betrayals, as well as for those who want to build authentic trust in their current and future relationships."

—Margo Adair
Author of *Working Inside Out*

"The gift of John Amodeo's book is that it gently invites the reader to participate feelingly, not just intellectually. By experiencing and understanding betrayal from a new and deeper perspective, the reader can access paths of healing and growth that are profound."

—Arnold Katz, Ph.D.
University of Washington

"A thoughtful, useful, readable book that sensitively addresses a topic touching all of our lives. This book helps us deal with the pain, loss, and disillusionment of betrayal in a way that can lead to a renewal of ourselves and our relationships."

—Aaron Kipnis, Ph.D.
Author of *Knights Without Armor:
A Practical Guide for Men in
Quest of Masculine Soul*

"John Amodeo addresses the too-long-neglected matter of failed relationships. He looks with the experience of a psychotherapist, researcher, lover, and friend, at the challenges faced by men and women who want to live with more love and less fear. *Love & Betrayal* fills a real need in the literature of self-help."

—Jean Liedloff
Author of *The Continuum Concept*

LOVE AND BETRAYAL

John Amodeo, Ph.D.

BALLANTINE BOOKS
New York

Sale of this book without a front cover may be unauthorized. If this book is coverless, it may have been reported to the publisher as "unsold or destroyed" and neither the author nor the publisher may have received payment for it.

Copyright © 1994 by John Amodeo
Foreword copyright © 1994 by Charles L. Whitfield, M.D.

All rights reserved under International and Pan-American Copyright Conventions. Published in the United States by Ballantine Books, a division of Random House, Inc., New York, and simultaneously in Canada by Random House of Canada Limited, Toronto.

Grateful acknowledgment is made to the following for permission to reprint previously published material:

Reggatta Music, Ltd.: Excerpt from the lyrics of "Fragile" by Sting. Copyright © 1987 Reggatta Music, Ltd. All rights reserved. Used by permission.

Spring Publications, Inc.: Excerpt from *Loose Ends: Primary Papers in Archetypal Psychology* by James Hillman (Spring Publications, 1975). Copyright © 1975 by James Hillman. All rights reserved.

http://www.randomhouse.com

Library of Congress Catalog Card Number: 93-90996

ISBN: 0-345-37856-3

Text design by Debby Jay

Manufactured in the United States of America

First Edition: May 1994

10 9 8 7 6 5 4

I dedicate this book to Peter Campbell and Edwin McMahon, who have inspired me with their commitment to heal the wounds of betrayal in our world. As founders of the Institute for Bio-Spiritual Research, they bring a depth of wisdom, vision, and compassion that offers realistic hope.

This book is also dedicated to all those who have tasted the pain of betrayal and, instead of giving up on life, have found the courage to love and be loved again.

Acknowledgments

This book owes much of its existence to the many caring teachers, mentors, and friends who have given me support and guidance over the years. Included among them are Bob Altheim, Pam Altman, Americ Azevedo, James Baraz, Don Booth, Rose Breda, Charles Brooks, Rich Byrne, Eileen Campbell, Peter Campbell, Ken Cohen, David Cory, Neil Dinkin, Jim Dreaver, Jim Fadiman, George Feldman, Martin Fortgang, Robert Frager, Charles Garfield, Eugene Gendlin, Meryll Gobler, Jay Goldfarb, Joseph Goldstein, Ignacio Gotz, Ed Graham, Arthur Hastings, James Hayes, Justin Hayward, Mike Heron, Elliott Isenberg, Robert Jones, Robert Kantor, Jack Kornfield, George Koury, Loren Krane, Steve Krause, Brian LaForgia, Bob Marcus, Ed McMahon, Robert Mendelsohn, Sandy Newhouse, Dan O'Hanlon, Brad Parks, Janis Paulsen, Ellen Pearlman, Ken Phillips, Kent Poey, Herbert Puryear, Soretta Rodack, Nick Rodin, Steven Ruddell, Maxine Scharf, Don Schwartz, Neil Selden, Charlotte Selver, Aaron Serah, Lisa Shapiro, Ernie Sherman, Jacquelyn Small, Bob Smith, Neil Solomon, Bob Spadavechia, Kathleen Speeth, William Staniger, Joseph Tein, Michael Toms, Ray Vespe, Ben Weaver, Michael Weisglass, Bernard Weitzman, John Welwood, Christopher Wentworth, Kris Wentworth, John White, Robin Williamson, Gordon Wolf, Dawna Wright, Fred Zarro, Bob Zelman, plus my supportive parents, Mary and Ben Amodeo.

I want to thank the following people who offered helpful feedback on the entire manuscript: Margo Adair, Pam Altman, Sue Amodeo, Charlie Bloom, Linda Bloom, Katie Byrne, Elliott Isenberg, Arnold Katz, Louise Robinson, and Steven Ruddell. I also greatly appreciate the helpful editorial assistance from Shepherd Bliss, Cara Brown, Meryll Gobler, Harriet Katz, Maggie Kline, Bob Manis, Francis Weller, Charles Whitfield, and Julie Garriott.

I want to express my appreciation for the caring and expertise of the Ballantine staff, and especially to my editor Cheryl Woodruff for believing in the book, and for her insightful commentary while nurturing the manuscript to completion. Thanks to her gracious and sensitive editorial support, I've gained a deeper appreciation for the art of writing.

Finally, I want to express heartfelt gratitude to my counseling clients, who have entrusted me with their confidences and inspired me with their commitment to self-understanding and personal growth. I also appreciate those strong and courageous individuals who allowed me to interview them for this book.

Contents

CONTENTS

Foreword

When I read John Amodeo's first book, *Being Intimate,* I was impressed by his clarity and warmth and the practicality of his advice. A few years later he told me that he was working on a book about love and betrayal—issues he often encountered in his counseling practice. Knowing how common, and often critical, this experience is in people's lives, I accepted eagerly when John offered to show me his manuscript. After reading it, I was even more excited because I knew he was breaking new ground. I know of no other work that offers such useful insights and guidance on dealing with this deep pain.

Who among us has not loved and then experienced the loss of some aspect of that love? Such a loss brings up many painful feelings, a powerful sense of having been betrayed being paramount among them. A number of core issues begins to rise to the surface—trust, the ability to love, a fear of intimacy, our inner sense of worthiness.

Our feelings of betrayal aren't limited to the relationships in our adult life. They go back to some of our earliest memories in infancy and remain with us all during our growing up years, becoming even sharper in adolescence. All we ever wanted was to love and be loved in return; to be accepted for who we are.

But growing up in an unhealthy family and an unhealthy world, few of us ever got the chance to give and receive the love we wanted and needed so much. As a result, most of us reached adulthood carrying a heavy burden of pain and old memories of past betrayals. What this means is that now, when we experience the loss of love, we're instantly pulled back into the intense feelings of those old wounds.

The way we respond to betrayal colors our entire outlook on life. It not only affects our relationships with others, it also affects our relationships with ourselves and the way we relate to every aspect of our world.

There are many ways people respond to the pain of betrayal. Some of us go into hiding when we're hurting. We're afraid to face the real pain inside ourselves, afraid to have others see us in pain. Others feel too ashamed to acknowledge and to talk about their disappointments or "failures." Sadly, by closing down inside, by failing to learn and grow from our experience, we're all the more likely to repeat old, painful patterns throughout our adult lives. At the very least, we severely limit our capacity for joy and freedom.

Another way many of us deal with betrayal is to collapse into our pain, to see ourselves as helpless victims of circumstance. Our hurts silently eat away at us, undermining our potential for living a happy life. Few of us know how to deal with emotional pain because our culture doesn't encourage inner exploration and authentic expression. Nor does it provide role models for courageously facing our hurts so they may heal and free us to love again.

And yet, each of us still longs for love and intimacy in our lives. But how can we respond when, one after another, our relationships fail to fulfill our hopes or expectations? How do we break the bonds of our old wounds, our old scars? How do we avoid becoming bitter and cynical? How do we avoid hardening our hearts and withdrawing from relationships because we don't want to take the risk of getting hurt again?

We discover this by learning how to finally heal the wounds of love when they arise in our current relationships. We can learn how to bring warmth and caring to ourselves during difficult times rather than reject that tender, hurting place inside us. We can find a way to embrace ourselves rather than get stuck in regarding others—and ourselves—with fear or contempt.

In *Love & Betrayal,* John Amodeo shows us a psychologically and spiritually sound way to heal the hurts and disappointments that arise in nearly every relationship. He feels that once we find healthy ways of dealing with betrayal, we can learn to face and resolve these painful feelings we've been carrying around inside us. Then, instead of giving up on life or ourselves, we can begin to develop a growing trust that enables us to deal with whatever life brings our way, even the most painful and difficult events. Through learning to trust, we can find the strength we need to deal with loss and disillusionment and move ahead in our lives.

John Amodeo offers us the guidance we need so we don't betray ourselves further when we feel betrayed by another person. Whether we've been deeply hurt in our family relationships, in romance, in marriage, in friendship, in business—wounds that still trouble us from years past—Amodeo shows us how to resolve these feelings, reaffirm our self-worth, reclaim our lives, and open ourselves up again to giving and receiving love. He reminds us that this takes time and patience and a willingness to accept ourselves rather than a desire to be perfect.

Love & Betrayal is a helpful, heartening guidebook for dealing with each of these issues, one step at a time. Amodeo has a rare and wonderful combination of skills: He is both a clear and able writer, and a respected front-line clinician with many years of experience in helping people free themselves from the crippling pain of betrayal. He speaks with accuracy, warmth, and compassion as he offers us a wealth of useful examples to help us recognize these old wounds, work through them, and finally heal them.

Amodeo shows us clearly and compassionately how to build trust in our relationships so that we can feel safer in sharing our true selves with others. He brings us an innovative perspective on what it means to be committed—both to ourselves and to our relationship partner. *Love & Betrayal* offers a groundbreaking method of dealing with adversity as an invaluable opportunity to learn more about ourselves and life. This process of growth and acceptance and love enables us to become stronger, wiser, more compassionate, and infinitely more joyful.

—Charles L. Whitfield, M.D.

LOVE AND BETRAYAL

Introduction

On and on the rain will fall
Like tears from a star   like tears from a star
On and on the rain will say
How fragile we are   how fragile we are
From "Fragile" by STING

Relationships are difficult. We want to feel cherished
and understood. And we want love and intimacy to endure—
for a lifetime. Sadly, love relationships often seem to fall short
of their tender promise, leaving us wounded, disillusioned,
and discouraged. Do we dare wonder if there is a sequel to the
bitter taste of disappointed love?

This book begins with the simple recognition that love
relationships can be tricky, if not treacherous. Despite our
sweetest vision of what is possible, intimacy can be hazardous
to our health. There is no ultimate safety or security in the
arena of relationship. Once we accept that, we're ready for the
good news: *There is a depth, delight, and richness that is truly
possible through love relationships.* There is no substitute for the
pleasure, fulfillment, and growth that come by relating deeply
to a wisely selected fellow human. Despite my own bruising
betrayals, I'm still a hopeless romantic at heart—though in a
different way than when I was twenty.

This book offers a means of dealing with love's shadow side, love's duplicitous polarity: betrayal. Only by bringing light to love's dark corners can we navigate our way through the beguiling traps that await our journey into love. Only then can we fulfill the promise of finding the radiant joy, delightful connection, and bountiful love that our heart and soul never abandon.

By courageously confronting the inevitable rejections and betrayals that life brings us, we can heal the hurts of our heart, discover new aspects of ourselves, and find a greater degree of safety in relationships. Betrayal in its many forms can become, in effect, the unwelcome rite of passage that ushers us toward a brighter understanding of what love is and what love isn't— what helps love grow, and what destroys it.

Sharing our heart, our tenderness, our hopes with another person exposes us to the painful possibility that our trust may be coldly betrayed or unwittingly undermined. This hurt touches each of us at one time or another. None of us will escape life without being betrayed in some manner by someone we have grown to trust and love. Betrayal is an equal opportunity misfortune.

Yet little has been written about this dreaded aspect of the human condition. Perhaps some people avoid the subject because they find it distasteful or depressing. Others may feel threatened by the discomforting feelings that accompany the very thought of betrayal. Nevertheless, unless we find the courage to look betrayal in the eye, we will continue to perpetuate situations that lead to our continued betrayal, as well as to our betraying others—while the promise of love slips away.

THE NEED TO HEAL OUR
BETRAYAL WOUNDS

The effects of a major betrayal linger long beyond its immediate sting. All too often, the pain of betrayal establishes a pattern of extreme caution in our relationships. Having been burned once, we hesitate to trust again. As a result, we withhold our real thoughts and feelings. We retreat from making genuine contact with others. We do not cry all of our tears; we do not surrender to the fullness of our joy. Instead, we shield our vulnerable core from the threatening presence of others. In the bargain, we deprive ourselves of the love we secretly want.

Betrayal's aftermath may manifest in other destructive ways. We may enter a new relationship with the crafty resolve to mold and manipulate our partner, bullying him or her to display the cooperation we expect, if not demand. We may sharpen a verbal sword that blames, shames, and attacks at the first sign of inattentiveness to our needs and desires. We may administer sly tests of loyalty to ensure that we're loved. We may adapt a subtle attitude of contempt that says, "You'll have to *prove* that you're trustworthy—that you're different from the rest!" Needless to say, these efforts to control our partner are likely to backfire. They reflect seething resentments, fearful suspicions, and unhealed wounds that linger from prior betrayals. Rather than make us safer, these attitudes and behaviors set the stage for a miserable relationship, and oftentimes another betrayal.

By not dealing with betrayal in a wise, effective way, *we carry our pain into our next relationship*. Our old hurts and resentments spill over onto our partner with the slightest provocation. By not resolving our prior pain we continue to suffer, as does our new partner. And we throw up our hands in resignation when it becomes apparent that yet another relationship isn't working out.

This book is a gentle invitation to stop, look, and listen so that we may alter the cruel cycle of betrayal that continues to hurt ourselves and others.

NOTICING THE SUBTLER FORMS
OF BETRAYAL

Betrayal is not limited to the more blatant forms of sexual deceit, broken promises, and outright desertions that normally merit this term. More subtle forms abound, ones that are easily overlooked yet can progressively sabotage our quest to love and be loved. These subtle betrayals can be even more insidious in the way they infect our partnerships and friendships. These seemingly harmless slights and oversights can lead to big hurts and account for much of the pain that exists in relationships.

This book is not just for those who want to understand and recover from sudden, life-shattering forms of betrayal. It is also for those who want to cultivate a climate of love and trust in their current relationships *so that little hurts do not grow into the quiet hostility and distancing that so often destroy cherished hopes and dreams.* Laced throughout these chapters are illustrations of the more subtle betrayals of trust, of how these "little" betrayals provide kindling for the larger conflagrations that can traumatize us.

What prompts us to break trust with people? Why do people break trust with us? Are there ways we contribute to a climate of mistrust that leads to big betrayals? Can we overcome the anger, pain, and bitterness that are left in the wake of a major betrayal and learn to trust again? Can we create a foundation for intimacy that would curtail the everyday betrayals that thwart our search for love, thereby minimizing the possibility of a larger, debilitating betrayal? Can we love others without betraying ourselves?

This book addresses these crucial questions. However, there are no simple answers to quickly relieve the pain of betrayal. It would be a betrayal of the reader to scratch lightly at the surface of this perplexing and multifaceted topic. The complex nature of this issue is well known to the betrayed individual, who wonders "What went wrong? How did love turn to ashes?" Real solutions require a fundamental transformation of how we view ourselves, relate to others, and understand life.

The subject of betrayal elicits our deepest emotions because it touches the very core of our humanness. Only by addressing the topic in a sensitive and in-depth manner can we transform devastating betrayal into greater self-understanding and serenity. Likewise, only by learning to deal wisely with the less dramatic, day-to-day assaults on our trust and innocence can we build loving, intimate relations with others.

Throughout the text I drew upon my own personal experiences and those of clients and friends. I also interviewed many men and women for this book and have included their illuminating comments (individuals' names have been changed).[1] Although the examples are of heterosexual couples, the principles apply to all significant relationships, whether gay, lesbian, or heterosexual. The hurt of betrayal spans a multitude of lifestyles.[2]

One final thought for those readers who have recently felt the anguish of betrayal: It is heartbreaking to be betrayed. It is scary to start over without the comfort of a once cherished friend or lover. I hope that by portraying the many dimensions of betrayal and offering creative ways to respond to it, this book can help you heal your hurt. Beyond that, my hope is that you will emerge with increased self-awareness, self-esteem, and compassion for yourself and others on your continuing journey toward trusting, satisfying partnerships and friendships.

NOTES

1. If someone seems recognizable to you, it is no doubt because our experiences of betrayal are quite similar.

2. If you have been betrayed in a gay or lesbian relationship and find that your experience is not consistent with what I've described, I invite you to share your views and feelings by writing to me at the address listed in the Guide to Resources on p. 273.

CHAPTER 1

The Many Faces
of Betrayal

The greater the love and loyalty, the involvement and
commitment, the greater the betrayal.

JAMES HILLMAN[1]

Most of us are unprepared to deal with betrayal in a
constructive way. Instead, we suppress the pain that it leaves
in its wake. We reel in confusion and bitterness, perhaps for
many years. We remain numb to our wound and distract
ourselves by keeping busy, seeking entertainment, or turning
to drugs, alcohol, or food. We become turned off to others,
concluding that the ill-defined path of love is not for us. We
abruptly abandon other people before they have an opportunity to abandon us. We devise cunning methods of getting
back at a formerly trusted partner or friend whom we believe
has wronged us, which may lead to a cycle of mutual vindictiveness that has no winner.

Betrayal occurs in all stages of life and on many different
levels. An infant may feel betrayed if his mother fails to bond
with him or is not immediately available to satisfy his many
needs. A child may feel betrayed when a trusted friend insults
her or when an admired teacher humiliates her in front of the
class for giving a "silly" answer. A teenager may feel betrayed
when his girlfriend no longer wants to date him. A young

adult may feel betrayed when she gets pregnant and is told by her partner that he does not want the responsibilities of parenthood.

As an adult, we may feel betrayed by an employer who fires us or mistreats us after many years of devoted service. We may feel betrayed by a friend who borrowed money without paying it back. We may feel betrayed by our profession because it uses intimidation to discourage us from speaking truth.[2] Or we may feel betrayed by the government for passing laws and regulations that we believe interfere with human rights and basic freedoms.

The Bible and classical literature depict many dramatic betrayals. The Old Testament story of Joseph and his coat of many colors describes a betrayal in which Joseph is cruelly left to die by his jealous brothers. In the New Testament, Jesus is betrayed not only by Judas but also by his other disciples, who pledged allegiance to his cause, then turned their backs during his critical time of need. Betrayals that lead to murder and emotional torment are a popular theme in many Shakespearean tragedies; the trusted Brutus plunges his knife as Caesar speaks the dying words "Et tu, Brute?"

Betrayal is rampant in the competitive business world. Driven by fear and greed, people often disregard their agreements, mislead others, and sacrifice their integrity in order to further their own security or dominance. Those who value honesty are disheartened by having to operate in an atmosphere polluted by deception and broken trust. As they enter middle age, many people who function in the business world turn cynical—an accumulative effect of bruising betrayals experienced in relation to competitors, partners, employees, customers, or clients.

The financial loss accompanying betrayal in business can impair our ability to support ourselves and our family. The hurt of betrayal in business can ominously pervade all of our close relationships by making us more cautious and bitter, less trusting and spontaneous.

The knife of betrayal cuts most deeply in our close friendships, intimate partnerships, and committed marriages. These relationships contain our greatest hopes, while being the source of our deepest hurts. This book focuses on betrayal that occurs in these love relationships.

No matter how many times we face betrayal, it is always painful and often shocking. Betrayal is not something we get used to so that it no longer affects us. Nevertheless, we can learn to deal with these rude affronts without drowning in despair and hopelessness.

By facing betrayal in an intelligent, conscious way, we can move toward greater self-understanding and healthy self-love. As we open to the experience of betrayal with gentleness and compassion toward ourselves, our injury steadily heals. We may then emerge as a wiser, stronger, and more loving person.

A depth of character and maturity grows as we courageously uncover our most dreaded fears and hurts, as well as reconnect with our deepest aspirations. As we live with opened eyes and develop an attitude of gentleness and kindness toward ourselves, we can discover a strength and resiliency that no one can take away from us.

THE BUILDING AND BREAKING
OF TRUST

The Gradual Growth of Trust

The meaning of *betrayal* may become clearer by comprehending the nature of trust. *Trust* is defined in the dictionary as a "firm belief or confidence in the honesty, integrity, reliability, justice, etc., of another person or thing." When we trust, we rest firmly in the knowledge that it is safe to be ourselves with a particular person. We trust that we are respected and cared about. We feel betrayed when our trust in another's honesty, reliability, or integrity is shattered, when what we thought was safe is not really safe.

11

Trust extends to three vital areas of our existence: trusting ourselves, trusting others, and trusting life itself. Trusting ourselves means that we are confident in being ourselves and affirming ourselves, as well as confident in our capacity to deal with conflicts and setbacks. Trusting others means that we feel safe and relaxed in their presence; we can be authentic and open without undue fear of negative consequences. Trusting life means having faith that we can learn from our experiences, and that, in some mysterious way, life supports our movement toward wholeness and self-actualization (though not always without struggle).

The process of building trust with another person is as fragile as it is complex. It can also be an exquisitely creative endeavor. We are asked to extend ourselves into another person's emotional, mental, and spiritual way of relating to the world—a world they may experience quite differently from our own.

Trust grows in different ways for different people. Let us look at one manner in which trust may develop.

Provisional Trust

If I want to develop close, trusting relationships with others, I need to give them a chance to show me who they are. A sound starting place is to hold the provisional assumption that what others say to me is true. There is little else I can rely upon as I meet a potential new friend or partner.

Through provisional trust, I give the relationship an opportunity to grow. In the past, I've had a tendency to be cynical and distrustful—perhaps because I've been hurt by people, or maybe because I grew up in New York City. Whatever the reason, I recognize that distrust generates distrust. No one enjoys the disempowered position of being tested, or having to prove themselves.

Intuition also provides invaluable clues into people's character and reliability, and I need to trust this sixth sense. Intuition provides an antenna that senses concerns and incongruities that would otherwise evade detection; it helps us sense the substance beneath people's words. One woman who didn't use her intuition faced a rude awakening in her marriage: "Who he purported to be was quite different from who he turned out to be. He dressed the part and talked the part. I didn't see who he really was until much later." A man who was later sexually betrayed expressed a similar sentiment: "I analyzed her words. That's how I was trained—I wasn't good at sensing her feelings."

Ultimately, intuition is the most reliable gauge of whether or not to grow closer to someone. However, my intuitive function is limited; at times I think I'm being intuitive when I'm really being judgmental, afraid, or cynical. Trying to figure people out before entering a relationship with them can be a defense against giving people a chance. Through triumphs and failures, I am becoming more adept at interpreting the vague fears and gnawing doubts that tell me something is not quite right.

Living with provisional trust places me in a somewhat vulnerable position. However, the very possibility that trust might grow with a particular person adds meaning and color to life. Therefore, I accept what people tell me until I have a reason to believe otherwise. By conveying a willingness to trust, my gift of trust may be rewarded with a positive response.

As trust grows, I am more inclined to take people's words at face value, rather than try to second-guess them. If people say that they like me, or repeatedly suggest that I take care of myself, I may begin to believe that they really mean it. I may conclude that they do not want to harm me—at least not intentionally.

My trust becomes firmer as people's actions match their words. For example, if they call me with some regularity, I may infer that they really do like me. If they volunteer to pick me up at the airport, I may feel a greater sense of being cared about.

Many people fail to trust because poor self-esteem does not

allow them to receive positive comments graciously or believe that someone might actually value their friendship. A pervasive sense of shame makes it difficult for them to imagine that anyone would find them likable, intelligent, or appealing. As a result, they never really trust. Or their trust is so tentative that they rearmor themselves at the first sign of conflict or disagreement.

The willingness to trust is not synonymous with blind faith or naivete. If someone seems to care about me, I don't immediately open up a joint checking account with her or mix our silverware together. Trust grows incrementally. I don't assume that I've found a lifetime partner just because she likes my homemade pasta or because we enjoy hiking together, or because she craves my body. But if we feel drawn to be together, I may relish the joyful anticipation of building some kind of meaningful relationship.

Some people trust too quickly. They gobble up others' lavish reassurances without recognizing that some individuals have their own hidden agendas. For instance, it is common for people to say pleasant things or offer gifts to procure sex. Or they may endeavor to please because they themselves are eager to be liked or loved in return.

We may so desperately want to believe someone loves us that we jettison our good judgment. But provisional trust is different from wishful thinking or a reckless surrender of our identity. It can swell into a sweet, stable trust between two individuals who have the willingness to be honest and forthright with one other when that willingness is combined with an even rarer desire to be honest with themselves.

The Quickening of Trust

Trust strengthens as we feel appreciated, rather than taken for granted, respected rather than denigrated, and understood rather than ignored or misinterpreted. As our feelings, thoughts, needs, and values are treated sensitively, we internally relax; we feel safer to be vulnerable, playful, open.

Once a credible degree of trust and affection has been established, a deeper trust and bonding may quicken as a result of the tender connection that accompanies sexual relations. We are somehow more connected to the deeper core of our being as we surrender to sexual feelings, especially if our sexuality is integrated with heartfelt love and emotional closeness. Through sexual contact, our defenses and boundaries tend to melt. Through some mysterious process, a powerful merging often occurs between two individuals who share the fiery energies of sexuality. When the relationship is going well, this may be a bond of love. If the partnership sours, there is often an equally strong, yet destructive, bond of hate.

There are many tests of trust throughout the course of a relationship, whether they stem from fear, from confusion, or from an inability to truly "see" and understand our partner. Stresses resulting from the daily demands of life may further strain our relationship. If we cannot resolve our conflicts, or if our differences become insurmountable, we face dissolution of the relationship—or the possibility of betrayal. But if we have built a strong foundation of self-awareness, trust, and communication, we may survive these trials and emerge as a stronger, wiser, and more fulfilled couple.

For many people, getting married further strengthens a bond of trust. Being offered the commitment to stay together during good times or bad helps many people feel more secure. They may then base important decisions, such as those related to career and family, on the trust-filled assumption that their partner's vows reveal an awareness of what he or she really wants.

Factors that lead to a quickening of trust vary for each relationship. Some people base their trust on the right chemistry, a shared worldview, similar goals, or common interests. For others, the growth of trust is guided by mutual caring, nonblaming communication, and steady commitment to be honest and open with each other.

The Breaking of Trust

Whatever leads us to feel safe with another person, *the agony of betrayal involves the sudden tearing of the delicate fabric of trust that has gradually united us.* The sobering discovery that what we thought was solid isn't solid, that what we thought was dependable isn't dependable, turns our world upside down. Betrayal overthrows our sense of what we considered to be true and trustworthy and hurls us into an emotional chaos in which we must reexamine the basis on which we have pursued love and built our lives. As one person put it, *"What* can I trust now? *Who* can I trust now?"

Betrayal happens in various ways. There may be clear and blatant violations of trust—the breaking of spoken agreements, such as wedding vows or sexual fidelity. Other betrayals shatter unspoken agreements that are prized by all people of good faith. Breaking unspoken agreements is more subtle, yet profoundly painful and insidious. At other times we may claim betrayal when there is simply an honest difference in our needs or vision, or we may simply be the victim of a painful misunderstanding. Sadly—even tragically—there are many opportunities for miscommunication in all spheres of life. Still other times we may betray ourselves. By recognizing this wide spectrum of betrayal, we may address the topic more fully.

BREAKING SPOKEN AGREEMENTS

Broken Promises

The most obvious form of betrayal results from a broken promise. Such betrayal comes in a variety of configurations—reneging on the promise to adopt a child, move to the countryside, or share decision making on expensive purchases, for example. Laurel, whose eager entry into marriage fulfilled a long-held dream, became disgruntled after several years of steady disappointments: "Before getting married, he said that whatever I wanted was fine—children, pets, moving to the country. But now whenever I bring up these subjects he hides behind the newspaper and television and tells me this isn't a good time to talk."

One of the most jarring betrayals is our partner's unilateral decision to separate. The shattered promise to love, cherish, and honor us can lead to a radical disruption of our lives. The pain of losing our spouse, lover, and, perhaps, best friend wrenches a precious connection that has grown in our heart, even if the partnership had its flaws or soured during its final months or years. Being abandoned against our will can severely jolt our self-esteem, leaving us wounded, powerless, and out of control. Dorothy, a fifty-year-old corporate executive who experienced several sudden separations in her life, expressed it this way: "My experience of betrayal is that I'm standing on a rug and somebody just pulls the rug out. And I'm falling, helpless, powerless."

Being deserted can also add severe financial worries, if not trauma. The urgent need to find new sources of income adds a dreaded burden at an inopportune time. The fear of survival may haunt us as never before, especially if we haven't pursued a career. One shell-shocked client who expected a lifelong marriage to a newly successful doctor put it as follows: "What am I supposed to do now? I took care of him through many years of college. I was patient when he spent weekends studying and didn't have time for me. Then I helped him get his business going. I was so involved taking care of *him* that I never developed my own career!"

If children are involved, we have the additional responsibility to care for their well-being at a time when *our own* is in serious jeopardy. As dreams crash, hopes crumble, and demands multiply, we are compelled to draw upon inner resources that we may doubt exist.

Affairs

Breaking a monogamous agreement is another common form of betrayal. Studies vary widely in their estimates of married men and women who have at least one affair during marriage, ranging from 15 percent to 75 percent. The truth probably lies somewhere in the middle. Breaking an agreement to be monogamous may sever a bond that was valued as special and sacred. Some people never recover from the hurt resulting from even one incident of sexual betrayal. Separation or divorce may occur immediately after the affair or, more commonly, sometime later as a result of smoldering resentments set in motion by the affair or exacerbated by it. If the couple stays together without dealing with this betrayal, one partner may make the other pay for the rest of his or her life.

Some partners try to preserve trust—and the partnership—by agreeing to suspend their commitment to monogamy, and doing so *before* being sexual with a new partner (whether or not they have a particular someone in mind). If each party consents to such an arrangement, then it is less likely to be experienced as a betrayal if one partner does proceed to be sexual with someone new. Although there may be pain and jealousy, there is no betrayal when consent has been granted.

In other instances, one partner may express the desire to have an affair, but his or her partner is unwilling to go along with it. As heated or hesitant discussions produce no resolution, the desirous partner may make the unilateral decision to go forward with his or her amorous plans, perhaps through some weak justification: "I have the right to take care of myself," or "I got married too early—before having enough sexual experiences," or "If she met my needs, I wouldn't have to do this," or "This will be good for our marriage."[3] Such a betrayal can be damaging, if not deadly, to a partnership. However, honest disclosure about the affair—talking about why it happened—may provide a basis for resolving this breach of trust.

Secret Affairs

Clearly, most affairs involve outright sexual deception, which is a more cold, calculated form of betrayal. Secret affairs are a glaring violation of trust in a partnership: We not only hurt our partner by desiring to be sexually intimate with another person, but we multiply the affront by being sneaky about it. The secretive nature of an affair is often more destructive than the affair itself.

Although we may attempt to conceal an affair, often we experience a marked shift in our emotional loyalties that is not easily hidden. A new sexual relationship is fresh and exciting. There is a new universe of sensations to delight us. If intimacy with our partner has receded, we may feel newly alive as a dormant part of us is reborn. One woman, who was feeling dissatisfied in her marriage, put it succinctly: "Something inside of me comes alive when I'm with this man."

Oftentimes, a betrayed partner can subtly sense that something has changed, that something is not quite right. He or she may detect that the other person has become emotionally distant, sexually disinterested, or inexplicably bored. Joseph, a thirty-two-year-old businessman who was in a two-year relationship (the longest he'd ever had), recognized that he wasn't being wholly successful in hiding his affair: "I swear my wife's psychic; she can sense it. She knows something's wrong, but she can't put her finger on it." When the issue was pressed, or if she made sexual advances, he was often irritable and distant, which covered up his guilt.

Although we may presume that we are successfully concealing an affair, the truth has a way of seeping out in subtle or dramatic ways. Our emotional distancing, mental distraction, withheld communication, and secret guilt may contaminate all aspects of the partnership. Also, it is difficult to orchestrate our affair so that it remains secret. Eventually, our partner may become suspicious about our absence from home at unusual hours. Or our partner may notice an odd scent of perfume on our body, or a stranger's hair on our clothes. Or a mutual friend may report to our partner that we were seen in public with our arm around a woman or man. Perhaps most haunting is that we live with the ongoing fear that we could be found out. As Joseph lamented: "I know in the back of my mind that someday I'll get caught and it'll bring things to a head."

Some affairs manage to escape detection, then abruptly end. In other instances, one person will be stunned to learn that his or her partner has been having a secret affair for years. When Stuart and his wife purchased a home in a nearby town, he was excited to begin a new phase of his life. Shortly thereafter, he learned of a three-year affair she'd been having. "It was an incredible shock," he said, "because I thought either of us would be able to tell if the other was having an affair." Suddenly, many things became clear: the emotional coldness, the lack of intimacy, the breakdown of communication. Perhaps what was most hurtful was that someone with whom he felt a sacred trust could break such an important pact with an apparently total disregard for how this would affect him. In addition, he felt foolish and ashamed that he could have let such a situation continue for so long without knowing about it. He harshly questioned his judgment as his self-esteem was seriously shaken.

Being sexual with someone other than our partner is not necessarily a betrayal. Whether this constitutes disloyalty and unfaithfulness has to do with the kinds of agreements entered into by a couple. British sociologist Annette Lawson found that 10 percent of married couples do not make a commitment to sexual exclusivity.[4] Needless to say, marriages that grant permission to be involved with other sexual partners can be fraught with difficulty. It is not within the scope of this book to explore the complex dimension of what have been called open relationships or responsible nonmonogamy.[5]

Couples who choose such a lifestyle must discuss the specific parameters of their agreements and operate within those limits if they are to avoid betrayal.

Negative Gossip

Negative gossip—the divulging of personal confidences—is another stinging form of betrayal. As we grow closer and more trusting, we feel safer revealing sensitive, personal details about our lives, without guarding our words or censoring ourselves. We might even ask our partner not to divulge our private sharings, although oftentimes we take this courtesy for granted (an unspoken agreement). An essential part of trust is knowing that our privacy will be honored, even if, for whatever reason, the relationship ends. We are slyly betrayed if our partner or friend lures us into a sense of security, then uses information gathered during intimate moments as a weapon to denigrate, humiliate, and hurt us. Gossiping behind people's backs after the partnership ends, or while it endures, is the methodology of choice for many betraying couples.

The current proliferation of "kiss-and-tell" books demonstrates the profit and fame that can accrue from this form of betrayal. Shrouding themselves in their right to freedom of speech, scorned lovers may offer graphic accounts of the intimate lives of their former partners. A sexual involvement with a tennis star, rock musician, or U.S. senator can create instant notoriety when the book contract is signed. Appealing to the public appetite for titillating tales and illicit escapades (emotional pornography), such individuals try to work through their personal problems at the expense of others.

Some may justify their treacherous gossip by insisting that they were betrayed first. Whether or not that claim is true, divulging confidences as a form of revenge offers only temporary satisfaction, one that may become addicting because of the momentary exhilaration it provides. In the end, these individuals may lose credibility among those who recognize that such gossiping represents an utter lapse of integrity, a violation of a right to privacy, an undignified way to try to reclaim their dignity. Even more menacing, their gossip may fuel a cycle of mutual retribution that brings out the worst in both parties. An extreme example of this is portrayed in Woody Allen's movie *Crimes and Misdemeanors,* in which a married man spurns his secret mistress. Her threat to divulge their affair to his unsuspecting wife, as well as expose a suspicious business transaction from years ago, prompts him to plot her murder.

Negative gossip is especially destructive when it contains distortions, if not outright lies. As Mark Twain once said, "A lie can travel halfway around the world while the truth is putting on its shoes."

Eric, a respected optometrist, was frequently passive and accommodating in his prior partnerships, fearful that his partner would abandon him if he expressed his own wants and needs. Entering a new relationship, he was determined to be himself. However, they didn't know how to talk about their differing needs in a way that would satisfy each of them. He described a scene in which she entered his room and angrily ripped a book from his hands, claiming that he didn't care about her. After this incident, she began spreading distorted gossip about him and proceeded to have an affair. She told people that she was being neglected and abused, and justified having an affair as a way to feel comforted as a result of his mistreatment.

Eric expressed the hurtful effects of her counterfeit claims: "The biggest betrayal was that she lied to her friends about me. She told these friends I was being abusive, which wasn't the case. She even said I physically abused her and that I broke promises. *I* got abused by those distortions and lies. It hurt to be rejected by all these people who were forming a clique against me. It was a sense of being outnumbered and not knowing what was going on. All these people just totally shut down to me."

Gossip and slander are destructive because once rumors spread, they're difficult to stop, even if they have no validity—

as politically savvy dirty tricksters well know.[6] Eric expressed his frustration as follows: "What do you do? How do you stop it? They're such lies, but you can't straighten out a lot of this stuff. It spreads. You can't go up to them at a party and say, 'You might have heard some weird things about me.' People won't tell you what they've heard. They just stop calling and that's it. It's very difficult to fight. Rumors go to people you don't know well, and it's too embarrassing to bring up. So it affects everything on a really oblique level. Once people believe it, they don't want to get close enough to talk about it and clear it up."

Secrecy versus Privacy

Respecting privacy is different from keeping secrets. Confidentiality is a key ingredient in building trust with a counselor or minister and is equally important in building trust with a friend or lover. If a person feels unsafe in revealing a vulnerability out of fear that it might be divulged to others, then a tender truth might be withheld.

Honoring people's privacy demonstrates respect and thoughtfulness. We betray an implicit trust by reading their private journal or by divulging private details that we can assume were shared confidentially, such as their sexual history.

On the other hand, by unwisely protecting someone, we may harm ourselves by keeping secrets. If our partner warns us not to tell anyone that he is physically abusing us and we comply with that demand, we may be betraying ourselves by not getting the help we need in order to stop the abuse. If we are confused, upset, or hurting, we may need to share the details with a trusted friend or counselor so that we can decide how to proceed.

Other Blatant Betrayals

Other overt forms of betrayal are never identified as such, perhaps because of the clever ways people justify their innocence. Nevertheless, any flagrant disregard of a mutual agreement might be experienced as a betrayal. For example, a couple may agree not to have children and proceed, as planned, to get married. Based on wishful thinking, the woman may presume that her husband will change his mind after marriage: "He just doesn't realize yet how wonderful it is to have children. He'll see what I mean!" The man may feel profoundly betrayed to discover her secret intention to get pregnant; he may be shocked to learn of her failure to use birth control when she had reassured him that she was using it. She might try to justify this glaring betrayal by insisting, "Once we have the child, I *know* he'll be happy." She would be betraying not only her spouse, but also her child by bringing him or her into an environment in which he or she may not be wanted. She is also betraying herself by creating a rift in the relationship as a result of plotting a secret strategy, rather than taking the risk to be honest.

BREAKING UNSPOKEN AGREEMENTS

Spoken agreements form a basis of trust, but relationships are sustained also by unspoken agreements—ones we assume, yet rarely verbalize. Such agreements, though not verbalized, are nevertheless vital for the growth of healthy relationships.

Divorce courts overflow with people who believed that their needs and wants should have been obvious, even if they were never stated. Clearly, it can be a pain-saving exercise to make our implied understandings more explicit as we advance toward deeper emotional investment and commitment. However, no matter how responsible and clear we try to be, there will always be some things that are not hashed out. No matter how thoroughly we negotiate agreements with our partner, we cannot hash out every possible contingency, as if we were signing a business contract. There will always be some elements of the relationship that must rest upon trust. *Partnerships often succeed or fail based on whether these silent covenants are honored or ignored.*

Physical Safety

From children's perspective, there is an assumption that parents, relatives, and other adults will not physically or sexually abuse us. We need and expect physical safety and nurturance, not violence and aggression. Similarly, as we enter partnerships, we assume that our mate will not physically abuse or threaten us.

Sexual and physical abuse are obvious forms of betrayal. They violate our need for safety. Since much has already been written on these subjects, I will not address them in detail here.[7]

Honesty and Deception

Honesty is another crucial factor that we often take for granted. A relationship based on good faith assumes that we won't be deceived or misled. The discovery of deception can quickly shatter trust and innocence. During a marital counseling session, Sherry complained to Walter that he wasn't giving enough to the relationship. There was little communication and even less emotional intimacy. She wanted to feel more connected, more appreciated, more supported. Surprised by her dissatisfaction, he replied, "But I always tell you what you want to hear!" Discovering this deception, Sherry was dismayed: "No! You don't tell me what *I* want to hear. You tell me what *you* want me to hear! You tell me what you think will please me. I want to hear the truth!"

Honesty also assumes that we will not withhold information that we know is important to our partner, even if potentially upsetting. For example, if we're asked about our sexual history, we might distort or lie about it so we don't expose ourselves to rejection. If we have a sexually transmittable disease, we may hesitate to disclose this to a potential sexual partner. Although we may feel scared or embarrassed to talk about it, failing to do so in a timely manner is an implicit betrayal—possibly even a deadly one. Having high-risk sex and failing to get regularly tested for AIDS might also be considered a betrayal of our current and future partners, whom we put at risk based on our own avoidance.

Giving another example of deception, if we renew an old drinking habit or run up the balance on our shared credit card, we would be inclined to divulge this unpleasant news if we value truthfulness. The commitment to honesty allows a relationship to sink or swim based on what is real. Fearing conflict or acting out of spite or resentment, we might hide or shade the truth, and so undermine trust.

Trust breaks down when we develop a habit of not being forthright, even about seemingly inconsequential matters. For example, if we get home late from work, we might offer the excuse that traffic was slow, although what really happened was that we worked late. Knowing that our partner resents our long work hours, we might distort the truth to avoid exposing ourselves to criticism.

Love and intimacy are undermined when deception about important matters is eventually uncovered. One woman felt betrayed when her partner "changed his mind" and no longer wanted children; she surmised that he had deceived her in order to get her to marry him. Another individual felt betrayed for the opposite reason. He had two children from a previous marriage and didn't want any more. His new partner assured him that she was comfortable with not having any children of her own. After marriage, she experienced a change of heart and pressured him to have a child.

It is not unusual for people to change their minds as they become clearer about what they want in their lives. We're all human. We are subject to unanticipated changes in our needs and preferences. However, we may be tempted to disguise our real intentions or, even more commonly, *hide them from ourselves* if they threaten the viability of a desired partnership. We might justify these misrepresentations by convincing ourselves that "it's not that important," or "I don't really know how I feel about it, so why invite trouble?" Gratified by the rewards of a partnership, we may be afraid to jeopardize our security. However, if we try to preserve what we have at the cost of honesty, we threaten the foundation of trust.

When today's seemingly trivial issue becomes tomorrow's hot concern, then the matters we have postponed dealing with may come back to haunt us. By offering solid reassurances on critical issues about which we secretly harbor reservations (such as entering a marriage) or by making firm agreements before being clear about what we really want, we may provoke bitter disappointment. We also set ourselves up for hurt. We invite future betrayal by contributing to a climate of suspicion and mistrust.

Deception and lying can assume devious forms. A currently popular and particularly hideous betrayal is to falsely accuse an ex-partner of abusing our children. Law enforcement agencies are required to investigate reports of physical or sexual child abuse, however frivolous or malicious they might be. This can cause emotional and financial trauma for years to come, not to mention the devastating effects that will linger in the lives of the children.

Wisdom in Ignorance

Being honest with ourselves and others involves a lifelong process of growth. Since our self-knowledge is always limited, we can expect that we will make mistakes. The important thing is to learn and grow from our errors of judgment. Failure provides the raw material for future success. Many of us who strive compulsively for perfection rarely take meaningful risks, because we believe if we're not successful, then a nagging inadequacy will be exposed.

Many of us feel ashamed or weak if we do not know precisely how we feel, or if we cannot provide answers on demand to questions about how we want our lives to look. This self-generated pressure to perform, please, or pacify sets the stage for disillusionment. The partnership may be in trouble when our actual wants and desires come crashing to the surface.

If we could be kinder to ourselves, we would feel less pressure to provide false reassurances that end up hurting everyone. In reality, there is nothing inherently shameful about not knowing. For example, there's no obligation to guarantee that we will want three children if, in fact, we're uncertain about it. We're being realistic, not pessimistic, if we can't guarantee that we'll be able to afford to buy a home or take an expensive trip. It is not a sign of weakness to say "I don't know how I feel about that right now," or "This is how I feel right now, but that could change," or "This is what I want and I don't expect that to change, but I can't guarantee that I won't feel differently later." Many betrayals could be avoided by not succumbing to the temptation to give false reassurances.

In a commencement address at the University of California at Berkeley, *San Francisco Chronicle* columnist Jon Carroll urged the graduates to "cherish your ignorance and husband it, because ignorance can quickly curdle into knowledge. . . . If you know something, you stop asking questions, and once you stop asking questions it's all over."[8]

The Risk of Sharing/The Risk of Not Sharing

We take a risk by being as honest as we currently know how to be. Our partner might leave us if they find our truth distasteful. They certainly have this right if their needs and wants don't match our own. However, if we fail to base our relationship on authenticity, we may be sowing the seeds of a much more painful separation when today's expedient reassurances lead to tomorrow's heartbreaking disappointments. We take a risk by being honest, but *we may be taking a much greater risk*

if we betray our partner by withholding our true feelings and wants:
We risk losing our partner's trust.

Many times, we have the best intentions to be honest with others. But until we are honest with ourselves, we will withhold our real feelings, thoughts, and wants. This is often due to a deep-seated fear and shame we carry in regard to our real experience. Having been taught by our heroic, individualistic culture that admissions of fear, hurt, or self-doubt are abhorrent, we may have learned to bury these shamed feelings. This is especially true of men. Believing we are weak or flawed for having normal human feelings, we may show only a false, fabricated self. For example, one client felt ashamed to reveal to his partner that he was scared to say no to his boss, which prompted his agreement to work late hours. Long ago he decided not to let others see his vulnerable places, since doing so was often met with ridicule ("Don't be a crybaby; quit your complaining!").[9]

Respect and Understanding

Another unspoken covenant that is all too frequently neglected is our commitment to respect and understand each other. Respect means holding others in high regard. We value them. We affirm their dignity as human beings. Being respectful is a vital aspect of building trust with another person. We cross an invisible border into betrayal when our initial respect turns into shaming and denigrating that person, such as through hostile name calling, cruel verbal assaults, or subtle sarcasm.

Trust strengthens as we support each other's autonomy and respect each other's boundaries. This means that we recognize that our partner and friends are not our property; they are not an extension of ourselves. They have their own unique set of beliefs, feelings, hopes, and preferences. They have their own lives to live. As our capacity to love matures, we do our best to further their growth on *their* own path. We betray an implicit trust when we trample on people's boundaries, such as by imposing our opinions and solutions when they are unsolicited. For instance, we might verbally badger our partner with the unwanted opinion that he should dress better, or that she should drive differently. These little gibes can undermine trust more than we realize.

Perhaps the most widespread, least intentional, and most subtle way we betray others is by not taking the time to understand them, or worse, by disrespecting their feelings, needs, and wants. Understanding others means recognizing the importance and validity of their feelings, values, goals, and whatever else is meaningful to them. Trust is nourished as two people become aware of what is significant to each other and use this knowledge to support one another.

Rather than truly listen, we may withdraw from making genuine contact with others. We may defend ourselves through the dubious art of arguing, as did Stuart, the man mentioned earlier whose wife had been having an affair. "I was always good at arguing," Stuart acknowledged. "I wasn't very good at just listening to her feelings." By closing off his heart and mind, Stuart realized how he contributed to a climate of distance and miscommunication.

Promoting Each Other's Well-Being

A related assumption in love relationships is that we are committed to furthering each other's happiness and well-being (while not overextending ourselves to such a degree that we neglect or betray ourselves). Conversely, we trust that our partner won't do anything to hurt us, although there are bound to be times even in the best of marriages when we're unintentionally hurt, or when our hurt is an unavoidable by-product of our partner's commitment to be true to himself or herself. However, we may be particularly confident that our partner would not deliberately injure us, an assumption that may prove to be fatally flawed.

When there is a growing relationship of love and tenderness it seems ludicrous to imagine that our devoted partner might harm us later, especially in some intentional way. Having basked in the glory of making love—whether several times or hundreds of times—it is preposterous to imagine that our gentle lover might later betray our well-being. Feeling close and connected, it seems absurd to promise that we will refrain from hurting each other. Such a basic commitment is implicitly assumed by all people of good will. When we feel "in love," the thought that our partner might turn on us seems out of the question. Yet that is exactly what happens in many partnerships, as affluent divorce lawyers well know.

Friendships are also based on the assumption that we will support each other as best we can. A painful and not uncommon form of betrayal is to have sexual relations with a friend's partner. Many friendships have been suddenly disrupted by such breaches of trust. Gary, who had been an open, trusting person, expressed this double-barreled betrayal as follows: "I not only lost my partner, I lost my best friend, too!" As a sad result, Gary was leery of introducing future partners to his friends.

Trusting the Sanctity of Each Other's Choices

Another subtle, unspoken agreement in trust-based relationships is that we're each making responsible, self-directed, free-willed choices. For example, if you choose to have a relationship with me or to have children with me, I assume that's what you really want. If together we agree to purchase a home or move to Montana, I trust that you have reflected upon the matter and that you are comfortable with that choice.

I would feel betrayed if you later tell me that you never really wanted to marry me, or that you really didn't want children, or that you never wanted to move to Montana or buy an upscale home. According to my understanding, we made those choices *together*. If I cannot trust you to be honest with me about what you really want (an honesty that must rest upon self-knowledge), then I will feel less free and trusting in our interactions. I'll be less free to be myself. I'll then become guarded, hesitant, and mistrustful, never knowing if your yes really means yes. Our relationship eventually suffers if you are merely pacifying me or acting out a script written by parents or society rather than being true to yourself.

Perhaps you acquiesced to my wishes because you were fearful of displeasing me. Perhaps you didn't know yourself well enough to make wise decisions at the time. Or maybe you simply changed your mind—perhaps you've discovered a growing satisfaction in your career that you're now unwilling to surrender. Although you never intended to betray me, I may nevertheless experience your lapse of self-awareness or change of heart as a betrayal of an important agreement. This common scenario points to the all-important commitment to be as clear with ourselves and each other as possible so that we do not unknowingly sabotage our cherished partnerships.

Perhaps I was manipulative in getting you to agree to have children or making an extravagant purchase. Perhaps I pouted and complained or withheld affection until you conformed to my demands. If so, I need to take responsibility for this. I need to accept my disappointment when our desires differ, rather than belittle or punish you when disagreements arise. I need to alter my habit of subtle coercion. I need to be more accepting of your preferences and limits.

Distinguishing the betrayer from the betrayed is sometimes not so clear-cut. Perhaps there is a way in which I betrayed you by not responding to your needs when you tried to share them. I may have subtly betrayed you by assuming I knew what was best for you and best for both of us, instead of respectfully listening to you. On the other hand, I may feel betrayed if you made agreements that came not from your heart, but from your wish to avoid conflict or abandonment. Relationships are a good place to learn the arts of humility and forgiveness, because we subtly betray each other more often than we realize.

Trusting the Choice to Be Together

Another agreement implicit in partnerships is that both parties continually choose to be together and to stay together. A partnership remains vital only if being together arises out of continual choice, not obligation. I would feel betrayed to learn that our ongoing partnership is based on convenience, duty, or a fear of disappointing your friends, rather than on an active choice and desire to be with me. I would feel betrayed to discover that you are staying with me when you really don't want to, perhaps for the sake of the children or to continue living at the elevated standard of living that I provide. Larry, who thought of himself as happily married for the past twelve years, felt such a betrayal when his divorcing spouse shouted, "I would have left you long ago if it weren't for the kids!" Concern for her children was one reason she avoided expressing her dissatisfactions more persistently.

If two people are dating, one might feel betrayed if the other stayed in the partnership while harboring serious reservations. After dating Bonnie for three years, Fred began pursuing other women without telling her. Being more honest with them than with Bonnie, he reassured them that he was willing to leave Bonnie: "I still go out with her because I don't want to be alone. There never was any passion in that relationship." When Bonnie expressed wanting a more committed relationship, he offered vague, evasive responses, such as "I'm not ready for that." In truth, he wasn't ready to be *honest*, fearful of losing the comfort of regular sex and companionship.

If you are choosing to be with me in a committed partnership, I implicitly trust that it's *me* whom you want to be with. I trust that you love me, that you like me, and that you are somehow connected to the essence of my being. This assumption might turn out to be inaccurate. I'd feel betrayed if you abandoned me simply because I lost my job or became ill. I would conclude that it wasn't me whom you married, but

33

rather the image of me as a successful, wealthy, or popular person. When that status disappears, then so do you.

It would be unfair to expect you to stay with me if I succumb to my misfortune—if I sit at home and watch television all day instead of taking the initiative to change my situation. But I would feel betrayed to discover that your love for me was based primarily on what you could get from me and did not include what you might offer during a difficult period in my life. I would feel betrayed to realize that you fell in love with your image of me, or your image of love, or worse, craved your own status and comfort alone and did not love me for who I am.

Trusting Each Other's Integrity

A growing relationship requires that we trust the integrity of our partner. Trusting his or her integrity means trusting our partner to be straightforward with us, at least to the degree that he or she can be self-honest. Trusting each other's integrity means trusting that we know ourselves to some reasonable degree, including our capabilities and limitations, so that we do not make pacts we cannot keep. It also means trusting that we are committed to a path of personal growth so that we will continually be more honest and familiar with ourselves: with our feelings, needs, hopes, values, goals, and motivations. Trusting each other's integrity means trusting ourselves to honor the unspoken agreements that all people of good faith hold dear.

Unspoken agreements can be difficult to pinpoint. Yet, when they are broken over and over again, they lead to more dramatic betrayals that drive couples to counselors' offices or divorce courts. Subtle betrayals have a cumulative effect. They are sometimes ignored but more often noted and stored, to be used against our partner at a later date. As we accumulate these IOUs—injuries owed you—without taking remedial action, we eventually succeed in destroying our partnerships.

BETRAYAL: A FINE LINE

The term *betrayal* is emotionally loaded. On the positive side, we may feel more empowered as we recognize the ways in which our love has been betrayed. Such recognition is especially helpful if we have the common tendency to blame ourselves when we're hurt by a partner or friend.

Many people who are betrayed multiply their misery by believing that this painful circumstance has been totally self-inflicted. The realization that indeed they *have* been betrayed can equip them with the empowering discovery that their human sensitivities have been violated.

On the negative side, for many people betrayal may mean a sacred right to fry the offender. We may then accuse and attack others whenever we don't get our way. We may derive emotional satisfaction by using the label in a strident, indiscriminate manner.

At times, stating that we feel betrayed may be helpful in drawing attention to how hurt or angry we feel. However, we must exercise discretion when using the *B* word. Generally, we are better off simply sharing our feelings in regard to others' words or actions. Furthermore, if we remain preoccupied with the notion that we have been betrayed, we may wallow in the self-perception that we are a victim. Even if we have been cruelly betrayed, *a prolonged identification with the self-image of being a victim prevents us from moving forward in our lives.*

Is It Betrayal, Self-Deception, or Poor Communication?

There is often a fine line between the deception that characterizes betrayal and the tendency toward self-deception that may prompt false accusations of betrayal. In addition, there are times when we may accuse others of betraying us when we are mutual victims of misunderstanding.

During the course of a new relationship, we may each be

35

motivated by totally different desires. A man may bring you flowers and take you out for a luxurious, candlelit dinner. He may gaze longingly into your eyes and act as if he is interested in a romantic relationship. In your eagerness to feel loved, you may assume that he wants to become your romantic partner. In reality, he may only have sex on his mind. If you are misinterpreting the signals you are receiving, you may be setting yourself up for a rude awakening.

Floating on your current high, you may not want to break the magic of the moment by initiating an uncomfortable or "boring" discussion about how you are each experiencing this new relationship. You may decide to "go with the flow" and see where things lead. This decision is fine if you are willing to deal with the possibility that he may not be as captivated as he seems to be indicating. Or perhaps you want to enjoy the newness and excitement of the relationship no matter where it leads. However, if you have a tendency to be deceived and hurt by men—if you often feel lured in and then abandoned—it may behoove you to move slowly, until you can make a clearer distinction between reality and wishful thinking.

There are a number of possible scenarios going on here. Perhaps this man is genuinely interested in the potential partnership that you also want. Another possibility is that he is meticulously leading you down the primrose path to his bedroom, without being interested in a full-fledged relationship. You would probably experience such deception as betrayal.

On the other hand, there may be no conscious deception, but rather major differences in your respective wants and expectations. For example, he may not be aware of how involved and attached you're getting. Or he may not like certain things about you but is too frightened to tell you. Or sex may mean different things to each of you. For you, sex might mean a trusting, intimate bond that has long-term possibilities. For him, sex might mean an enjoyable release of tension and physical rejuvenation. Perhaps he has had many sexual partners but has difficulty forming close emotional ties. You may be looking for marriage, while he wants to date different people. Even if you have been reassured that he wants a long-term partnership, it may not be clear whether he wants this with *you.* In short, each of you may be experiencing the relationship on very different levels.

Your partner may fail to communicate as clearly and directly as you might like. For example, your new friend may not volunteer that he does not see you as a potential partner. He may not be aware that you're looking for a mate if marriage is far from his mind. Or he may sense that you're growing attached to him but may be telling his friends: "She's great in bed, but I'd never marry her." It may come as a distressing surprise to discover that you were each operating out of totally different desires and assumptions. If you want to understand his real wants and intentions, you must take the responsibility of asking the right questions, then hear his response through the receptive ear of your intuition.

Of course, being so direct can be scary. The fear of hearing an unpleasant truth may dissuade you from broaching sensitive topics. You might rather live with the uncertainty of not knowing what he really wants than face the hurt of knowing that you are not wanted. You might retreat from inquiring about potential differences because you fear that the raw truth might spoil your hopes and aspirations.

The disquieting discovery that your wants and expectations have been discordant might lead you to claim betrayal when there was mutually poor judgment and communication. Understandably, you may feel a gut-wrenching hurt if you are not wholeheartedly embraced. You may feel bitterly disappointed or angry if someone fails to satisfy your deepest longings. However, your legitimate burden of hurt, anger, or disappointment does not necessarily mean that you have been deceived or betrayed.

What we call betrayal is sometimes our own tendency toward self-deception. We may so much want to be loved and cherished that our longing overrides our heart's deeper knowing about the relationship. Our own wants may be so pressing that we neglect to comprehend that others may be in a very different place. They may have needs that clash with ours. They may have different goals for their life. Or their own personal peculiarities may prevent them from being truly intimate with anyone.

What seems like a betrayal may reflect a larger wound from our dimly remembered past. Our current disappointment may reactivate painful memories of being hurt or abandoned. We may then need to acknowledge and embrace the wound of our past betrayal—whether in our original family or earlier partnerships—so that we may identify and heal the deeper source of our hurt and anger.

BETRAYING OURSELVES

Life invites us to grow in a direction that has been variously termed autonomy, wholeness, and self-actualization. We become depressed or anxious when we fail to respond to this quiet call of our inner being.

Early in life, our natural needs and inclinations may have been thwarted by parents who failed to provide a safe and secure environment. They may not have responded in a timely manner to our desire for physical comfort, caring attention, and tender affection. They may have undermined our self-esteem by being critical and cranky, rather than warm and nurturing. They may have demanded submission to their will as the high price for love and acceptance. They may even have abused or neglected us.

However negative or positive our childhood endowment may be—however we may have been betrayed in those early years—we must, at some point, take charge of our destiny so that we do not perpetuate the legacy of betrayal by now *betraying ourselves*. Whether this requires some recovery work or a moving forward from the healthy foundation we have already established, we must affirm, respect, and love ourselves if we are to find fulfillment and meaning in our lives. We must resolve the fears and negative self-image that swindle us of a positive future. We must get clearer about what we want in life—our career choice, lifestyle preference, and the kinds of relationships that we find rewarding. We betray ourselves if we are not moving toward a life that is congruent with our unique inner calling.

There will never be a shortage of people who confidently and persuasively tell us how to live our lives. However, such individuals are not compelled to live with the consequences of *our* choices. We are ultimately accountable for these choices for our lives.

Many people stay in partnerships or friendships that have become routine and unsatisfying. Fearful of surviving on their own, they may never acknowledge the full depth of their dissatisfaction. They may tell themselves, "Things could be worse," rather than asking, "How could they become better?" Such individuals betray themselves by not pursuing the "more" that is possible in their lives, whether that means working to improve their partnerships, leaving them, or broadening their base of nourishment through caring friendships, an enriching career, or other creative pursuits.

We betray ourselves when we ingratiate ourselves to others, rather than be ourselves and be willing to accept the consequences. We forsake ourselves when we make choices to impress others, rather than to satisfy ourselves. We misdirect ourselves when we fail to pursue our own unique destiny, or, as mythologist Joseph Campbell often said, "follow our bliss." We deprive ourselves when we ignore these words of Rumi, the Persian poet: "Let yourself be silently drawn by the stronger pull of what you really love." We disserve ourselves when we allow fear of the unknown and fear of rejection to lead us off our path. We defraud ourselves when, instead of listening to the meaning-filled guidance that whispers within us, we go astray by trusting another's version of reality. We cheat ourselves when we are unwilling to explore for ourselves, make our own mistakes, and find our own special way.

Betraying ourselves is the very essence of what has been

called codependence. According to psychotherapist Charles Whitfield, codependence occurs when

> we focus so much outside of ourselves we lose touch with what is inside of us: our beliefs, thoughts, feelings, decisions, choices, experiences, wants, needs, sensations, intuitions. . . . Co-dependence is the most common of all addictions: the addiction to looking elsewhere. We believe that something outside of ourselves—that is, outside of our True Self—can give us happiness and fulfillment.[10]

By looking elsewhere, by not trusting ourselves, we betray ourselves. By manipulating and adjusting ourselves to please, accommodate, or satisfy others in order to win love, acceptance, and approval, we display a curious kind of contempt for ourselves. Whatever "love" and acceptance is gained is then precariously perched upon our continued disclaiming of our true feelings, thoughts, and aspirations. Henry, who could never understand why he felt anxious and ungenuine in his relationships, expressed it as follows: "I'm always playing to an audience rather than living from my real self. I'm always busy taking care of other people rather than seeing how I feel and what I want." This is self-betrayal, and it leads to chronic dissatisfaction, if not rampant misery, disconnection, and miscommunication in our relationships.

EMBRACING OUR DEEPER IDENTITY

Personal growth and happiness spring from sturdy self-affirmation and self-esteem. This is often initially based on achieving a positive sense of meaning and identity in our lives. For example, our self-image as a successful professional, parent, provider, or spouse helps us feel a sense of adequacy and strength, a surer sense of connection with ourselves, others, and life itself. Personal growth involves a certain degree of mastery over our lives and destinies so that our well-being is not disrupted whenever the winds of change blow from an unforeseen direction.

However, our well-being is jeopardized if we cling to an excessively narrow self-image or purpose, one that provides a comfortable, though limited, sense of self. We may then become so competent or powerful in our role—so bolstered by the "success" or control we have achieved—that we cut ourselves off from the rest of life. We may solidify into a role identity that becomes so gratifying that we may never grow toward a larger, more expansive vision of life. We then betray the deeper calling of our being that would inspire us to go beyond the predictable, the secure, the dutiful. We become diminished as a person. As Bob Dylan put it, ". . . he not busy being born is busy dying."

Many people we envy as being successful, energetic, and confident are troubled in their quieter moments by a sense of emptiness and meaninglessness. What appears to be enthusiasm and vitality is oftentimes compulsive drivenness and anxiety. What seems to be a search for excellence is often the concealment of a well-hidden fear of failure. The power, victories, and fortune that flourish in the board room are often shadowed by conflict, betrayal, and impotence in the bedroom.

Many high-powered, high-achieving individuals think they are maturing and growing, when all that is really growing is an inflated sense of their power—a will to dominate and control whatever threatens their security, be it a competitor, a colleague, or a partner. On a larger scale, this tendency may be observed as a determination to upgrade our standard of living while ignoring the effects on the natural world around us, which may mean environmental ruin. The nearsighted pursuit of personal gain and comfort, whether in the personal or environmental sphere, is ultimately self-destructive.

In his insightful book *Betrayal of the Self*, psychotherapist Arno Gruen offers the broad view that ideologies of domination, power, and control are

> antithetical to human nature and [are] the cause not only of
> "the betrayal of the self" but of almost all else that is morally

41

and politically evil or reprehensible in the world. The quest for power and control (and the corollary tendency to overvalue abstract thought) dehumanizes us, causing internal dissociations and denying us access to such elementary human urges and tendencies as love and empathy.[11]

Personal growth involves integrating a full range of feelings and needs into our overall sense of self. Doing so means being flexible and resilient enough to embrace qualities that appear to be in opposition: our strength *and* our tenderness, our need for autonomy *and* our need for love and intimacy. Rather than further our own power and self-importance—the isolationist goals of the "Me Decade"—we are invited to integrate our human limitations and vulnerability into our overall sense of self.

We betray ourselves by splitting off parts of ourselves that we find distasteful or threatening, especially feelings that may prompt us to feel helpless or weak, such as our fear, sorrow, and shame. By excluding such emotions from awareness, we stifle our life of feelings, thereby unwittingly denying ourselves access to the experience of tenderness and intimacy. We become rigid, self-righteous, and disconnected. We subvert our journey toward wholeness and love. We betray our emotional and spiritual development. We impoverish our soul.

This disconnection from our authentic self is almost inevitable in a culture that extols the pseudo virtues of perfection, certainty, and control (the veneration of an image), while ridiculing imperfection, ambivalence, and messiness—in short, our humanness. As a sad consequence, our society unwittingly encourages a climate of self-betrayal, one in which we are cajoled and pressured to live up to an idealized image of a human being.[12] Our challenge is to find the courage to discover what it truly means to be human—to swim against the current of social shaming and to declare to ourselves (and appropriate others) that we have strengths *and* weaknesses.

42

BETRAYING PEOPLE AND OTHER
LIVING THINGS

We betray ourselves by disowning our true nature. Perhaps less obviously, we simultaneously develop a way of being that lends itself to the betrayal of others. By squelching the more delicate side of our being, we develop a corresponding aversion to the sensitivities of others. When others display pain, hurt, or fear, we are ill-equipped to respond with empathy because we dread these feelings when they arise within ourselves. When people express affection and tenderness, we may notice in ourselves a faint repulsion, perhaps bordering on nausea, that relates to feeling out of control. Even worse, we may mistreat those who display their softer, "weaker" side, perhaps by ridiculing, judging, or manipulating them.

Gruen warns of further destructive effects when people split off their helplessness, then sustain this split by continuing to

> seek revenge on everything that might recall their own help-lessness. That is why they scorn it in others. Scorn and contempt conceal their fear and at the same time encourage a general attitude of contempt for helplessness and the need for a compensatory ideology of power and domination. In this way, victims join the ranks of their oppressors in order to find new victims—an endless process by which human beings become dehumanized.[13]

Few people suspect that they are motivated by emotions of which they remain unaware. Few admit to themselves that their personal pursuit of autonomy and freedom regularly leads to hurting, if not betraying, others. Sadly, many individuals misunderstand autonomy as being freed from their more vulnerable feelings, rather than living in harmony with them.

True autonomy and freedom remain forever unattainable

43

whenever we do not first seek self-understanding and wisdom. For when we treat our vulnerability as the enemy, then, as Gruen astutely points out, freedom takes on "an entirely different, unexpressed significance: it means deliverance from, not harmony with, our own needs. In this way the wish for freedom is perverted into a struggle for power, a struggle to gain mastery over things outside our rejected self."[14]

As a result of this perverse search for a freedom that is alien to our true nature, we heartlessly manipulate our world and become desensitized to others. Pursuing our immediate gratification, we remove ourselves more and more from a healthy sense of relatedness to people, nature, and community. We become more and more cut off from the healthy freedom, the autonomy, and the love that we really want. We create institutions that further the alienated agenda of a false, disconnected self. We enjoin others to find their "freedom" and "dignity" in the same questionable ways that we do, such as by worshiping success or pursuing personal wealth, notoriety, and achievement—or even personal growth—at others' expense. In essence, we persuade others to betray themselves and join hands as we walk the well-worn path that leads to futility. Henry David Thoreau, who tried in his own way to live a life true to himself, observed over a century ago, "Wherever a man goes, men will pursue him and paw him with their dirty institutions, and, if they can, constrain him to belong to their desperate oddfellow society."

As our vulnerability becomes an aspect of our strength, we create a self that is more readily responsive to the sensibilities of other people, as well as to those of the larger environment. Without this broader awareness, we make ourselves the center of the universe. Pursuing a distorted, self-centered version of personal growth, we may hunt for happiness regardless of the effects that our efforts visit upon other people or the world of nature, which are viewed as instruments to further our pleasure and reduce our pain. Nested in our egocentric and species-centric viewpoint, we may claim our constitutional right to the pursuit of happiness without considering whether other people, as well as the world of nature and other living creatures, have rights, too.

An ill-boding consequence of being disconnected from ourselves is to remain impervious to the sensitivities and needs of other living beings who cohabit this planet. In our quest to be the sovereign species, we may fail to fully recognize that our very existence depends upon the health and well-being of other life-forms, that we are interdependent with them. By living in an antagonistic relationship with our natural self, we view our relationship with nature *as a competition to be won, rather than a partnership to be worked out.* Being clever human beings, we are bound to beat the competition, which, of course, will mean that we lose.

Since the natural environment is the very source of our own sustenance, we indirectly betray ourselves by being inattentive to its needs. By destroying biodiversity, clear-cutting the ancient forests, and destroying the ecosystem, we are actually uprooting ourselves from life. We are amputating a part of ourselves. The poisons we spew into the air, water, and soil are recycled into our tissues and organs whenever we breathe, drink, and eat. For many philosophers, this raises the curious question: How intelligent are we as a species?

Our personal well-being, in fact our very survival, requires that we live in harmony with three interrelated domains of life—ourselves, others, and nature—rather than betray any of these dimensions out of arrogance or ignorance. As we heal the wounds of betrayal in our personal lives—the trauma of sudden disconnection, the disruption of our longing to love and be loved—we are better positioned to heal our relationships with people and the natural environment. Recovering from broken trust not only restores our personal well-being, it also provides inspiration to live with greater sensitivity toward our fellow human beings. In the latter stages of recovery from betrayal, we not only get back our own life, we are propelled toward a deeper, more trusting connection with life itself.

NOTES

1. J. Hillman, *Loose Ends: Primary Papers in Archetypal Psychology* (Dallas: Spring Publications), 1975, 66.

2. For example, Catholic priests have been forbidden from "publicly dissenting from church teachings on artificial birth control, papal authority and other controversial matters or face disciplinary measures." *San Francisco Chronicle*, "Vatican Forbids Academic Dissent," 27 June, 1990, A 11.

3. The old adage "For every rule there is an exception" may apply here. I've spoken with several people who insist that their affair ended up being helpful to both them and their marriage.

4. A. Lawson, *Adultery* (New York: Basic Books, 1988), 75.

5. See Deborah M. Anopol, *Love Without Limits: The Quest for Sustainable Intimate Relationships* (San Rafael, CA: IntInet Resource Center, 1992).

6. Early in his political career, Richard Nixon accused his opponent of being a Communist. He later was reported to have said that he *knew* this man wasn't a Communist, but that the important thing was winning.

7. Interested readers may refer to *Adult Children of Abusive Parents* by Steven Farmer (New York: Ballantine Books, 1989) and *Outgrowing the Pain* by Eliana Gil (New York: Dell Publishing, 1983).

8. J. Carroll, "On Not Knowing," *San Francisco Chronicle*, 2 June 1991.

9. This theme of disconnecting from our natural self will be explored more thoroughly in my forthcoming book, *Let's Stop Hurting Each Other*.

10. C. Whitfield, *Co-Dependence: Healing the Human Condition* (Deerfield, FL: Health Communications, 1991), 3–4.

11. Quoted in Leo Goldberger, review of *Betrayal of the Self—The Fear of Autonomy in Men and Women*, by Arno Gruen, trans. Hildegarde and Hunter Hannum, *New York Times Book Review*, 10 July 1988, 16.

12. An example of these destructive values is found in the presidential campaign of 1972, in which candidate Edmund Muskie shocked the nation by crying in public. This "horrid" display of "weakness" contributed to the demise of his political career. Until we value the honest expression of feelings in our culture, we will continue to elect those who successfully fabricate an image, rather than embody the genuine honesty and integrity that we say we want from our political leaders.

13. Gruen, *Betrayal of the Self*, 9.

14. Gruen, 22.

CHAPTER 2

Common Reactions
to Betrayal

Threatened by something terrible that may overwhelm us, we contract like the narrowing spiral of a
whirlpool. Just as we begin to honor our pain, our
reasons for avoiding it grow stronger, giving us the
illusion of control. We point accusing fingers.
We strike out verbally at others. We accuse ourselves. . . . Blame is clever at finding logical reasons
for our nameless sadness.

GABRIELE RICO[1]

THOSE who are shaken by a serious betrayal may undergo
a process of grieving that is akin to the stages of dying outlined by psychiatrist Elizabeth Kubler-Ross, who worked with
people facing life-threatening illnesses.[2] Recovery from betrayal may also be compared to the life-wrenching readjust-
ment that is forced upon us when a loved one dies. We may
experience a similarly stunning distress when confronted with
the loss (or potential loss) of a cherished relationship,
whether through betrayal or death.

What we experience as a serious betrayal and how we react
to it vary from person to person. It is vital that we allow
ourselves to experience whatever is true for *us*, without minimizing or exaggerating our response. People react differently
to similar events.

Still, I have observed a common pattern among those who are struggling with betrayal. When our world is turned upside down by a blatant betrayal of trust, such as sexual infidelity or desertion, we are likely to be thrown into grief. Subtler betrayals such as dishonesty and disrespect may be experienced as a less traumatic, but nevertheless painful loss of trust and connection, especially when they persist over time.

The first encounter with a serious betrayal in our adult lives often remains the most painful and insulting. Whether the relationship was brief or long-lived we are jolted by the sudden undermining of hope, trust, and innocence. The first blush of betrayal radically alters our perception of ourselves, our partner, and, oftentimes, life itself. The way we deal with this initial betrayal is pivotal. It sets a pattern for how we will handle future disappointments in life. As one woman put it as she emerged from a period of grieving, "After dealing with so much pain and loss, I feel like I can handle anything now."

If we do not deal with betrayal in a healthy way, we will learn to protect ourselves against the possibility of being betrayed again. We'll shelter the tender place in our heart that longs for connection, but which dreads the prospect of being hurt. When fear overshadows hope, we become cautious and guarded in our relationships. We become less open, less available for a full, rich relationship. However, it is never too late to deal with betrayal in a way that leads to healing and growth, even if the betrayal happened long ago.

There are no wrong reactions to betrayal. We must accept and embrace whatever *we* experience during this time of crisis if we are to overcome our injury. However, we can easily get lost in the throes of betrayal. It is common that we find ourselves overwhelmed, or stuck in a narrow band of reactivity. By recognizing common reactions to betrayal, we may feel less alone in our struggle. Also, we may better distinguish between those responses that are steps toward healing and those that may perpetuate our pain and confusion.

48

SHOCK AND DENIAL

When we are deserted by a spouse or partner whom we have grown to love and trust, we experience the pain of betrayal. This betrayal may be so sudden, so unexpected, that our initial reaction may be to deny the depth of our pain. Even if we anticipated the desertion, we may feel jarred when it actually happens. Just as we may have difficulty accepting that we have a terminal illness, or that a loved one has died, so may we avoid the full realization that our partner has really left us. Just as we may have denied indications, which, in retrospect, were clear warnings of an impending rift, so we may deny that our mate, our companion, has really abandoned us.

We might try to prop ourselves up with self-soothing reassurances, such as "She'll be back soon" or "This can't last long." We might attempt to pacify ourselves with the spiritualized belief that all will work out for the best. Or we might busy ourselves with activities in order to divert attention from intolerable pain.

Many of us experience emotional shock as our first reaction to betrayal. This initial shock has to do with sudden loss combined with utter disbelief. Our mind cannot comprehend the magnitude of our loss. Being betrayed is not consistent with our image of the other person, nor with our view of how life is supposed to work. We might believe that this type of thing happens only in bad dreams or B movies; or to pitiful people we have known. How could someone do this to us, especially a person with whom we've shared our heart, our bed, and our dreams. Shock is our body's way of cushioning us from the devastating impact of a life-altering event. It protects us from the unbearable pain that might result if the truth were absorbed too quickly.

Our body will nevertheless register the event of betrayal and manifest its displeasure in various ways, depending upon our makeup and the severity of our loss. We might feel weak or shaky. Waves of anxiety may lead to restless sleep, if not serious sleep loss. We may have little appetite due to a jittery stomach. We may have difficulty concentrating at work and functioning in our daily lives for some period of time. We might ask larger questions about human nature and the meaning of life, as did Robin, a graduate student. She was coldly deserted by a partner who shut off his heart and leaped into the arms of a new woman. Even more agonizing for her was his refusal to talk about it: "I was totally disillusioned with humanity. Is this what human beings do to each other?"

One aspect of Robin's initial shock was to get caught up in unending questions about what happened: "I was trying too hard to know why. I got into a groove. I had to step outside my usual thinking to see it in a new way. It was sort of like giving up—letting go of *my* approach, *my* definitions, *my* concepts of what happened. My intention to understand is still there—so I can grow in my awareness—but I had to let go of my old ways of *how to get* to the why." By releasing the repetitive, circular thoughts in her head, she was able to tend to the hurt in her heart.

Denying the Pain of Sexual Betrayal

We may also deny the pain that accompanies sexual betrayal. We might tell ourselves that we shouldn't be so rigid. We might forgive too easily. Mindy, whose partner had a string of affairs that he sloughed off as "meaningless flings," put it this way: "I was too idealistic. I knew he kept screwing up our agreement, but I always thought he'd still come through for me. So I hung in there."

Other people avoid their pain by having an affair themselves. This often postpones or prolongs their pain, while creating more distance and alienation in the relationship.

One man who broke his monogamous agreement with a new partner justified a series of betrayals in a lighthearted, yet shallow way. He explained to her, "You know me. I just get out of control when I'm with a beautiful woman. I can't do anything about it. But I really love *you. You're* the one I really want to be with. I just get seduced by these glamorous women for one-night stands." Years after the relationship ended, she reflected somewhat humorously on why she tolerated this situation: "I would say to myself, 'Okay, I guess that's what it's like to be a man. You're at the mercy of all these women seducing you.' So I would forgive him for these 'mistakes' and we'd go on."

Rather than recognize her pain as a message that there was a crisis of trust in the relationship, she turned against herself. She avoided the signals her feelings were trying to give her. She chose to believe the words "I love you" (which she had longed to hear) rather than trust what her heart was telling her.

Loss of Betrayal versus Loss Due to Death

Desertion can be every bit as disturbing as losing a loved one to death. In fact, there are ways in which the effects of such betrayal may linger more insidiously than when a friend or partner dies. When a loved one dies, we are likely to be shaken to our core. However, there is nothing more we can do about it. Our organism has little choice but to grieve the loss and gradually adapt to a new life. As one man put it, "That person is gone; it's done."

When we are deserted, there is not the same kind of finality; there is no dead body to view at the funeral parlor. We are haunted by the knowledge that our betraying partner is still out there, somewhere. In fact, we may know exactly where this person lives and works. We may maintain a common tie to the same friends and acquaintances. We may be unable to avoid encountering an ex-partner who lives or shops nearby. Even more foreboding, a common commitment to parenting or an ongoing business relationship may require exposing ourselves to unwanted contact. We may be emotionally restimulated through planned or unplanned encounters. These gut-wrenching episodes may trigger persistent emotions of longing, loss, and rejection, thereby disrupting the process of letting go.

In contrast to losing someone to death, betrayal can pierce to the core of our self-esteem. When someone dies, we don't accuse them of hurting us intentionally. We're not prone to question our worth and value. We don't say, "What's wrong with me?" But if someone deserts us or has an affair, we are hurt by the awareness that it was their *choice* to do so.

Lingering Confusion, Doubts, Denial

Reeling in the confused and sometimes tormenting aftermath of betrayal, we may suffer a procession of nagging thoughts and self-doubts regarding how things might have been different: *If only* we had said such and such on one occasion, or *not* said this or that on another occasion. *If only* we had spoken less hastily, expressed love more wholeheartedly, taken more vacations, invested in couples counseling, or been more tolerant of differences that now seem petty. *If only* we had been less inflexible and stubborn, and more mature and aware. Then, we tell ourselves, we might have stayed together.

Our mind may be plagued by repetitive fantasies of how we might reunite, coupled with fears regarding this chilling prospect. Is it possible to get back together? Do we really want to—or would things only get worse? Should we write that letter we've been contemplating? Should we mail the one we've already written? Should we make the phone call that we've been considering? Or should we call just to hear his voice on the answering machine, then hang up? But what if he answers the phone? What excuse would we give for why we're calling? What if we learn that she's with a new partner? Do we really want to know? As we live week after week, month after month, or year after year with the Hollywood fantasy of a poignant reunion, our life slips by. We live in denial of our loss.

When suddenly left by his partner of three years, Phil was

52

tormented by unanswered questions and tenacious hopes: "She hates me now. I don't know why she hates me. She just ignores me now." Not yet accepting what happened to him, Phil would visit places where he might run into her. "I'm hoping that if I see her, then somehow we'll talk and she'll remember that I love her. I'm still hoping she'll turn around."

Maureen was tormented by similar longings for the man who left her. Like many people, she was quick to blame herself for a failed partnership: "I kept thinking, 'What am I doing wrong here?' I kept wanting him back. I thought if I could figure out what I was doing wrong that he'd come back."

Trying to get someone back is similar to the stage of dying that Kubler-Ross calls bargaining, during which people try to strike a deal with God, or promise to be "good" in exchange for a few more years of life. Similarly, the betrayed partner might promise that if he or she is given another chance—or if the relationship is given a new life—then things will surely be different. Or the betraying partner might make overtures to reconcile. This may excite us with new possibilities, while raising the frightful prospect of yet another round of betrayal in the future.

The fantasies that preoccupy us about our lost yet mentally present partner can take a cruel toll. Zelda's experience with her fiancé is common. She had a daughter from a previous marriage. A loving, cozy connection was growing between all three of them when a sudden conflict caused him to bolt from the relationship. One year later she reflected, "In one part of my mind it's never really over. The longing is still there—the possibility of reconnecting is there, whether it's real or imagined. But if I see him or hear his voice, I kind of have to start the process of grieving all over again."

Mathew, whose partner left him for another man, voiced a similar sentiment: "I can't get her out of my mind. I think about her all the time. It even interferes with my work. I never realized how much I took her for granted, how much she really meant to me."

Although our will is often weak after a serious betrayal, we perpetuate our own victimization and "stuckness" in life by indulging our tempting fantasies to reunite, rather than seeing our fantasies for what they are and letting them pass without acting upon them. It is sometimes more gratifying to swim in a vague sea of possibilities than it is to see reality clearly and face the deeper hurts and fears that accompany loss (more about this later).

The attempt to get our partner back may have more to do with our lost sense of dignity than actually wanting to be together again. If we succeeded, what would we do with him or her? Do we really want to reconnect, or do we just want to salvage our wounded pride by coming out of all this without looking bad?

Oftentimes, we do not recognize that we have been so hurt by the whole ordeal of being betrayed that we may have difficulty reopening ourselves to this person. We may be sexually closed-down and emotionally hostile or withdrawn. Our trust may have been so wounded that it may take many grueling months, if not years, to process our hurt feelings and relevant issues in order to rebuild trust and intimacy (especially if there has been repeated physical abuse or sexual betrayal). In our eagerness to confirm our adequacy and desirability, we may not carefully consider what it will take to heal the relationship, or whether we really want our partner back.

Accepting that a once prized relationship has ended requires a willingness to conclude one stage of our life and walk toward an uncertain future. If we release our partner, will we meet someone new? Will anyone else find us appealing and desirable? Can we make it on our own? Perhaps never before have we been so challenged to test our faith in ourselves and our trust in life.

If our self-esteem is slipping, we will have an especially difficult time letting go of the past and finding the strength to face the present with renewed hope and openness. Even if we feel good about ourselves, completing the past is never easy, especially if we fear for our financial viability without our ex-partner. Gradually, as our initial shock subsides and our icy denial begins to melt, we may notice unpleasant emotions that must be faced and embraced on our sputtering path toward acceptance and healing.

REACTIONS OF SHAME AND SELF-BLAME

Seeping through our shock or denial may be a heavy sense of shame and self-loathing. We may feel self-contempt for a variety of reasons. We may blame ourselves for not sizing up our partner properly, or for not anticipating the betrayal and taking steps to counteract it ("How could I have ignored all the warning signs? I should have seen it coming!"). Or we may regret having become sexually involved with that person or marrying him or her ("How could I have been so dumb?"). We might now admit to ourselves that the relationship was largely unsatisfying, and berate ourselves for settling for so little, year after year ("All I ever got were crumbs, but I kept hoping I'd get more someday").

Shame might come in the form of believing it's our fault that we were deserted. If our partner had an affair, we might criticize ourselves for not being sufficiently attractive, interesting, sexy, or loving. Familiar feelings of being worthless and inadequate might be amplified, especially if we were sexually, physically, or emotionally abused and betrayed as a child. For Marla, who was verbally abused as a child, her current betrayal pricked an old wound she'd carried for many years. She described her shame as follows: "I feel that I don't deserve to be alive; I don't deserve to take up space." That gnawing shame subsequent to betrayal led to depression, emotional fatigue, and feelings of worthlessness.

Due in large part to parenting that was overly protective, critical, and solicitous, Marla had never developed her own stable center. Instead, she learned to be dependent upon others for her sense of self. As she later expressed it, "I had nothing inside myself that was separate from other people's reactions to me." Because she possessed little inner strength and no locus of self-evaluation, whatever her partner said became automatically true for her. When she was treated poorly, she felt that she was bad and defective. When treated kindly, she felt uplifted and worthwhile. Her moods would sway according to how others related to her in any given moment.

It is not unnatural that we feel bad when we are mistreated and feel good when we are loved. The point is that if our well-being is so dependent upon the changing moods of our partner, then we are not fully living our own life. If our sense of self is enmeshed with how our partner views us, *then our life is animated not by our own self-view, but rather by the capricious whims and opinions of another.* Betrayal can become a wake-up call to overcome a pervasive sense of shame and inferiority.

Many men experience more shame than they like to admit, as it vaporizes their image of being the independent, suave Marlboro Man. Eric, the optometrist whose partner had an affair and spread negative gossip about him, expressed his self-blame this way: "I kept thinking, 'There's gotta be something wrong with me. What am I doing wrong here?' I kept wanting her back even though she was hurting me. I got really strung out."

The shame we experience from being betrayed may magnify the shame we carried into the relationship. This commingling of past and present shame poisons our well-being and inhibits our interplay with the world. We recoil from people when we're convinced that they will find us repugnant or unworthy. Driven by shame, we avoid making contact. We avoid others' glances, fearful that they might see our fundamental flaws. Or we stare with eyes that are cold and hardened, rather than softly reflective of our tenderheartedness and goodness.

When our perception is colored by shame, we fail to see things clearly. We assume too much responsibility when a relationship fails. We neglect to recognize the shortcomings of others. Being gripped by the deluded belief that others are more substantial, important, or powerful than ourselves, we condemn ourselves to a fate of inferiority and inequality—they're okay and we're not okay.

When old shame is restimulated by a current betrayal, it comes into a clearer, more conscious focus. We are then presented with an unsought opportunity to allow it to slowly heal. Instead of being debilitated by shame, we can learn to find compassion for ourselves amidst our shame, perhaps with the help of supportive friends or the guidance of a skilled counselor who can help us validate ourselves during a time of crisis. By getting stuck in the stranglehold of shame, we may permanently retreat from close relationships. But if we find the courage to heal, we can once again open our heart, hopefully a little wiser than before.

ANGER, HOSTILITY, AND VENGEANCE

Surging waves of rage and anger are other common reactions to betrayal. We may experience a bloodcurdling resentment upon discovering that our partner has had an affair, or is indeed serious about leaving us. Acting out the impulse to lash out is often a desperate, though impotent attempt to coerce our partner to conform to our wishes or reassert our failing dominance. Oftentimes, we regret the words that fly loosely during frenzied moments of rage and hostility.

Robin, the graduate student whose partner left her for another woman, left a venomous message on his answering machine shortly afterwards. Later, she regretted it. Dumping her hostility on him alienated him so much that further communication became more difficult and torturous, which ended up hurting her. On reflection, she noted, "One thing I learned was not to talk to someone or leave messages when I'm in an angry state, even though I want to so badly. That old adage about counting to ten . . . we hurt each other so much when we don't stop and think."

Expressing our anger can facilitate our recovery from the

pain of betrayal, especially when communicated in a direct, straightforward manner, free of the hostile name calling and shaming accusations that often erupt from anger. Experiencing our anger and expressing it in a responsible, nonblaming way can be a sound step toward healing, as Robin later recognized: "It was important to realize that I was angry, but I could have expressed it differently. I could have said, 'I'm angry!' Period. I wouldn't say, 'You did this and you did that!' I wouldn't make any accusations. Instead, I'd go pound some pillows or run five miles or talk it over with someone. It hurt more in the long run to vent on him. It marred any communication we tried to have for many months after that—so it hurt *me* more than it hurt him."

In a curious way, discharging our anger may also allow us to contact a deeper level of sadness, which enables us to release our deeper pain. When Robin allowed herself to feel and express her anger in a counseling session, she tapped into a whole new level of hurt. After a long session of crying, she exclaimed, "I didn't know *that* was there! It felt good to get in touch with it."

Many people refrain from expressing anger directly because they are reluctant to evoke further negative consequences. Caution is sometimes well advised, such as during delicate divorce proceedings. However, we more often withhold anger because we fear the energy contained in it, or because we deny our right to experience this powerful vehicle of self-affirmation and self-transformation, perhaps because we were punished or shamed for being angry as a child.

In reality, anger itself is not what is so detrimental. In fact, it can be helpful in restoring self-esteem and dignity. It is the unhealthy ways we vent anger that injure others and eventually return to haunt us. Anger becomes toxic when it slinks into vindictiveness and revenge, and is then used to gain emotional gratification at others' expense. And so the cycle of hurting continues.

The Impulse to Punish

The impulse to harm and punish is especially common when we feel betrayed (or think we've been betrayed). Having been hurt, we may want to hurt back to "even the score." We might glibly say to ourselves, "I've been wronged! I'll show them! I'm going to seek justice!" This impulse is as human as it is destructive. Yet, as Martin Luther King, Jr., soberly warned, "That old law about 'an eye for an eye' leaves everybody blind."

Unless we deal with these emotions wisely, rage and hatred lend themselves to a variety of inventive ways to seek revenge. For example, when Cathy learned that her partner had an affair, she felt infuriated: "I went to his house and went through his drawers and threw his stuff on the floor and took all my clothes I had left there. He never treated me or my stuff with respect, so why treat him that way?" Other people have been even more violent in their reactions. One frantic man smashed his former lover's car window. An irate woman cut up her ex-partner's clothes. Others have expressed their violence and vengeance through the courts, usually leading to a drawn-out, debilitating battle that cripples both partners. The more that trust is damaged, the harder it is to repair.

The book and movie *War of the Roses* graphically portrays the lethal effects upon a couple of an escalating war of reciprocal retaliation. *Mutually assured destruction of our emotional and spiritual well-being is the all-too-frequent outcome when vengeful impulses race out of control.* On a larger scale, there are ample examples of the tragic waste that ensues when feuding ethnic groups engage in devastating contests of revenge and counterrevenge.

Vengeance is legitimized in our culture by such popular expressions as, "Don't get mad, get even!" Such was the reaction of Dorothy, a fifty-year-old corporate executive, as the result of a series of painful relationships with men, culminating in the sudden dissolution of her engagement with Don.

He had invited her to spend a weekend at his parents' home in a nearby state in order to announce their marriage. She arrived with excitement and anticipation, only to be stunned by Don's revelation that he didn't think he was really ready for marriage.

Dorothy's relationships with men were never the same again. "I really isolated myself and didn't have that degree of intimacy for years," she acknowledged. "When I started being with men again, I said, 'Okay, this is a game to see who can get the most goodies and be the less damaged.' And I made sure *I* did. I made sure *I* was controlling the show. It was like I took on this mission of getting even—in one form or another. I'd seduce these men into falling in love with me, and when I got bored with them—which didn't take very long—I'd just discard them and go get the next one. I would lure them into my spider web and chew them up and spit 'em out. I didn't know I was doing it out of revenge. I only know that looking back. It never occurred to me that I was punishing these men for what others did to *me*. I left a lot of dead bodies in the path as I went through life."

Through her new commitment to personal growth, Dorothy courageously allowed herself to recognize how she, as the betrayed, became the betrayer: "I would be going along in a relationship and then just walk away. There was always some great excuse I'd give for leaving. The truth was that I never allowed myself to be emotionally involved with any of these men. They must have experienced real betrayal by me. I had become the armored Amazon and didn't let anyone get close." As Dorothy began to feel her sorrow and remorse for having hurt others, she could begin to forgive herself for it.

Subtle Vengeance and Spite

Vengeance and hostility can be enacted in a subtly devious form that is difficult to detect, leading to a cold war between the sexes. For example, Les was angry at Janet for not giving him the amount of sexual affection he wanted. He acted out his anger by having a secret affair, distancing himself from Janet both emotionally and sexually. When she asked why he'd become less interested in having sex or cuddling, he would sneakily say, "I'm too tired." When further questioned about why he was always so tired, he deflected responsibility through the hostile remark, "Don't you ever care about how *I* feel?" These frequent spats led to much pain and confusion for Janet. Feeling shunned, she would retaliate by buying expensive clothes, which she knew infuriated him, thereby furthering a downward spiral of mistrust.

Psychologist Susan Campbell describes spite in this way:

> You hit me (or I imagine that you have), so I hit you back. Tit for tat. Do unto others what they've done to you. Have the last word. But do it subtly, as passively as possible, so you can't be held responsible for it. . . . Spite arises from the pits of the lowest, the most selfish and competitive, aspect of human nature.[3]

Another popular way to seek vengeance or act spitefully is to use children as a pawn in a destructive game of revenge. Therapists call this triangulating—coaxing the kids to take our side and portraying their mother or father as the bad, incompetent parent. Feeling powerless to affect our partner emotionally, we may play our last desperate card by preying upon our partner's attachment to the children. In some instances one of the parents may indeed be incompetent, but usually each possesses strengths and weaknesses as a parent. Of course, it's a lot easier to see others' flaws when we're caught in a struggle to recapture our self-worth by proving that we're right and claiming the high moral ground. Needless to say, yanking at the children's heart strings can create a profound disruption in their emotional development.

Lawyers thrive on people's taste for vengeance and retribution. Legal action as a socially sanctioned form of violence and revenge is especially prevalent in the United States, which has one lawyer for every 360 people, in contrast with Japan, which has one for every 10,000.[4] Perhaps more than others,

Americans believe they have some inherent, God-given right to get their way.

Nursing Hate Hurts Us

We often fail to recognize that the hateful impulses we carry inside ourselves are injurious not only to others but also to ourselves. The hate that we nurse within ourselves and hold toward others *eats away at our own heart and soul.* The vengeance we inflict on others has a curious way of rebounding upon us in one way or another: What goes around comes around.

Acts of revenge hurt us in yet another way. We often violate our own ethical standards as we plot and scheme to get back at people. Jungian analyst James Hillman notes that

> it is a strange experience to find oneself betraying oneself, turning against one's own experiences by . . . acting against one's own intentions and value system. In the break-up of a friendship, partnership, marriage, love-affair, or analysis, suddenly the nastiest and dirtiest appears and one finds oneself acting in the same blind and sordid way that one attributes to the other, and justifying one's own actions with an alien value system.[5]

This discrepancy between our deepest values and retaliatory impulses creates an inner disturbance, a self-alienation that disables us from finding abiding peace, stability, and maturity. If we are to rediscover our integrity and realign ourselves with the ways of love, we must reconcile ourselves to the fact that we have not only injured another but have violated our own ideals and standards.

Each of us possesses a shadow side containing emotions and urges that may be acted out in hurtful ways. But how do we tolerate the perception that there is hate and vindictiveness in us? How do we live with ourselves knowing that we are spewing ill will toward another? Most of us deal with this by disavowing these shadow parts of ourselves. A lethargy in our soul prevents us from courageously recognizing our hate and cruelty so that we may deal with them constructively.

The defense mechanism known as reaction formation enables us to conceal our real impulses from ourselves. We do this by covering up our actual intentions and motivations with the opposite impulse. For example, if hatred and malice are inconsistent with our self-image, we might persuade ourselves that our real motivation is a noble one, such as "teaching them a lesson for their own good." We then turn to "supportive" friends who validate the self-perception that we are a kind, good person without a mean bone in our body. Acknowledging how we've hurt others may be one of the most difficult and courageous discoveries we make in a lifetime because it requires letting go of a stubborn self-righteousness of which we're each capable.

Origins of Our Destructive Inclinations

One difference between maturity and immaturity is *not* that we no longer experience destructive impulses. Just the opposite. Personal growth involves fully identifying these impulses, rather than disguising them. Only then can we find some distance from our pernicious inclinations. Gaining a clearer perspective provides the precious moments we need to recognize their origins and deal with them in a healthier manner.

Vindictive impulses often originate from a desire to know that we're important to someone, that we make a difference in his or her life. We want to know that we have the power to affect someone. For example, one client who became vindictive toward her spouse, and later regretted it, explained that "the worst thing was that he didn't want me—that's what made me so angry. But now I feel guilty about how badly I treated him. He didn't deserve that." The fear of losing a precious connection triggered her reaction of rage.

When we are betrayed, we are disheartened by the sudden knowledge that we are no longer important to someone. We're no longer special (at least to that person). We are no longer cherished for being unique, or appreciated for what we have to offer; we're no longer wanted.

Even worse in some instances, our humanness is blotted out and obliterated by the other. Our soul is squashed and invalidated. A serious betrayal is the ultimate disrespect of the dignity of our existence.

Rage and revenge are often reactions to feeling powerless to affect others' predilection for caring about us, wanting us, and validating us. Such rage is a vehicle through which we try to control others by *demanding* that they value us. If we are snubbed, our vengeful actions will ensure that our presence will be felt in one way or another, such as by making life as miserable as possible for our ungrateful partner. If we can't make this person feel *love* for us, we can make him or her feel something else—*pain and misery*. Then our ex-partner will suffer just the way we have—by stripping him or her of value and dignity. Then we'll know that we've had an impact, even if it isn't the one we preferred. But at least we will be back in control—we will feel significant—although in a most temporary and twisted way.

We are especially driven by the need to feel validated when our self-esteem is shaky. Uncertain about our own self-worth, we struggle to show others that we have clout. When our self-esteem is weak, we may employ an emotional form of vandalism for self-validation.

The Healthy Function of Anger

If we can distinguish the emotion of anger from the related, destructive impulses of hateful vengeance and retaliation, we may respond to betrayal more sanely. On the positive side, anger can be an early (though vital) step toward helping us differentiate ourselves from others. It is often a healthy response in situations in which we have been physically abused, verbally ridiculed, or cruelly deceived. Rather than sink into a debilitating shame, we can extract the power contained in our anger to stand up for ourselves. Through a firm and clear self-assertion, we can recover our dignity, proclaim our rights, and reaffirm our worth and value as a human being.

Experiencing anger can provide an impetus for wanting more for ourselves and more out of life. Through anger we define our limits regarding the unacceptable behavior of others. We establish a boundary that boldly says, perhaps for the first time, "This is me, this is how I really feel, this is my viewpoint." Positive changes sometimes ensue from an appropriate, well-timed expression of anger. If we realize later that our anger was inappropriate or excessive, we can clarify our position—or apologize.

Some people suppress their legitimate anger when they're betrayed. They claim it is beneath them to express such "base" or "vulgar" or "unspiritual" emotions ("He's not worth getting upset about" or "I'm not gonna let her get to me!"). A hearty spurt of anger might help such individuals release powerful energies that might otherwise remain pent up within themselves. Stifled anger can lead to a self-contempt and self-hatred that damages not only their emotional well-being but their physical health as well.

Just as those who are prone to anger and blame are often covering up their deeper hurt, those who easily sink into a shame-laden hurt, self-blame, and depression may benefit by tapping their legitimate anger, while also embracing their real hurt.

When Beth's husband announced that he'd fallen in love with a younger woman, she was angry but held herself back from experiencing its depths. Instead, she tried to be as sweet and open-hearted as his new lover, hoping he'd then find Beth more desirable. But this charade only made her feel worse. She felt better letting herself feel as angry as she wanted, but without being vengeful. As she put it, "My challenge was to let myself feel all that anger, but without inflicting more pain."

The Limits of Anger

On the negative side, anger is perhaps the most addictive and intoxicating emotion due to the euphoric burst of power and energy it arouses. Like unspent fuel, anger can keep feeding on itself, until we get some satisfaction. Unbounded anger can quickly get out of control. Discovering that angry outbursts daunt and intimidate others, we may use that anger as our chief ally whenever conflict arises—at least until someone finally stops us, or leaves us.

Self-righteous anger can produce the illusion of invulnerability and invincibility. It can help us feel good by making others look bad, or by making them suffer. We may become accustomed to getting our way when we are enraged, just as we may have manipulated our parents into surrendering to our demands when we yelled and stomped our feet. Having an adult temper tantrum helps us feel secure when we believe that it will deliver what we want.

Those of us who fly into anger during stressful times but who have a low tolerance for more vulnerable emotions will eventually receive convincing feedback from the world that violent expressions of anger do not get us what we really want, and that we must go further in our growth. When we come to believe that venting our anger is the method of choice for dealing with betrayal, we betray ourselves by not taking a further step that is necessary for many of us: embracing our deeper fear and pain. Sadly, well-meaning friends and even some therapists might lead us astray at this critical juncture by encouraging us to "regain our power" by verbally attacking, if not abusing, a partner, friend, or parent.

This is not to suggest that we deny our legitimate anger toward others. Nor is it to propose that we wallow in self-blame, while being protective of someone who has hurt us. As previously mentioned, a clean, nonhostile expression of outrage is often a necessary step toward restoring our well-being. However, anger is oftentimes an early stage in the process of grieving.[6] At some point, we must look deeper into the source of our pain in order to transform confusion and misery into the possibility of being touched by some kind of redemption.

JEALOUSY

The rage, anger, and venomous impulses resulting from betrayal are closely associated with the emotion of jealousy. The dictionary defines the word *jealous* as "fearful or suspicious of being replaced by a rival in affection or favors." Fearing that we may lose a cherished partner to someone who is better, cuter, smarter, or more accomplished, we may plunge into a self-esteem tailspin. One man who had few friends and a strong fear of being abandoned put it this way: "Just watching her look at other men reinforces my insecurities—the feeling that I'm not good enough."

Our fear or suspicious vigilance may be particularly strong if we imagine that a rival is more sexually desirable than ourselves. We may be dejected by the suspicion that we are no longer the special object of our partner's amorous desire. Sexuality binds us in a deep and mysterious way to another person; some portion of our jealousy is a very natural fear that we are losing (or have lost) a precious connection. The emotion of jealousy reflects the real or imagined loss of a deeply sacred, emotionally rewarding, and physically satisfying union.

Fits of jealousy are especially common among those whose self-worth is excessively tied to their body image and sexual attractiveness, values that the entertainment media unabashedly promote. Those who are strongly identified with physical beauty and sexual prowess may experience a new kind of vulnerability and helplessness when these powers to draw others toward them begin to wane.

Jealousy is amplified when our autonomy is poorly established. If our identity is enmeshed with our partner, we experience him or her as an extension of ourselves. We claim him or her as our personal property, while refusing to extend our love into the world in some creative fashion. This intertwining of identities and destinies has been hailed in modern times as the culmination of romantic love. This mythology has generated massive pain and confusion in our search for genuine love.

Although we're unlikely to totally transcend the deep-seated emotion of jealousy, we may loosen its grip by sorting out the unrealistic beliefs that are fueling it. For example, if our partner prefers to be with someone else, we may feel undesirable or unattractive. But that preference does not verify that we are indeed an undesirable, unattractive person. If we can find the wherewithal to continue affirming our worth during such a difficult period (as well as seeking out people who affirm us), our jealousy may subside.

SEEKING REFUGE IN JUDGMENTS AND INTERPRETATIONS

No one is beyond the temptation to judge and criticize others, especially when a relationship goes awry. It can be emotionally satisfying to enumerate the faults of others, while retaining a self-view that is beyond reproach. However, arming ourselves with clever judgments rarely helps us in the long run. The most astute analysis is unlikely to relieve the anguish of betrayal. Even if our partner is guilty of having a secret affair, deserting us, or slandering us, our retaliatory accusations are unlikely to soften the betrayal in any real and lasting way. Although the impulse to lash out with judgments can be compelling, we only distract ourselves and eventually bore our friends by indulging in a tiresome litany of our partner's faults.

Enshrouding ourselves in judgments and interpretations insulates us from the pain we refuse to face within ourselves. For instance, by proclaiming that our parting partner is "on a power trip," we avoid the hurt of being rejected. Or, if we accuse our partner of being "a tease," then we deflect attention from our painful loss. Curiously, we probably didn't think that our partner was on a power trip the week before he or she left us. We probably didn't believe that he or she was a tease while we were enjoying sex.

Diagnosing others is often an attempt to gain some immunity against the heartache of having been betrayed. Our internal antenna is well poised to pick up others' limitations. We possess an uncanny ability to perceive the faults of others, while being far less perceptive when surveying our own shortcomings.

When Sally's partner broke off their engagement, she aired judgments, such as "He's an egomaniac, irresponsible, and immature." Then her judgments grew more sophisticated: "He's cut off from his real feelings. He's in denial. He's not aware of what he's doing." These criticisms gave her some distance from her pain, but they didn't help for very long.

Unfortunately, our most clever and caustic analysis grants only temporary relief at best. The deeper pain that is masked by our interpretations lives on. We must eventually face this underlying pain if we are truly to heal. We must understand what really happened so that history does not repeat itself.

While our judgments and perceptions are sometimes accurate, oftentimes they are distorted by emotional reactivity. When we are reeling in hostility, jealousy, and fear, we see things not as they really are, but as we prefer them to be. When we view events through the lens of our sagging self-esteem, we reach for explanations that bolster our fragile self-image, which typically means that we search for foul interpretations of others.

When we feel hurt by others, we tend to magnify and exaggerate their faults. We may then convince ourselves (and persuade others) to believe this skewed, self-serving version of their flaws. Even if others do have serious shortcomings, we may neglect to balance our viewpoint with a realistic assessment of their positive traits, coupled with an acknowledgment of our own weaknesses.

The Hazards of Judgmental Thinking

Becoming attached to our judgments disrupts our growth by closing our minds to other perspectives. The word *judge* derives from the Latin term meaning "to declare the law." Our judgments are often accompanied by the conviction that truth and justice are solidly on our side. This perception may be valid from a certain vantage point, but when we're spinning in the pain of betrayal, we may overlook the less visible possibility that both we and our partner have pieces of the truth.

The danger of judgmental thinking becomes more apparent if we compare it to the way some fundamentalists convince themselves and each other that they are right, good, and special, while all unbelievers are misguided infidels who are not "saved." By labeling large masses of humanity as "other," or the "unfaithful," if not "the evil ones," they feel justified in distancing themselves from people whose perspectives clash with their own. They then continually fortify themselves against new information that might challenge their inflexible perceptions and beliefs. Such rigidity spells calamity for genuine emotional and spiritual growth.

One of our hidden agendas in forming judgments of others is to make sense out of a painful experience in a way that does not seriously undermine our current self-view. Noticing the speck in our partner's eye protects us from the unsettling discovery that our perceptions may be clouded by the log in our own. Our defense mechanisms of denial, avoidance, and intellectualization shield a brittle self-image from potentially damaging revelations. Unfortunately, these defenses also prevent us from examining the milieu that led to betrayal so that we might learn and grow from acknowledging our own shortcomings.

Judgments may serve the additional hidden agenda of propping up support among friends and garnering sympathy among acquaintances, many of whom have yet to work through their own pain and resentment from past betrayals.

We may turn to those people who arm us with the most cutting interpretations. We may associate with those friends who reinforce a blind reactivity, while feeling indignant toward those who might challenge us. We certainly need care and empathy when we are hurting, but there's an important difference between supportive empathy and misguided sympathy.

Anne Wilson Schaef, a former psychotherapist, explains that "we may become so insecure about ourselves and our place in the world, we feel compelled to convince others to agree with us. We become self-righteous and adamant about our perceptions, and we become judgmental of people who do not share them because we so desperately need their support to feel good about ourselves."[7]

Our campaign to align ourselves with like-minded individuals may be instigated by a deceptively frail and rigid sense of self, a self that cannot withstand too much truth. It is difficult to live with self-deception without being supported by those who share our misconceptions. Larry, who was very hurt by childhood criticism, developed a tough shell that guarded his well-hidden sensitivity. The possibility of being "wrong" or limited in some way raised the prospect of being human like everyone else, rather than "special" or better than others: "By surrounding myself with people who agreed with me, I got to feel that I was right—that the truth was on *my* side. I was more interested in being right than in getting to the truth. I never learned anything from past breakups because I wasn't strong enough to look honestly at what really happened. Having to be right all the time covered up my fear and shame of being criticized."

Often there's no need to try to persuade our friends to agree with us. Jennifer, who was in an on-again, off-again partnership of six years, would be propped up by eager friends during the times she believed the relationship was over: "It was *easy* for my friends—my fan club—to get sucked into my viewpoint: 'Yeah, he's a jerk. He doesn't deserve you anyway.' It felt good to hear that, but I later realized it wasn't

71

really true. And it wasn't helpful. It only got in the way of really understanding what happened. They meant well, but they didn't help me look deeper."

By bolstering their position of being "right," both Larry and Jennifer avoided the pain that often accompanies seeing a deeper truth—a pain they needed to face in order to heal and grow.

The Comfort of Victimhood

There is a dubious form of self-satisfaction that comes from portraying ourselves as a victim in various arenas of life. The essayist Shelby Steele astutely points out that "being a victim delivers to you a certain innocence."[8] Writer John Taylor further suggests that "victim status not only confers the moral superiority of innocence. It enables people to avoid taking responsibility for their behavior."[9] By achieving victim status, individuals are given a license to blame and accuse without exploring how they may have contributed to their own unhappiness.

This current social trend to avoid accountability has its roots in the legitimate refusal to accept responsibility for the effects of social injustices (such as racism) or physical and psychological atrocities (such as child abuse and rape). Unfortunately, major strides in our social sensibilities are often exploited by those with hazier vision, leading John Taylor to comment that

> what began as a well-meaning attempt to acknowledge the plight of previously ignored victims has developed a momentum of its own. In their rush to establish ever more categories of victims, lawyers and therapists are encouraging a grotesquely cynical evasion of the ethic of individual responsibility. . . . While much has been made in recent years of the syndrome called "blaming the victim," less attention has been paid to another syndrome, the "don't-blame-me-I'm-a-victim-syndrome."[10]

72

Our real challenge is to be free of blaming ourselves and blaming others, which are always two sides of the same coin. If responsibility and blame are fused in our minds, then our defenses will marshal to avoid any responsibility. However, the self-contempt of blame is quite different from the self-empowerment of responsibility. By suspending self-blame, we can look more calmly and soberly at how we may be responsible for our choices and accountable for our actions. Only then will we become wiser and stronger. Only then can we grow emotionally and spiritually.

A Positive Aspect of Judgments

For some individuals, judging and evaluating others may have a positive feature *if used sparingly.* Perceiving the flaws of others may enable them to experience themselves as equals of those others. It may supply the evidence they need to confirm that they are indeed valuable and worthwhile. Those leaning toward self-blame may more easily relinquish destructive judgments toward themselves by recognizing that others have shortcomings also. In enumerating others' real or imagined faults, they may find it easier to accept their own—especially if their self-esteem is somewhat tenuous, which it commonly is after betrayal. As one woman put it, "My judgments helped me to see that it wasn't all my fault, that it wasn't just me, that he had his part in it, too. Usually, I would take all the blame. But we *both* had blind spots."

Judgments provide a way of differentiating our own beliefs and values from those of others; they can be a step toward forming a healthy sense of identity and personal boundaries. In addition, some portion of our postbetrayal exploration may be helpful in clarifying aspects of our partner that we had ignored or misperceived. To be more precise, these perceptions are really *discernments,* not judgments. Taking time to discern what happened to a dying or defunct partnership may increase our understanding not only of our partner, but also of ourselves.

Perhaps we realize that we'd overlooked our partner's well-hidden sensitivity. Or we may recognize that our partner never really listened to our concerns and that we had given up on the relationship a long time ago. Or we might realize that we deliberately ignored many subtle deceptions—little betrayals—before discovering the sexual deception that finally tore us apart. Although these bitter discoveries may come late, they can serve us in future relationships.

The hazard of judgmental thinking is that we may become intoxicated with self-righteousness. We may cling to our interpretations as a weapon in an internal debate to prove that we really are right, virtuous, and honorable. Or we may adhere to our judgments in a haughty attempt to dodge responsibility, or to feel morally superior. We cannot grow in wisdom until our judgments are infused with a hearty dose of self-doubt. Gradually, we can learn to make wise discernments without indulging in judgments.

What is necessary in our struggle to overcome the pain of betrayal is to ask ourselves the right questions. What will facilitate our healing? What must we learn in order to reduce the possibility of future betrayals? How can we grow from this experience so that we can make wiser choices and communicate more effectively? What underlies and perpetuates our initial reactions to betrayal? Can we go more deeply within ourselves when we feel the urge to retaliate?

LOOKING BEYOND OUR IMMEDIATE REACTIONS

Some people who are betrayed may not want to look beyond their immediate reactions, such as those of shame, anger, and blame. They may believe that they really are inadequate and that being betrayed is further proof of their undesirability. Or they may feel justified in discharging their periodic spasms of hostility and rage because they were so cruelly betrayed. They might then redefine vindictiveness as "taking care of myself." They might reinterpret revenge as "teaching them a lesson" and describe their belligerent judgments as "telling it like it is."

Let me emphasize again that such reactions are not wrong or reprehensible. They are often part of a normal grieving process; they are steps toward acceptance and resolution. However, healing and growth are arrested when we overly identify with such responses—when we fail to do our deeper work.

Those who get stuck in shame may find a curious kind of gratification by resigning themselves to the self-image of being a loser. They may find a peculiar solace in giving up on themselves and on life.

Other individuals may find some measure of satisfaction in their sanctimonious anger and hostile judgments toward their betraying partner. They may tell themselves, "I've been wronged. *I* was faithful and loyal. *I* was committed to the marriage." Such individuals see themselves as sincere, trustworthy, and mature, while viewing their partner as vile, irresponsible, and infantile.

You have probably met people who, years after a bitter divorce or separation, continue to talk about their ex-partner as if their showdown happened yesterday. Sadly, their lives have failed to move forward. They remain preoccupied with the past, thereby *betraying their own journey toward greater love, joy, and wisdom.*

It can be emotionally gratifying to hold a position of being right and virtuous. However, as Caesar was warned by his wife, Calpurnia, in Shakespeare's play *Julius Caesar,* oftentimes our "wisdom is consumed in confidence." Our smug, shortsighted positions disable us from seeing reality clearly and overcoming the arrogance of certainty.

Deeper dimensions of growth become possible once we set aside our preoccupation with issues of right and wrong, or good and bad. After all, *even if we are right, the point is that we are still hurting.* Even if we are good, we are the ones who continue to suffer by nursing our grudge, living in the past, and sharpening our mental arguments in a feeble attempt to reassure ourselves that we really are okay.

Whether or not we are right is largely irrelevant. If we seek refuge by clinging to our cherished beliefs, as though fondling a revered source of life-sustenance, we foster an insidious thought addiction that removes us from any lasting source of healing and growth. Being right is of little consequence. Discovering the *right manner of inquiry*—into ourselves and into the truth—is what will really help us heal and grow.

Oftentimes we are treated cruelly and unjustly. Life sometimes seems unfair. Even so, it is more productive and empowering to embrace our hurt, investigate how we may have contributed to the betrayal, and discover avenues of growth amidst our pain. Doing so is the surest way to restore self-esteem, ease our hurt, and build more satisfying, trusting relationships in the future.

NOTES

1. G. Rico, *Pain and Possibility: Writing Your Way through Personal Crisis* (Los Angeles: Tarcher, 1991), 101, 104.

2. The stages of dying outlined in Kubler-Ross's classic book *Death: The Final Stage of Growth* (Englewood Cliffs, NJ: Prentice-Hall, 1975) are (1) denial, (2) rage and anger, (3) bargaining, (4) depression, and (5) acceptance. Individuals do not necessarily go through such stages sequentially. Likewise, those experiencing betrayal do not necessarily experience each of these responses. However, many people dealing with betrayal experience a process that partakes of many of these stages. Also, it is quite common to flip-flop between these various stages, such as between anger and sadness.

3. S. Campbell, *The Couple's Journey* (San Luis Obispo, CA: Impact Publishers, 1980), 43.

4. *San Francisco Chronicle,* 17 Feb. 1991, This World section.

5. J. Hillman, *Loose Ends: Primary Papers in Archetypal Psychology* (Dallas: Spring Publications, 1975), 73.

6. An exception is made here for those who tend to repress anger and become depressed as a result. For example, those who have endured physical or sexual abuse as children may have a difficult time affirming their anger.

7. A. W. Schaef, *When Society Becomes an Addict* (San Francisco: Harper & Row, 1987), 123.

8. John Taylor, "Don't Blame Me—The New Culture of Victimization," *New York Magazine,* 3 June 1991.

9. Ibid.

10. Ibid.

CHAPTER 3

What Underlies Our Common Reactions?

> No one ever taught us how to be in our hurt so that
> it could unfold into a better place. . . . We became
> masters of distracting ourselves from pain. . . . We
> hold at arm's length and try to control what we can-
> not accept. . . . Can I find some way to be a little more
> friendly with my feelings that are so hard to deal with?
> PETER CAMPBELL AND
> EDWIN MCMAHON[1]

EXPERIENCING shock, shame, depression, and anger and making blameful judgments are common steps along the path of recovery from betrayal. Sadly, many people find a seemingly comfortable resting place in one or more of these reactions. They take shelter in one narrow band of emotions, laden with skewed interpretations arising from the particular emotional responses toward which they gravitate. Those who leap into anger and rage might view their loss as a confirmation that men or women are indeed untrustworthy; those leaning toward shame and depression might repeat the forlorn refrain "I'll never have a good relationship."

When we get stuck in circumscribed reactions to betrayal, we choke off our more subtle inner experience. We circumvent the unexplored ground that must be traversed if we are truly to heal and grow. It's like turning back on an unknown trail. We do not know what lies ahead and the weather appears unfavorable. Being frightened, we retreat to the apparent security of the known. And yet, if only we could gingerly walk a few steps forward—just up ahead the weather suddenly clears and the path graciously opens.

In order to heal from betrayal, we must take the next step of uncovering the factors that underlie, if not drive, our immediate reactions. What propels us to seek revenge? What prompts us to sink into shame or become lost in unproductive judgments? Can we get our life back? Can we open ourselves to loving someone new in due time, rather than betray ourselves by abandoning life and love?

Our initial reactions to betrayal, which so often injure others and ourselves, are propelled by complex factors. The major areas I will address include unrealistic expectations and romantic fantasies, disowned hurt and grief, the fear of abandonment, and the shame of failure. The first category involves cognitive factors—beliefs that distort our feelings and shape our behavior. The other categories involve emotional factors—feelings that control and dominate us when they remain split off from awareness, rather than embraced.

UNREALISTIC EXPECTATIONS AND ROMANTIC FANTASIES

Distinguishing our own beliefs from those imposed by our culture is as meticulously challenging as microsurgery. The ideas and values we internalize through spending thousands of hours with parents and teachers become an integral, seemingly "natural" part of us.

This process of adaptation and acculturation happens to children in all cultures. We may observe it in the political "brainwashing" of children in other societies. Watching television, we may be astonished to observe malleable children in developing countries engage in fervent, nationalistic marches and sing political songs hailing their leaders. The ways our own children are shaped by society may appear less obvious.

Children develop their sense of self through contact with their social environment. There is no other way for human beings to form an initial sense of identity. Much of what is internalized is a confused composite of the cultural norms and romantic notions that dominate our search for acceptance and love. Chasing after distorted images of love can lead to pain and confusion. Hearing the quiet call of what is really possible can inspire us with a richer, fuller life.

One of the more difficult arts of living involves a continual assessment of whether our expectations *exceed what is reasonable* or *minimize what is possible.* Excessively high expectations set us up for a hard fall when reality rudely intrudes on our plans and designs. Excessively low expectations rob us of a greater personal joy and happiness.

In my view, the Western notion of romantic love that blossomed in medieval Europe was an evolutionary advance over the attitudes of earlier millennia. Then, the selection of mates was arranged by elders to fulfill duty and obligation, rather than to satisfy personal tastes. However, this advance was accompanied by assorted fairy tales and fantasies, which on the one hand sparked the imagination, but on the other hand saturated our consciousness with fanciful, grandiose hopes.

On the positive side, quixotic myths and romantic musings awaken us to the possibilities of erotic pleasure, exalted love, and deeper fulfillment. But the distorted way that romantic love is presented in our culture (the absence of struggle, pain, and work) impregnates us with a host of related beliefs and notions that distort and overstate what a partnership can provide. It is when we swallow these Disney-tainted myths whole, without realizing that they are meant only to offer inspiration and guidance—a taste of possibilities, not a detailed map to our destination—that we oversimplify what it takes to build a satisfying relationship.

Some of these romantic notions—distorted offshoots of mythopoetic tales—are explained in *Being Intimate.* Included among them is the notion that there is only one other person we can love deeply in this life and that once we marry this special person, we'll be forever happy. This belief deludes us into thinking that our salvation lies merely in finding the *right person,* rather than doing the *right kind of work* within ourselves and within the relationship. Or we may believe that if someone really loves us, then it becomes his or her job to intuit all of our needs and give us exactly what we want whenever we want it—regardless of what our partner's feelings and needs might be. Accepting a romantized image of "easy" love, we might also assume that emotions of anger and hurt spell doom for the relationship, rather than use pain and conflict to learn more about ourselves and our partner, thereby growing closer.

A flight into betrayal is a common reaction to our frustrated romantic longings. When Katie's marriage reached a new depth of exasperation, she hoped for a romantic rescue through secret affairs. She became involved with men whom she believed really cared about her, unlike her distant husband. Later, she discovered they were only interested in sex. In retrospect, she realized that "I was looking for a fantasy, for someone to take care of me. It would have been wonderful if Prince Charming came along and said, 'All you have to do is sit around and look gorgeous.' I was looking for someone to rescue me and protect me, to take me out of that miserable situation."

It is one thing to intellectually recognize that romantic fantasies are indeed fantasies. It's a more formidable task to relinquish our emotional attachment to them. Like a jack-in-the-box, they have a way of rearing their alluring heads when least expected. Reversing the effects of these tenacious beliefs requires a continual act of recognition. We can then gently challenge these beliefs whenever we notice them arising and replace them with more accurate understandings—ones that may not be as comforting, but that will better prepare us for the sometimes uplifting, sometimes unnerving journey of love.

Revising Our Romantic Beliefs

Outmoded presumptions must be supplanted by a bodily felt recognition of what it really takes to create meaningful relationships. For example, those pursuing personal growth realize that building intimacy requires showing our feelings, accepting our differences, and communicating effectively. Such goals are vitally important, yet they may appear trite after a while. It remains a herculean task for those of us who "know" these things in our minds to *really* know them—that is, to grasp these truths deep within our body and soul, or as the poet Yeats put it, to "think with the marrow bone."

We may appreciate the notion that a maturing love can withstand the expression of "negative" feelings. We may realize that expressing our feelings and needs is vital for the growth of a healthy partnership. We may recognize that we need to respect our partner's feelings, wants, and boundaries. And yet all this sounds like gobbledygook when we are seized by our own compelling desires and emotional reactions that are spurred by romantic beliefs and unrealistic expectations. "I was just desperate," I often hear from people whose needs outpaced their clarity, "I felt out of control. I lost myself in the relationship."

Beliefs shape behavior. Operating out of enticing romantic ideals and expectancies makes us more likely to betray our partner when reality fails to coincide with our socially ingrained images of how a partnership is "supposed" to be. When the reality of our daily lives fails to match the unreality of our impelling images, we have a clear choice: We can either reevaluate those images and beliefs, or, like Madame Bovary, we can betray our partner and continue the mythological search for the "perfect" mate. Sadly, many of us choose the latter course, roaming from relationship to relationship without knowing how to create a connection of depth—an enduring intimacy.

It takes more than reevaluating outmoded beliefs if we are truly to change. An intense emotional charge infuses our romantic notions, creating an alloy that isn't very malleable. An expectation to be cared for, if not adored, may be fueled by the fierce fears and hurts stemming from our past deprivation. If in our earlier years we didn't sufficiently experience the emotional balm of being accepted and affirmed for ourselves alone, we never internalized a sense of being acceptable and lovable. We may then be on the lookout for the perfect, all-giving mother or father we never had, the prince or princess who can certify that we are indeed precious and good.

Once we find someone we're attracted to, we may vigilantly scour for signs that we cannot trust this person (or anyone) to be supportive and understanding. Of course, whether or not we are inclined to extend support and understanding is irrelevant to our hurt, neglected "inner child," who is enveloped in its own narcissistic world within us. But the point here is that we may turn people away when they fail to match our romantic notions of perfect love.

In order to move forward in life, we need to acknowledge our fears and reevaluate our beliefs, and we may need to grieve the loss stemming from broken trust and insufficient love in childhood. Otherwise, we will never break our attachment to the painful past. Instead, we'll tenaciously behold our partner as a parent substitute. We'll unwittingly place our partner in a role that he or she never signed up for, and that can never be fulfilled. When the inevitable happens—when our hopes and longings are frustrated—we may feel betrayed, which may prompt us to betray our partner in turn. In reality, it may be only our fear-based attachments and distorted fantasies that have been betrayed.

Our resulting disappointment can provide an opportunity to update our view of reality, as well as *embrace our grief and pain with the same kind of compassion and understanding that we seek from others.* Unless we use our hurt and disappointment as an impetus to look more deeply into ourselves and life, we are destined to repeat the same tired patterns; we are condemned to continually confirm the erroneous premise that there's no love for us.

DISOWNED HURT AND GRIEF

When we are betrayed by a partner, we may further betray ourselves by abandoning the hurt inner place within us that needs gentle, caring attention. For a time, we may need to distance ourselves from an overwhelming torrent of hurt. But at some point, we must accept our hurt if we truly want to recover from betrayal.

Many of us find it easier to brace ourselves against our hurt than to embrace it. We find it more convenient to avoid our hurt by holding others responsible for it than to turn responsively to our hurt and hold it lovingly. It is more gratifying to diagnose what's wrong with our partner than to explore where we may have gone astray. It's easier to poke rudely at our ex-partner's tender spots than to turn tenderly toward the center of our own pain so that it might heal through kindhearted attention. By seeking solace in outer-directed maneuvers, we keep our attention off our pain; we distract ourselves from ourselves. Meanwhile, by defying our pain, we deify it—we support its continuation and make it all-powerful over us. As one client put it, "I keep finding ways to push away my hurt, but it always comes roaring back. I guess it's finally time to look at it."

Fearing Our Hurt

It is a platitude to suggest that betrayal hurts. Yet there's a striking difference between knowing that we've been hurt and *allowing ourselves to experience the full depth and breadth of that hurt.* Fearful of opening to the varying layers of our hurt, we might try to rationalize it away or distract ourselves from it. We may succumb to resignation. Or we may fight against our pain by grasping destructive hatred, as writer James Baldwin explains: "I imagine one of the reasons people cling to their hates so stubbornly is because they sense, once hate is gone, they will be forced to deal with pain."[2]

People distance themselves from their pain for many reasons. For some, experiencing hurt might remind them of the unspeakable pain and isolation of childhood. Others might fear that if they allow their hurt to stream forth, they might unleash a flood of never-ending tears, or, even worse, go crazy. They conclude that it's too painful to experience hurt, that it will destroy them. In reality, this hurt must be accepted and felt if it's ever to be released—and beyond that, if they want to be free to love and trust again.

I've never met anyone who has gone crazy by embracing their hurt. To the contrary, I've worked with many people who have become deeply troubled due to an inability to feel the hurt that stirs within them. Such individuals remain chronically angry, arrogant, bitter, or depressed as a result of disassociating from their hurt, a hurt that lingers despite heroic efforts to suppress it.

Still others maintain that it is masochistic to feel their hurt. Men in particular often believe it's morbid to hurt. I've often heard men say, "What do you mean, let myself feel hurt? That sounds ridiculous!" Instead, their heart becomes cold and rigid; they become armored in anger. Other people try to replace pain with positive thinking or affirmations. Although these efforts have value at times, we remain disconnected from ourselves if we do not simultaneously embrace our authentic feelings.

Others mistakenly equate hurt and sadness with depression. In reality, a state of depression is quite different from experiencing the enormously rich and vitally alive emotions of hurt and sorrow. Depression occurs when there is a dire *lack* of feeling. It is a condition in which we remain numb and anesthetized to life. Our soul shrivels.

Allowing ourselves to experience whatever hurt may be present can actually feel good. As Beth discovered as she faced the pain of being left for a younger woman, "I kind of enjoyed the intensity of the pain. I know I was fully alive. I wasn't covering up anything. As much pain as I was in, I also knew how vitally alive I was."

Self-Compassion versus Self-Pity

Some people who are repulsed by their hurt hold the conviction that they're only "feeling sorry for themselves" if they grant their hurt the space to be present. Taking refuge in a distorted pride, they maintain that they don't want to "wallow" in their hurt. So instead, they push their hurt away and live with the self-deception that they're done with it. Of course, *it* isn't done with them. They do not realize that betrayal represents a cataclysmic loss that takes time to heal.

Self-compassion is vastly different from self-pity. Self-pity means feeling sadness for ourselves. Self-compassion means feeling love for ourselves as we feel our sadness. Self-pity means standing outside ourselves and lamenting our despised condition. Self-compassion means sitting in ourselves and embracing our sorrow, a sorrow that we may gradually recognize as a part of the human condition. Self-pity pulls us into a soppy sinkhole of self-absorption and despair. Having self-compassion for our pain leads us out of pain; it provides the salve we need to heal.

Self-pity means holding our pain with fear and judgment. Compassion means embracing it with love.

Other Reasons for Fleeing from Our Hurt

Some people flee from hurt because they do not want to appear too different from the mass of humanity, whom they fantasize as "having it all together." They assume that everyone but themselves is frolicking in success and merrily enjoying life. In reality, most people are adept at hiding their blunders, heartaches, and dissatisfactions. They feel ashamed of their vulnerability and pain, which they interpret as meaning that they're defective or imperfect. They tell themselves to "snap out of it." They find inventive ways to evade and elude their sorrows and discomfort and not let others see it.

Of course, if we feel ashamed of our pain, we will want nothing to do with it. But there is a huge difference between being *responsible for* our pain and being *responsive to* it. If we believe we are responsible for it—that we caused it because we're a jerk, etc.—we'll shut off our feelings because that burden is too much to bear. Or we'll fervently blame others as an alternative to saddling ourselves with such a heavy responsibility. Finding the strength and clarity to relinquish self-blame enables us to acknowledge and embrace our pain without accusing ourselves or blaming others. Accepting our legitimate pain frees us to be ourselves.

Perhaps men in our culture are especially prone to hide their hurt. After volatile breakups, I've often heard women say, *"He* seems to be taking it fine. When I want to discuss things to feel more resolved, he says he already feels resolved!"

Some hurting men try to dilute their pain through fervent requests to get back together. Others are more willing to acknowledge and experience the same kind of gut-wrenching pain that women often experience.

Both men and women who take a "practical" position insist that nothing positive can be accomplished by experiencing hurt. They ask incredulously, "What good does it do to feel hurt?" They maintain that hurt simply hurts and they willfully refuse to tolerate it. They seek fast relief by redirecting their energies toward more "productive" pursuits, such as work, hobbies, or television. Or they distract themselves by drinking, eating, or shopping. Remaining oblivious to their pain, they persuade themselves to "put on a happy face" or "look at the brighter side" as they forge ahead into life's next adventure. At times, we may need some relief from unrelenting pain, but if this becomes a habit of avoidance and denial, we betray ourselves.

Others shun the hurt of betrayal due to false pride or stubbornness that says, "I won't give him the satisfaction of knowing that he hurt me!" Those who hide their hurt to spite others are only lengthening their own sentence of isolation and suffering, even if their stifled pain is experienced only as a vaguely felt numbness.

Displacing Our Hurt

Many people have been so hurt in their past that they've never felt safe enough to allow their pain to surface. Experiencing childhood hurt was not an option if insensitive parents or teachers punished them for crying, or humiliated them for feeling weak and vulnerable. Then, instead of discovering a source of healing and strength by embracing sadness or hurt, they had few alternatives but to circumvent their pain or futilely rail against it by condemning, blaming, and manipulating their world.

Such individuals may carry a latent fury that they periodically unleash upon the world, or, more specifically, upon innocent others who are unwitting representatives of the world. They are oblivious to their neglected hurt, which is the driving force that energizes their cleverly justified fury toward innocent individuals. They are unaware that by offending and attacking people, they're surreptitiously acting out their hurt—in effect, *coercing others to feel the hurt that they themselves refuse to face.*[3]

Object relations therapists refer to this dynamic as projective identification, in which people unknowingly act in ways that transfer unwanted feelings onto others. As explained by therapist Sheldon Cashdan, "Without realizing it, the target unwittingly becomes a repository for the feelings . . . of the person doing the projecting. . . . It is as if one individual forces another to play a role in the enactment of that person's internal drama."[4] Rather than embrace such feelings as fear, hurt, and anger, these people act in ways that induce others to experience the feelings they find distasteful or threatening. Such individuals will never achieve a stable sense of maturity until they embrace the hurt they so desperately fear, rather than continue to criticize and assault others, delivering onto them the feelings that they reject within themselves.

These pain-spreading reactions neglect to consider the transformative power of hurt when approached in the right way. As we soften into a certain quality of pain that we've resigned ourselves to endure, *we may discover a precious pearl within the deeper chamber of our hurt.*

FEAR OF ABANDONMENT

Another factor fueling our typical reactions to betrayal is the fear of abandonment that operates just beneath our conscious awareness. To be abandoned means to be deserted, to be cast out, to be utterly alone in the universe, adrift in the twilight zone of isolation and emptiness. This fear of being alone is closely related to the fear of dying, the fear that we may suffer in some indescribable way or that we'll no longer exist.

The fear of abandonment is the primary terror of the helpless infant. This fear subsides as the mother provides ample time and caring attention to reassure the infant that it is not alone in this environment that we call the world. This world becomes less hostile when the infant is fed when hungry, physically comforted when frightened, and encouraged to sleep when tired. As the infant internalizes the consistent presence of the mother, it feels safer in the world—it begins to trust.

When, as infants, we have not received adequate nonverbal reassurances, we remain uncertain about our value and desirability. Adult relationships become troublesome when serious doubts linger about our worth and lovability. As we enter relationships in which we begin to experience the acceptance we've always wanted, we become especially susceptible to the terror of being abandoned or betrayed.

Betrayal and abandonment are allied concepts, but there are subtle differences in their meaning. Betrayal implies a breach of trust. When we are betrayed, that trust is shattered. Abandonment has a broader meaning. We can be abandoned without being betrayed. For example, a friend may decide to move out of state. A man might feel abandoned if his partner makes love with someone else, despite their earlier agreement not to be monogamous. In both instances, there may be a painful sense of abandonment, but there has been no betrayal, no broken promises or agreements.

Some portion of the hostility, anger, and rage that are common reactions to betrayal may be generated by our fear of being abandoned and alone. For example, our rage and anger may be a plea for our partner to stay bonded to us, or a furious protest against the dreadful prospect of being deserted. By discerning whether this fear of abandonment is operating, we might better understand what's really happening in our inner world. We can then address our more primary fear of being alone (as discussed later in this book), rather than get lost in our secondary reactions.

The fear of abandonment and isolation underlies many of our attempts to control others through subtle forms of deceit and manipulation. For example, we may administer secret "trust tests" to detect whether others are really committed to us, or we may devise strategies to make others dependent upon us. A man may encourage his partner to quit her job, or he may withhold validation or actively criticize her, thereby keeping her preoccupied with earning his approval. A woman may go out of her way to please her partner, such as by offering sex when she's not in the mood or by withholding opinions that might clash with his. In time, the deceit and manipulations that stem from fears of abandonment can undermine trust and create conflicts, which could lead to betrayal.

THE SHAME OF FAILURE

The tendency to associate pain with failure is another major reason we minimize our hurt and deny our grief. Having been betrayed, we surmise that we are a glaring failure, that we're not good enough. Neil, whose wife walked out of the relationship, typifies the American male who is bred to succeed and excel: "I have a hard time accepting failure. It's hard to accept that I failed in my marriage. I didn't want the relationship to end. It made me feel so powerless." Having conquered many obstacles on his path toward enormous success in business, he had difficulty accepting the fact that he couldn't conquer the problems in his marriage.

If we associate the pain of betrayal with failure and defeat, it is no wonder we refuse to fully acknowledge our pain. Through a curious twist of logic, we believe that if we can swindle our hurt out of its right to exist, we have not really failed. Then, instead of facing our disappointment, we may cynically complain, offer excuses, or become bitter and withdrawn.

When betrayal has shaken our self-worth, we may be paralyzed by the shame of failing. We may be unable to embrace our shame as a normal part of being human. We may believe that it's wrong to feel shame, or we may be afraid that if we allow our shame to be felt, we'll remain its permanent prisoner. We may imagine that letting down our defenses and allowing ourselves to be washed over by shame would lead to our demise. But if we could allow ourselves to experience the emotion of shame without being ashamed of our shame, then rather than disintegrate, we could begin to reintegrate this emotion into our overall sense of self. This would enable us to feel more whole, as well as safer in the world. As one client expressed it, "It's becoming more okay for me to feel my shame, my fears, and my hurts. I guess it's becoming more okay to see that I'm human. I'm becoming stronger, but in a way that's different than what I thought strength was."

Shame and fear are especially gripping when we believe that we should be able to control everything in our lives. But life keeps trying to teach us that there are things we cannot control. Being a control freak is a cruel setup for shame and humiliation when reality fails to conform to our wishes. As Anne Wilson Schaef puts it, "When we believe that we can and should be able to control our world and it turns out that we cannot, . . . we experience failure."[5]

The possibility of resolution and redemption arises as we realize that our failing in any relationship or enterprise does not mean that *we* are a failure. It only means that we are learning some painful lessons on the road to greater wisdom or a more satisfying endeavor. Just as bankruptcy is often a common step toward success in business, divorce can be a common step toward more rewarding relationships.

Experiencing failure or shame is nothing to be ashamed of. We are not a failure when we fail. There is a plaque in my office that reads "It is a mistake to suppose that people succeed through success; they much more often succeed through failure." The artist Nicolaides reminds us that "the sooner you make your first 5,000 mistakes, the sooner you will be able to correct them." If we can disentangle our shame and pain from the insidious thought that we are defective, then we speed our recovery from betrayal. If we can learn to embrace our natural grief and sorrow, these emotions gradually pass, leaving us emotionally freer and mentally clearer to make wise choices.

NOTES

1. P. Campbell and E. McMahon, *Bio-Spirituality: Focusing As a Way to Grow* (Chicago: University of Loyola Press, 1985), 15–17.

2. Quoted in *Sunbeams: A Book of Quotations*, ed. Sy Safransky (Berkeley, CA: North Atlantic Books, 1990), 91.

3. Psychotherapists might especially recognize this dynamic in those who are characterized as having borderline or narcissistic conditions.

4. S. Cashdan, *Object Relations Therapy* (New York: Norton, 1988), 56–57.

5. A. W. Schaef, *When Society Becomes an Addict* (San Francisco: Harper & Row, 1987), 45.

CHAPTER 4

Befriending Our Hurt

The deeper that sorrow carves into your being, the more joy you can contain. . . . When you are sorrowful look again in your heart, and you shall see that in truth you are weeping for that which has been your delight.

KAHLIL GIBRAN[1]

Many people have learned to avoid uncomfortable or difficult emotions because they've been so heavily burdened with painful feelings from their past. There may have been so much fear that they no longer feel it. There may have been so much hurt that they may not recognize the mechanism by which they become anesthetized to it. I often hear clients say, "I've had enough hurt!" Growing up with a steady diet of hurt, they no longer allow themselves to experience it. Doing so would restimulate the anguish endured during a time when there was meager support and insufficient awareness to deal effectively with pain.

Instead of acknowledging the pain and hurt that arises in life, many people create an appearance of being cool, cheery, or "together." They present a forced smile that betrays hidden discontent. Others go through life with few displays of emotion. They don't allow themselves to get enthusiastic about anything, except perhaps, while taking in Sunday football games or buying a new car.

If we grew up in an environment where there was repeated shaming by parents, siblings, peers, or teachers, our survival depended upon deadening ourselves to the shame of being ridiculed, the fear of being rejected, and the hurt of being criticized and controlled. But if we continue the once necessary habit of stifling pain, we remain alienated from ourselves. In our continued attempt to dodge pain, we create a false self that we present to the world, one that buffers us from direct, and potentially unpleasant, contact with others. At the same time, we fail to avail ourselves of our body's natural facility for grieving the loss that betrayal is.

SOCIAL CONSPIRACY TO AVOID HURT

In our quietly desperate attempt to evade hurt, we adopt behaviors that dull our sensitivities to the natural hurts that accompany being alive. We develop the habit of overeating in order to fill a gnawing emptiness in our soul. We use alcohol or drugs to replace our discontent with more pleasant sensations. We drink coffee to get us going in the morning and keep us motivated throughout the day. We pursue activities that distract us from our underlying discontent, such as watching television, working excessively, and gambling on lotteries or the stock market. More subtly, we may weave sophisticated systems of thought that make us feel better by bolstering the illusion that we are good, important, and right, and that others are less than noble.

These activities, substances, and beliefs mask our pain or make it more bearable. They become, in effect, the addictions of modern life, ones that pass as natural because almost everyone else seems to agree that they are normal, even necessary, to modern-day fulfillment. Nevertheless, the emotional aches that are part of life persist. By cleverly dodging them, we pay the tragic price of betraying ourselves.

Those reluctant to feel their hurt are here advised to remember that their choice is clear: Either they suffer some pain now, or they will suffer now *and* suffer later. The sooner they gently embrace the natural grief that is theirs, the sooner they can begin to attain some peace in relation to a painful event. The more they postpone opening to their hurt, the more sharply it will arise in the future.

Psychotherapist Maggie Kline makes a useful distinction between pain and suffering.[2] According to Kline, we can release our pain only when it is honestly faced; this frees us to experience joy. Chronic emotional suffering is the consequence of not facing our pain. It is a self-victimization through which we avoid the uncomfortable feelings that are a necessary part of emotional and spiritual growth. In short, opening to our legitimate pain frees us from pain; avoiding pain leads to long-term suffering.

The False Hope of a Pain-Free Existence

Society conspires to brainwash its members to believe that they're not supposed to hurt. This view is seductive; we are enticed by the prospect of a pain-free existence. The part of us that fears pain (or is ashamed of it) is eager to believe that there is a cure readily at hand. So we take an aspirin or sleeping pill, or get a stronger prescription. Sadly, we may then become oblivious to the fertile feelings that teem with important messages regarding how best to live our lives.

Drug companies spend billions of dollars each year researching the latest ways to help people escape the natural pains of life. They spend even more training consumers to believe that if they hurt, modern chemistry has the remedy.[3] This is not to condemn the selective use of drugs and medication to help alleviate human suffering, but it is to expose a culturally conditioned mentality that sends us fleeing to the drug store or the liquor store or the refrigerator to deal with our daily dose of pain.

Society has so conspired to dull us to the natural pains of life that we may be persuaded to believe that all forms of discomfort are unnatural and unnecessary. And so we seek technological solutions to the discomforts "inflicted" by nature. We install climate control devices in our home, office, and car that keep us from feeling too hot or too cold. We store our food supply in energy-guzzling refrigerators and freezers. We use microwave ovens to satisfy our hunger instantly. We rely on cars and airplanes to take us wherever we wish to go. Future generations will pity those poor humans, living before the twenty-first century, who survived without fax machines, garage door openers, and satellite dishes providing 120 channels of entertainment.

The attempt to subdue and dominate our natural pain— rather than use it to discover a deeper part of us, or awaken to something that needs attention in our lives—creates a split in our soul. Rampant consumerism is a modern-day response to an empty, fragmented existence.

The Hidden Price of Comfort-Seeking

In our determined dash for a life of ease, we pay little attention to the long-term cost that will be exacted. By blindly pursuing comfort and convenience, we're on a galloping course toward destruction of the planet itself. If we continue this self-aggrandizing trend toward exploiting and betraying nature rather than befriending it—as we deplete the ozone, cram the atmosphere with greenhouse gases, and destroy the rain forests—we will pay a collective price for our appetite to gain pleasure and avoid pain. In precisely the same way that we increase our suffering by denying our personal pain, much of humanity (not to mention scores of innocent species) may eventually sacrifice their lives for the immediate comforts demanded by the ever-growing, resource-hoarding haves of the world.

How dependent have we become on sheer physical comfort? How bitterly do we complain when electrical power failures remind us of the artificial lifestyle we have become dependent upon? How isolated have we become from people living in less affluent countries, or from the have-nots in our own neighborhoods, who have yet to join the social campaign to eradicate pain?

Can we be responsive to others' cries of hurt when we have become callous to the pain in our own lives? We can never learn and grow from our pain when we treat it as something to conquer and control.

This is not to propose that we live in huts and wash our clothes by the river, nor is it to suggest that we seek out pain or idealize it in some perverse way (it will find us, ready or not). Instead, it is to remind us that pain is a natural part of life and that if we go to extremes to eradicate it, we diminish our humanness, as well as our capacity for compassion (as I will explain later). Pain is inherent in living and loving.

When we defy the feeling-encoded messages our body is trying to give us in the best way it knows how, our body, in its never-ending creativity, will soon deliver a much stronger message. Just as nature eventually rebels when we dominate it, our inner nature rebels when we mindlessly manipulate ourselves. The personal pain that we so desperately try to suppress inexorably rises to the surface, perhaps in the form of a headache, hypertension, or some debilitating illness.

If we ignore our personal pain, we can never uncover the real source of our dissatisfactions, just as we can never reverse ecological disasters if we remain oblivious to the silent cries in the animal and plant kingdoms. By blotting out pain, we will never awaken to the fact that life is trying to tell us something. Although we may defy reality by temporarily obliterating that dreaded enemy pain—perhaps by distracting ourselves or erecting firmer defenses—our pain will eventually be heard.

Pain is nature's way of getting our attention. When we're hurting, *there's something we need to notice.* If we can welcome the life messages that speak through our body and find the wisdom to decipher them, then we can move forward in our lives. We can heal and grow from betrayal. We can learn lessons that lead to greater wisdom and more fulfilling relationships. But in order to do so, we must look and listen. If we betray ourselves by ignoring the whispers of life, we will eventually encounter its deafening roars. As one man put it, "I finally had to look at myself. I couldn't put it off any longer. My life was going downhill fast."

TAMING THE FEAR OF BEING HURT

We are born into the world equipped with a self-regulating capacity to respond to the painful events of life. Young children exemplify this natural ability to respond to life's insults. The natural reaction of a child hurt by the cruel words of a friend is to cry. Children release much of their pain through their body's mechanism of crying; then they reenter the playground. Somewhere during the process of earning our adult credentials, many of us forget how to cry. Our capacity to deal with hurt is then seriously impaired.

When we deaden ourselves to emotional hurt and grief, we have not eradicated these emotions. We have merely relegated them to some dark corner within us, where they operate secretly and insidiously. For a time, these emotions may appear to be contained. But just as toxic wastes eventually leak from their sealed containers, so will the "emotional wastes" that we retain within our bodies eventually rise again.

Some Ill Effects of Suppressing Grief

The effort required to seal off threatening feelings creates an inner disturbance of being, which generates such symptoms as emotional distancing, compulsive joking, insensitivity, irritability, anxiety, depression, and hostility. These symptoms lead to strained relationships. The energy we require when we distance ourselves from threatening feelings may also create a background feeling of fear and agitation, one that we may find barely noticeable but that often irritates those who interact with us. Although some people may not detect that we're ill at ease with ourselves, they may feel uncomfortable in our presence because we are painfully disconnected. We are quietly driven by a pain we refuse to face.

Another ill effect of repressing our natural hurts is that we may unknowingly be creating disease within ourselves. Some studies suggest that when pent-up emotions are not released through our innate capacity to cry, these emotions may find outlets in stress-related diseases, such as colitis, ulcers, and hypertension.[4] Biochemical analysis has shown that crying may be a chemical release for emotional stress. When we cry, we also release a chemical known as leucine enkephalin, which is one of the brain's natural opiates associated with pain relief.[5]

Finding Relief and Strength by Attending to Our Hurt

Today it is almost antisocial to suggest that it's okay to hurt. Many people wonder, why should I feel pain if I don't have to? Why should I expose myself to potential hurt or let others get away with hurting me?

Central to our recovery from betrayal is our willingness to feel the hurt that we have been intently avoiding. Our pain needs a certain kind of attention, which Peter Campbell and Ed McMahon, who are psychotherapists and Catholic priests, refer to as a "caring-feeling presence."[6] Just as a hurting child needs attention and caring, so do our hurting heart and knotted stomach need the healing power of our loving presence— persistent, gentle, nonjudgmental attention.

Opening to our pain can lead to a subtle, if not dramatic, transformation of how we experience ourselves and relate to others. As our vulnerable core begins to thaw, we awaken to an inner center that is vibrant with our hurts and joys. As we no longer struggle against our hurt, we witness a stilling of the turbulent waves of our mind and emotions.

We cannot enjoy true self-esteem and autonomy when our life is subtly animated by the fear of being hurt. As we tame this fear, we live more in harmony with life; we discover more peace within ourselves and become less defensive and protec tive. Other people disturb us less as we become less troubled by the fear and hurt that they may trigger in us.

As we find our way to embracing our hurt, it loses its dreaded sting. Just as a hurting child stops crying when enfolded in the arms of a caring, understanding parent, so does our own hurt subside in the very process of our loving and understanding ourselves. A calm center of vitality may then emerge—an inner peace that's always there, but that we experience more tangibly as we accept what we cannot control. Hurt becomes less disturbing as we learn that not only does it not have to destroy us, it can actually make us stronger and more open to life.

Discovering Meaning in Our Pain

By turning to the core of our pain, we may come to understand its hidden meaning. This meaning is accessible if we can patiently attend to its felt quality. As our pain feels warmly welcomed, it may be able to reveal precious gems of wisdom, or a clearer sense of what we've lost or what we overlooked in the partnership.

As we focus on the pain of betrayal, we may remember past losses that are reminiscent of our current one ("This has happened before"). We may feel sad to recall the good times that are now a thing of the past ("I miss holidays and special times together"). We may long for the rich moments of companionship or sexual union we once enjoyed ("I miss the lovemaking; he was a very gentle lover"). We may be disappointed with ourselves for not noticing the early signs of trouble in the relationship ("I can't believe I didn't see it coming!"). We may regret not having been more communicative or more understanding ("I thought our communication was pretty good"). We may be sad to have come so close to finding love, only to be coldly deceived or rejected ("Everything was fine as far as I knew; life had never been better"). We may feel hurt that someone with whom we've been so close has taken a divergent path, or has shown contempt for our well-being; we may feel wounded because a partner who once seemed to cherish us is now intentionally harming us. As one distraught client put it, "Sure, there were problems, but I thought we *had* something together. But she's so cold and calculating now. It makes me wonder how much we ever meant to each other." As we experience the various dimensions of hurt and sorrow that are relevant for us (and perhaps share them with someone who cares), we take a further step toward freeing ourselves from the pain of betrayal.

Life invites us to experience the full flavor of its richness, including its triumphs and disappointments. The experience of hurting is closely connected with the experience of loving. Hurt is our natural response to our frustrated desire to love and be loved in its many variations. If we choke off our hurt, we simultaneously extinguish the awareness of our need to give and receive caring and tenderness. We smother the subtle awareness of our soul's longing to be lovingly united with another person.

Our hurt can educate us about ourselves and point us toward new, creative directions. As we discover the unique meaning of our hurt, we are reminded of what we need to be happy. We may discover new pathways ahead that would never have appeared unless we had used our hurt to help us find them.

NATURAL GRIEF

By allowing ourselves to experience our hurt and grief, we release past attachments. We disengage from former loyalties and reorient ourselves to a new life situation. Similar to the experience of grief when a loved one dies, the grief associated with betrayal is our body's way of letting go and readjusting. Through the process of feeling the pain of our loss, as well as whatever this loss means to us, we simultaneously release our hurt. Of course, recovering from betrayal takes time, often a year, two years, or even longer depending upon the severity of our loss, our history of past hurts, our capacity to deal with loss, and the frequency with which we are restimulated by unwanted or unhelpful contact.

When someone we love or desire betrays us, we are submerged in an unwelcome torrent of change. It hurts to realize that someone has lied to us, broken an agreement, or deserted us. We do not heal and readjust through a mere intellectual acceptance and matter-of-fact understanding, as Mr. Spock from "Star Trek" might attempt to do. Understanding and acceptance take root only as we tend caringly to the hurt that accompanies loss and betrayal.

As we anticipate a radically altered reality, we experience emotions. Fear is an emotion that alerts us to real or imagined danger. Anger is an emotion that provides protection or calls us to action. These emotions prepare us for change, for some kind of adaptation.

Sorrow and hurt tend to be emotions of release. As we experience them, and perhaps listen to what they have to say about our life situation, we begin to relinquish our pain and release the past. Experiencing our loss and hurt in a caring, feeling way ushers us toward acceptance of things as they are, which prepares us to welcome a new phase of our life.

Our evolution as individuals and as a society requires that we awaken to our body's natural mechanism of grieving. If we have no effective outlet to deal with the natural losses of life, then we'll desperately cling to well-worn defenses while circumventing situations that might lead to disappointment or abandonment. We'll be too afraid to risk reaching out, sharing how we really feel, asking for what we want, or giving our best. Instead of being our real self, we'll parade an inauthentic self to others. Rather than move toward more rewarding relationships, we may rest content with stagnant, abusive, or dissatisfying ones. Refusing to deal with the possibility of losing a relationship, we may let others exploit or mistreat us.

Unless we learn to grow through our hurt by bringing warmth and love to it, we will continue to act in ways that hurt ourselves and other people. We'll judge and condemn others and find fault with the world. Or we'll try to persuade others to change or conform to our viewpoints, perhaps so they can serve us better. In short, we'll scrutinize and dominate our outer world rather than attend to our inner world.

Focusing: A Way to Embrace Pain

Myriad techniques and approaches can guide us to an honest confrontation with pain and hurt. The educational approach known as Focusing, developed by Eugene Gendlin at the University of Chicago,[7] is one of the most direct and useful tools I've found to help individuals embrace the depth and richness of their own experience. Focusing provides a structure that supports us in welcoming the personal concerns, vague fears, and ill-defined hurts and sorrows that we so easily bypass in favor of the allure of quick fixes, such as formulas for positive thinking that are disguised forms of denying our feelings. By practicing the art of resting our attention on what is alive and real in our bodily-felt experience, we become less preoccupied with self-critical, unproductive efforts to "fix" ourselves. Instead, we foster an inner climate that lends itself to fresh perspectives and new directions. We're empowered to find *our* way toward *our* own truth.

Unlike our usual effort to solve problems in a purely mental way, we cultivate that same attitude of allowing that is central to meditation.[8] However, we do not go beneath or beyond the personal issues of our life. Instead, we allow them to "simmer"[9] in the warm embrace of our loving attention. We ask relevant questions and allow them to incubate in the deeper chamber of our being until a new shred of understanding, a welcome wave of relief, or our next small step forward in life is revealed.

More specifically, we might use an image of being with a hurting child as a way to find compassion toward our own pain. Or we might gently place our hand on the part of our body that experiences hurt, sorrow, or fear. Or we might consciously remind ourselves to be gentle, caring, or tender in relation to a hurting place inside ourselves.

However helpful any approach may be, we need to remember that techniques alone are not the answer; they are not cure-alls. They're helpful insofar as they provide an orientation, an aid to awareness. They direct us toward the general vicinity where healing and growth occur, but they do not guarantee that we'll find our way there.

Methods of personal growth that uncover our real feelings, needs, and motivations do not bestow magical cures, but they can provide a helpful structure if we simultaneously summon the courage to embrace these authentic—though potentially discomforting—experiences. At first, we may feel unsettled as we uncover new truth that can disturb our status quo. Experiential approaches such as Focusing are helpful insofar as they provide guidance in rediscovering our balance based on an ever-firmer grounding in what's true and real for us.

In his bestselling book, *Care of the Soul,* Thomas Moore invites us to add depth and spirituality to everyday life by nurturing our soul. He proposes that "Eventually, we might find that all emotions, all human activities, and all spheres of life have deep roots in the mysteries of the soul, and therefore are holy."[10] Focusing offers gentle guidance and caring reminders to embrace the mystery of our feelings, sensations, and intuitions that arise in response to life situations. By cultivating an interior "sacred space" or "safe space" to accommodate the hurts of our heart—as well as our joys—we are caring for our souls; we are doing soul work.[11]

When Celeste was left by her lover, she felt deeply hurt and confused. As I invited her to focus on her hurt—simply being with it in a gentle, heartful way—she began to acknowledge and accept feelings she'd been pushing away. Rather than telling herself that "I should be over this by now" or "I shouldn't let him get to me this way," she was able to find a place within herself that could be kind and caring toward her pain. She began to find the courage and compassion to say to herself, "It's okay to be with all this; I can be open to this hurt.

I know it won't destroy or debilitate me." By embracing her hurt over and over again, her tears softened the sting of her sorrow. She began to feel stronger, more alive, and more peaceful as she allowed herself to gently connect with what was real for her.

Allowing our soul to rise out of the ashes of betrayal is difficult to do alone. To help us feel safe, we may benefit by seeking the presence of a caring person who can extend empathy toward us and offer acceptance of the very feelings that we dread, and therefore reject. Betrayal means we've been hurt by another person. Rather than continue the betrayal by now betraying ourselves—closing down and vowing never to trust and love again—we need people, or at least one person, with whom we can share our pain openly. Sharing our story with a trusted counselor, spiritual guide, mentor, or good friend who can simply listen with kindness and sensitivity, we maintain a bridge to humanity, and to life. We gain great strength by feeling less alone and isolated. Also, by assimilating nurturance from outside ourselves, we may more easily give it *to* ourselves. And we may more easily put into practice our good ideas and noble intentions.

By relating to ourselves in a kindly manner, we begin the pivotal process of replacing inner criticism with self-acceptance. We affirm that we're okay just the way we are; our pain does not mean that we are ugly, flawed, or repulsive. By turning toward our pain in a gentle, caring way, we create conditions that awaken our latent compassion. As we love ourselves in this more tangible way, our defensiveness yields to a greater ease of being.[12] We rediscover a place of peace within ourselves. We gradually heal.

Finding Strength through Our Grief

By softening into our grief, we can become more compassionate toward ourselves and others. By being more kindly disposed toward our pain, we become a more whole, loving person; we grow toward our more bountiful human potential.

Rather than manipulate people and external circumstances, we can find the strength to trust that new directions will emerge as we "rest" within our hurt. For those new to this path, much faith is required to embrace what is normally cast off, whether we refer to this as having faith in ourselves, faith in the life process, or faith in a higher power to guide our way forward.

Unless we are willing to face loss, we will overlook opportunities for growth and enjoyment that present themselves on a daily basis. Until we learn how to grieve, we will forsake our journey toward a psychologically sound spirituality. The potential for our collective evolution lies in taking intelligent risks, being creative, and exploring new pathways. If we're unwilling to deal with potential loss or failure, we will shun new ventures because we dread facing disappointment. As one client put it, "If I take no risks, I can't be defeated. It's safer to sit on the fence." As we become confident in our ability to experience sadness and grief without being debilitated by them, we develop an essential foundation for our growth.

If we fear loss, we will feel inhibited in expressing ourselves fully. We'll ignore the more subtle feelings and thoughts that we fear will earn us condemnation. Rather than being ourselves fully, we will cower inwardly, thus bypassing opportunities to connect more deeply and genuinely with people. Fearing rejection and loss, we'll withhold the tender part of us that longs to be warmly united with others.

The willingness and capacity to grieve provides a needed flexibility in our lives and relationships. Without the ability to ease into our grief, we become brittle in the face of loss or failure. We may break when life doesn't go our way. By surrendering to our grief we release deeply held pain which enables us to remain supple and resilient.

The very act of opening to our grief enables us to release our pain. Feeling our legitimate hurt *is* the letting go of that hurt. Such grieving enables us to recover from loss with our self-esteem, inner resources, and aliveness fully intact, if not stronger than before. We are more free to be ourselves when we know that if we're rejected or abandoned, our resulting hurt will not be catastrophic.

The Courage to Face Our Demon

When our automobile is skidding out of control on an icy road, the way to regain control of our vehicle is to turn the wheel in the direction of the skid. Our initial impulse is to do the opposite, which only worsens the skid. Similarly, it is only by going with our pain—experiencing it exactly as it is, without exaggeration or minimization—that it loosens its grip on us. By meeting this demon face to face, we find that it becomes less terrifying, less powerful. We are freed to continue our life journey.

Some of us want to open to our pain yet have difficulty doing so. Old patterns of fear and shame shield us from it. It may then be especially helpful to confide in a trusted friend or counselor. Talking about our situation may help us release our deeper hurt. Shared pain is more bearable.

A caring human presence has a curious way of eliciting what is most real for us. In addition, various forms of "body-work," therapeutic massage, even exercise can be helpful in softening the body armor and defenses that protect us from discomforting feelings. Most important, however, is our own continuing courage and intention to face what is scary or unfamiliar.

It is a curious mystery how we continue to attract hurtful experiences when we have refused to confront and embrace the pain that accompanies betrayal. We tend to repeat destructive patterns in our lives until we uncover the hidden motivations, disowned feelings, and unhelpful thoughts that propel our troubled relationships. In a way, life invites us to befriend our hurt and learn from painful experiences so that we may learn to live and love more wisely.

When approached in a caring, feeling way, the hurt of betrayal can become an entry to a dimension of life that many spiritual traditions have termed the sacred. One woman who dealt with a gut-wrenching betrayal that happened five years earlier described it as follows: "The betrayal catapulted me to a new spiritual stage as I wrestled with all the pain. My husband has his own problems, but he was a catalyst for me." When this woman was first deserted, she experienced fierce anger and overwhelming hurt. She spent several months sleeping four hours a night and crying nearly every day. Fortunately, her willingness to open to the depths of her pain enabled her to heal to the point at which she could say, "I now see that there was wisdom in parting. My soul grew in ways that I could never have foreseen by facing my pain and coming through the other side."

Embracing our hurt can lead to a more tangible connection with our very life force; we uncover a new source of strength, energy, and well-being. Being less troubled by the hurts of life, we can live more nakedly in the world, without the lies and pretensions that we thought we needed to protect us from potential hurt. When hurt no longer looms as a dreaded adversary, we become more confident and relaxed within ourselves and with others. We can take more chances. We can live with less fear and hesitation, more presence and dignity.

Opening to the hurt of betrayal provides no instant cure. Waves of hurt and sadness may come at unpredictable and inconvenient intervals, such as during a date or when we need to concentrate at work. As one impatient man expressed his feelings about being deserted by his partner: "I thought I dealt with this once. How come I'm getting another wave of pain that feels the same as the last one?"

If our hurt is big, we may need to open to it incrementally, slowly over time. As we find the faith and courage to welcome what is real for us, the waves of pain gradually subside. We become more accepting of what is.

Embracing Grief: Rediscovering Joy

Being willing to face and deal with loss does not mean that we invite pain or hold on to it. Facing loss means that if hurt or rejection happens to come our way, we have the inner resources to deal with it, then move on. If we are so afraid of loss that we avoid situations that might result in our being abandoned or betrayed, then at the same time we will avoid circumstances that might also further our well-being and joy.

Strangely enough, feeling our hurt can actually be satisfying. We feel good when we can be intimate with all aspects of ourselves, rather than deny what is real for us. Once fully accepted, hurt can assume a bittersweet quality, one that reflects a mature awareness of life's pains and pleasures. As one woman who prevailed in her trial by fire expressed it: "Joy comes just on the other side of allowing the pain to be there. The depth that I'm willing to experience the pain—to allow it to come up and out—is also the height to which I'm able to experience the joy." Sadness and joy are close allies on our journey toward a rich and fulfilling life.

EMBRACING PAIN:
AN ENTRY TO SPIRITUALITY

This capacity to walk vulnerably in the world—being as we really are—is a key to what it means to be spiritual. Rather than adhere to narrowly defined behaviors, we grow spiritually by being our unarmed, spontaneous, multidimensional self. At times, this means relishing the joy and wonder of being alive. In other instances, it means allowing ourselves to embrace our grief and sadness. We can be childlike and open while also cultivating adult wisdom and discernment. We can gracefully flow with the changing currents of life.

The word *spirituality* comes from the Latin meaning "breath of life." Genuine spirituality involves connecting with this life force within us, then living in a manner that is increasingly animated by it. Unfortunately, many religions throughout the centuries have maintained a damaging split between our spirit, which has been held as pure and good, and our body-life of feelings and pleasure, which has been viewed with suspicion, if not contempt.

Many of us who find meaning in the term *spirituality* persist in trying to connect with our sense of the sacred by disassociating from our emotional life. As one man expressed this soul-splitting spirituality, "I always thought spirituality meant getting beyond my feelings, transcending them, detaching from the pain and sorrow of the world." However hard we try, we can never achieve lasting peace by holding down our feelings or remaining disconnected from the fear, shame, and hurt that silently drive us. Opening to our hurts, as well as to the pain in the world, can deepen our soul and help us feel more connected to people and other living creatures. What Christianity calls grace and redemption cannot enter a heart that is busily protecting itself from unwanted emotions. These can enter our lives only to the degree that we are unguarded, receptive, and open.

Being aware of our feelings does not mean that we wear our feelings on our sleeve or view feelings as the sole goal of personal growth. Living in harmony with the changing rhythm of our feelings means we are not unconsciously dominated and controlled by them. As we move toward a more harmonious relationship with our life of feelings—as we courageously ride the waves—they become less turbulent, less distracting, less overwhelming. As the waves subside, we can see more clearly to the silent core of our radiant essence, which includes qualities that all the great spiritual traditions cherish, such as love, beauty, strength, and joy.

A Spirituality of Embodiment

Many people try to become spiritual by doing favors for others, by participating in rites and rituals, or by just being nice. Those taking a more contemporary approach might surround themselves with crystals, practice affirmations, or chant. These activities and practices may be helpful if they lead to greater self-awareness and mindfulness. However, they do not necessarily make us more spiritual.

Some proponents of the New Age try to embark on a "vertical" path of spirituality. They reach for the stars and higher chakras without developing a breadth of emotional awareness that would provide the grounding for spiritual aspirations. *They pursue a spirituality of transcendence, rather than a spirituality of embodiment.* Without this broadly based grounding, many spiritual aspirants subtly shame themselves and others for having natural human feelings—for not being enlightened enough, which amounts to a cynical betrayal of their humanity. As a result of this pressure to be a spiritual person, they unknowingly—and with truly pure intentions—cultivate the self-image of being spiritual. They fall short of developing an authentic, embodied spirituality as would be evidenced by a compassionate presence to people as they are and a committed caring for the environment and other living things.

In my work as a counselor, I encourage people to let themselves experience bodily felt emotions such as fear, shame, and anger with an attitude of acceptance and self-caring. I've noticed that these feelings, once embraced, often yield to an underlying wound of sadness, hurt, or grief. People often use the generic word *pain* to refer to this mix of feelings. The possibility of deeper healing and self-transformation dawns as people can accept and embrace these hurts.

There is nothing spiritual in itself about sadness or hurt. The possibility of spiritual awakening lies in our approach to these deeper emotions. It is the way in which we hold our hurt, sorrow, and grief that makes the crucial difference between drowning in them and being unexpectedly lifted to a new level of well-being, wholeness, and connectedness.

Welcoming Emotions Rather Than Bypassing Them

I am not suggesting that people bypass other important emotions in order to get to their hurt. More specifically, those overcoming abuse often need to experience emotions of empowerment (rage and anger) as a vehicle for honoring their rights and establishing personal boundaries. However, these individuals will never find peace by permanently relying on anger as a way to allay the hurts of their heart. They must eventually open to these deeper layers of hurt if they want to heal and grow, or go back and forth between hurt and anger many times.

Many of us brace ourselves against the deeper hurts that terrify us. There is often little support and assistance for welcoming our hurt. Friends may try to divert us from it. Therapists who have not yet embraced their own deeper pain may unknowingly betray us by "empowering" us to avoid it. It takes a vivid understanding of the positive power of warmly accepting our naked hurt in order to guide others on this precarious path. This triumph of personal growth is not required for graduation from psychology programs or for procurement of a counseling license. It is learned only in the school of life.

Psychotherapist Francis Weller offers the astute view that "it takes a lot of self-worth to begin embracing our pain."[13] We must hold ourselves with respect and esteem in order to honor the pain inside us. We must tap into our courage and affirm our value in order to acknowledge and feel the real pain within us. If our self-worth has been weakened through years of being shamed, ridiculed, or neglected, it can become stronger in the very process of opening to our pain.

The field of psychology remains in its infancy regarding how to deal with betrayal in a healthy way. Rather than view it as a pivotal point in one's personal development, traditional psychology often sees betrayal as a regrettable tragedy with which one must cope. Those psychiatrists and psychothera-

113

pists who remain pain-phobic fail to offer guidance in the art of embracing deeper feelings as a vehicle for growth. They see their job as protecting people from pain. Oblivious to the transformative power of painful emotions, they may quickly locate their prescription pads, offering medication as their treatment of choice for dealing with the inconvenience of strong feelings. Less medically oriented therapists might advise engaging in new activities or socializing more. Although these pursuits may have their place, they often distract a client from the deeper soul-searching that can deliver him or her to a new level of self-understanding.

When counselors and therapists have not yet embraced their own vulnerability, they fail to embody a depth of compassion that would enable their clients to safely experience and explore their deeper feelings. Unaware of the redemptive power of painful feelings, they apply methodically elegant techniques that usher clients away from the tender core that is the source of both their vulnerability and their spirituality.

James Hillman writes about the transformative possibilities of betrayal when approached in a constructive way: "As analysts we have not worked [betrayal] through to its significance in the development of feeling life, as if it were a dead end in itself out of which no phoenix could arise."[14] By maintaining a bleak view of betrayal, we become shut off in the world of the cynical, which, according to Hillman, prevents us from working toward a positive meaning of betrayal: "Cynicism, that sneer against one's own star, is a betrayal of one's own ideals, a betrayal of one's own highest ambitions."[15]

The sorrow, hurt, and grief of betrayal affords a unique opportunity to awaken us to a new depth of our feeling life. By flowing with these emotions rather than resisting them, we are able to nestle into a deeper place in ourselves. Our pretenses, defenses, bitterness, and inner rigidity soften as we surrender with faith to our hurt and sorrow. Our sense of self changes; our protective self-image yields to a more fundamental sense of who we are. In short, our hurt and sorrow become vehicles of inner transformation.

NOTES

1. K. Gibran, *The Prophet* (New York: Knopf, 1972), 32–33.

2. Personal communication during a discussion in August 1992.

3. More specifically, drugmakers spend up to twice as much on sales and marketing as they do on research and development. B. O'Reilly, *Fortune*, 29 July 1991, 48. "Drugmakers under attack."

4. See K. Pelletier, *Mind As Healer, Mind As Slayer* (New York: Dell, 1977).

5. Ronald Kotulak, "Why Tears Aren't a Crying Shame," *San Francisco Chronicle*, 1 Jan. 1984.

6. See P. Campbell and E. McMahon, *Bio-Spirituality: Focusing As a Way to Grow* (Chicago: University of Loyola Press, 1985) and E. McMahon, *Beyond the Myth of Dominance* (St. Louis: Sheed and Ward, 1993).

7. This approach is based on extensive research conducted over many years. See Eugene Gendlin, *Focusing* (New York: Bantam Books, 1981).

8. Focusing and meditation are close companions. By helping us empty our mind of its repetitive, unhelpful thoughts, meditation sharpens our attention so that we can focus more clearly on what is really going on.

9. In his inspiring book *Fire in the Belly*, Sam Keen refers to his teacher, Howard Thurman: "His rule of life, which applied to cooking, fishing, sipping bourbon, and puffing his pipe, as well as to thinking, was to savor his time. 'Simmering' he called it. 'When you wake up in the morning,' he told me, '*never* get out of bed—simmer. And when you go into bed at night, *never* go to sleep—simmer.'" (New York: Bantam Books, 1991), 159.

10. T. Moore, *Care of the Soul* (New York: HarperCollins, 1992), 242.

11. See *Being Intimate—A Guide to Successful Relationships* for a description of the Focusing Steps as I teach them, and how Focusing helps us develop intimacy skills with ourselves and others. (London: Penguin Group, 1986.)

12. Spiritual teacher Jean Klein has written a book aptly entitled *Ease of Being*. (Durham, NC: The Acorn Press, 1984.)

13. Quote is from an illuminating audiocassette series entitled "Healing Shame," by Francis Weller. Available through Healing Arts Media, P.O. Box 840, Occidental, CA 95465.

14. J. Hillman, *Loose Ends: Primary Papers in Archetypal Psychology* (Dallas: Spring Publications, 1978), 72.

15. Ibid., 73.

CHAPTER 5

Understanding
Betrayal

In order to enter into a committed relationship, we
both must have already made peace with the fact that
there are no guarantees.

SUSAN CAMPBELL[1]

WHY do people break their agreements? Why do people
offer promises and reassurances that turn out to be empty?
Why do people deceive, have secret affairs, or suddenly leave
us? What leads to intentional or unintentional breaches of
trust?

Betrayal—breach of trust—is the result of a complex set of
internal and interpersonal factors, and each school of psychology has its own vantage point in dealing with such rup-
tures in our relationships. Some counseling approaches take
their cue from the Gestalt Prayer of Fritz Perls: "I am not in
this world to live up to your expectations, and you are not in
this world to live up to mine." Therapies that prize emotional
release might encourage us to vent legitimate rage toward the
betrayer, perhaps by beating a pillow with a tennis racket. In
this manner, we are expected to release tension and regain
our power. Psychoanalysts and object relations therapists
might help us explore early childhood factors that tend to
lead us into reenacting, later in life, relationships that end

disastrously. Client-centered counselors might offer empathy and understanding and encourage us to experience the full range of feelings elicited by the betrayal. Jungian analysts might explore the disowned parts of the self that we projected onto our partner with the expectation (usually hidden) that he or she would, in return, somehow bestow certain qualities of being that we need to integrate within ourselves. Adopting this perspective, we may then be able to see betrayal as a potential impetus for our further growth and individuation.

No one viewpoint can account for all of the human variables and complexities that play themselves out in the arena of betrayal. Nevertheless, each of the above has its place, and I will try to integrate the various perspectives in these pages.

Betrayal is rarely a planned, calculated event. Of course, some troubled individuals do consciously use trickery and deceit to win hostages for obedient servitude. Unaware of the possibility of finding personal satisfaction by being their authentic self, they deliberately manipulate others to achieve power and foster dependency. Their betrayals are conscious, but rationalized. They know it will hurt others, but they do it anyway, justifying it with an arsenal of self-serving positions ("He hurt me, so it's my right to hurt him back" or "She'll never find out if I have an affair"). They prey upon people who love too much, or more accurately, those whose personal needs and longings overshadow their good judgment. Such manipulators are prepared to denigrate or drop their unwary partners at the first sign of rebellion against the dependent role they originally agreed to play (tacitly in most cases).

However cruel men or women may appear, most are not intentionally malicious; they do not mean to hurt others. Crippled by a negative self-image, they do not realize the power they have to affect people. Lost in a sea of self-concerns, they do not see things from others' viewpoint; they do not sense others' feelings or needs.[2]

More commonly, it is the half-conscious lies that we feed ourselves and others that create an emotional climate leading to betrayal. There are the seemingly innocent deceptions through which we hope to win love and acceptance. For example, during the early stages of a relationship, we may project an image of being a "cool" or "unruffled" person. We may hide our interest in pursuing a closer partnership. We may conceal our fear and vulnerability through a stylized or domineering way of talking. We may tell small lies when we could just as easily tell the truth. We may hide our blemishes and weak spots. We may conceal our discontents and pretend that everything is just fine. Such ways of deceiving others can become such a familiar part of us that we may be wholly unaware of our emotional dishonesty, or only partly aware of its extent. These little betrayals can create significant hurts, which can lead to bigger betrayals.

These bigger betrayals may result when our partners realize the extent to which they have been quietly misled. The discovery of deception, dishonesty, or indirectness may prompt an abrupt exit from the relationship. Or these little betrayals may set up a pattern in us "little betrayers"—a pattern that can lead to bigger, more hurtful betrayals. Since we were allowed to get away with breaching trust and breaking faith in small ways, we may feel little compunction in betraying in a bigger way. As Mark, a thirty-year-old accountant, said, "She puts up with a lot of stuff from me. I know she won't like it if she finds out I'm having an affair, but she can deal with it."

I will first explore how our tendency to betray others has roots in early childhood experiences that continue to haunt us. Betrayals are also fostered by our making unrealistic commitments, especially if we are unable to tolerate ambivalence and lack of control. Hopes can also sour when we fail to be consciously committed to the "process" of relationship—a process essential to our building a foundation to support a deepening love and intimacy. Finally, betrayal can be an indirect result of an inability to gain access to our actual inner experience and to communicate that experience in a respectful, nonblaming way.

Of course, the factors leading to betrayal are enormously

complex. The following discussion is not meant to exhaust all the whys and wherefores of betrayal.

CHILDHOOD LEGACY

The predisposition to betray others often has origins in early childhood experience. Similarly, our childhood legacy may lead to personality traits that predispose us to being betrayed. We may better understand some of the psychological factors leading to betrayal by identifying patterns of thought, feeling, and behavior that originate during our earliest years. Understanding how our past has shaped our present, we are better positioned to move toward a positive future.

While reading the following, you may find that some descriptions fit your experience, while others do not. As always, I suggest an attitude of self-compassion as you consider how your past—through no fault of your own—may have impeded your ability to form satisfying relationships.

The Wound of Unmet Needs and Shame

According to object-relations theory, a currently popular school of psychology, the first three years of life play a crucial role in our ability to form satisfying, sustainable relationships as adults. The emotional wounds carried from this period can make trust and intimacy precarious.

In order to feel relatively safe in the world, a child must form a durable physical and emotional bond with the mother. Experiencing reliable relief from discomfort, whether through the breast, the bottle, or physical contact, reduces the anxiety of being alive; this sense of comfort and security enables the infant to proceed to more complex developmental tasks. The mother's physical availability, comforting voice, and caring presence are especially vital during the first year of life.

Even the most dedicated mother cannot possibly meet all of the infant's needs. At times, the infant's desperate cries of hunger, physical discomfort, and loneliness will go unheeded. However, if the mother is generally attentive, loving, and responsive (if she has provided what D. W. Winnicott has called "good enough mothering"[3]), the child is likely to emerge from this crucial developmental period with what psychoanalyst Erik Erikson refers to as basic trust.[4]

If we were inadequately nurtured—if our mother was unable to comfort us and connect with us—we become severely handicapped in our ability to trust others. We feel inwardly anxious, guarded, and disconnected. Not having received enough love, we are unable to give it. If we do not take steps to strengthen trust with ourselves, others, and life, we remain predisposed to betraying people.

We will also have difficulty with adult intimacy if we were overprotected and overindulged as children and adolescents, although this may be more difficult to see. If our parents catered to our every whim and then some, we may never have developed the healthy sense of autonomy and inner strength that grows through a certain amount of struggle. Even more importantly, we may still experience a hidden emotional and spiritual hunger if our *authentic needs* were not met. For example, Kurt, a lawyer with political ambitions, was showered with approval and rewards for his academic achievements, sports success, and musical talent. This satisfied his parents' need for social status (to showcase a "special" child), not his need to be supported in his own budding interests.

Marjorie, a real estate agent who was partially supported by her parents, was shaped by similar forces. As a child, she was showered with material gifts and given special schooling, but she was not offered the more precious gift of knowing she didn't have to be special, superior, or perfect to be lovable. She learned to associate love and acceptance with the realm of doing and achieving (good grades, singing lessons), rather than the realm of being (being loved for simply being human). This set up a troubling pattern of not wanting to accept challenges that might end in failure, since failing would undermine the flow of parental approval, which still secretly motivated her. By being pampered and "loved" for fulfilling the parents' image of goodness and perfection, she missed a vital lesson—that life imposes limits and that *she* has limits—and that she is lovable even if she fails at times, or feels lost, hurt, or angry.

Having been so spoiled (yet still deeply deprived), Marjorie was accustomed to getting a copious flow of rewards from outside herself. She expected the world and other people to provide the living and loving she couldn't or wouldn't give to herself, then complained when others didn't satisfy her. A low tolerance for frustration, limitations, and conflict led to blame, withdrawal, and betrayal when life (or her partner) failed to conform to her wants and desires.

Interestingly, this childish, temper tantrum mind-set describes the typical yuppie mentality, which reached its peak during the Reagan–Bush era of leveraged buyouts, corporate takeovers, and wild speculation. According to most economists, the overindulgences of the 1980s—the attempts to amass wealth without contributing anything real or valuable to society—helped precipitate the major recession of the 1990s.[5] Substituting personal ambition and material accumulation for the persistent hungers of our soul, we perpetuate our own self-betrayal by overlooking our deeper needs. We also betray those we exploit to get ahead, as well as future generations who must clean up our mess, in the form of runaway budget deficits and environmental degradation.

As children we were frequently yelled at, humiliated, ignored, or smothered by our parents, relatives, teachers, or siblings.[6] As a result, we often have difficulty with intimate relationships in our adult lives. This is especially true if there had been no adult "guardian angel" present—perhaps a grandparent, a teacher, a friend's parent—who provided approval, affection, reassurance, and nurturance. Without heartfelt support and guidance from family, extended family, or community, we probably concluded that we were unwanted or unlovable. The fear, anxiety, and shame generated by rejection and mistreatment have short-circuited our process of becoming a coherent, confident, mature person, one who can meet challenges and handle disappointments. As a result, we experience the world as unsafe and hostile. Losing hope that our real self is acceptable, we experiment with constructions of a self that we hope will win us the comfort and connection we seek.

The Expectation of Rejection

One result of our childhood legacy may be that we live in a high state of readiness to be criticized and rejected. We prepare for the worst, even in relationships in which we are treated kindly. We subtly or not so subtly test people's loyalty and commitment, as if to say, "You'll have to *prove* to me that *you're* different from all the rest," or "You'll have to keep showing me how special I am." We become apprehensively alert to any signs of rejection or disapproval. Constantly on guard, we are ready to flee from (or pounce upon) those who pose a real or imagined threat to our fragile sense of security and identity.

Relationships become volatile when we cannot live confidently and peacefully within ourselves; we then make it difficult for others to satisfy us. They can never quite do enough or be enough for us. *Our expectations of conflict generate the very conflict we fear;* ultimately, whether through an affair or callous abandonment, we may readily betray those who cannot meet our needs.

Conversely, we may be betrayed by others, because our chronic anger, cynicism, and distrust, as well as our ineptitude in extending and receiving love, make us unpleasant company. One man who was frequently critical of his wife, which led to her leaving him, put it this way: "I can see now that I was no fun to live with anymore. I didn't realize that I saw her as my mother in many ways, someone I expected to take care of me all the time. I had to learn how to take care of myself!"

Still whirling from our troubled childhood legacy, we may live in chronic disconnection from our authentic, natural self. This state of self-alienation results from our rejecting our real feelings, needs, and wants. As a result, we may experience unwarranted suspicion and paranoia. Our moods may shift radically and unexpectedly. Our relationships may be intense and short-lived. We may have poor self-esteem, which often includes an inflated sense of self-importance. We may rarely feel guilt, remorse, or responsibility for the pain we cause others. We have little to *give*. We may rarely display empathy because our own needs press so heavily upon us. Not having felt sufficiently loved and wanted, we cannot relax enough to extend real warmth, understanding, and appreciation to others. We are afraid of getting close for fear that rejection is inevitable, as past experience has proven. Preoccupied with our own emotional wounds (whether consciously or not), we're disinclined to extend good will toward people.

The Creation of "Enemy"

Our childhood legacy may keep us preoccupied with a desperate search for certainty and predictability, which prevents us from appreciating the complexity and fluidity of our life experience. We then remain stuck in a child's way of comprehending ourselves and others. We demonstrate a self-righteous reactivity when life fails to gratify us. We speak in absolutes and think in simplistic categories of black or white, good or bad: "You're either for me or against me! Either you love me or you don't!" We have little patience to discern fine shades of meaning and little tolerance for personal differences with others. Life is experienced as a competition or battle. The goal is being right and winning, or, at least, surviving.

As adults who are wounded, even if worldly successful, we may remain ill-equipped to deal with conflicts and differences that arise in relationships. When we feel hurt, embarrassed, or frightened in relation to someone, we may employ a complex mental operation to protect ourselves from experiencing feelings that have proven in the past to be so painful. Those who injure our pride or threaten our security may be given derogatory labels that identify them as less than human. By dehumanizing and demonizing others, *we disconnect from any awareness of their worth and well-being.* It is then a short step toward hurting or betraying them—without a shred of self-doubt or guilt.

Some people use religion to deny others their dignity, while proclaiming their own virtue. They may claim that it's God's will that women serve men, or that there's no right to consider divorce under any circumstances. As Thoreau reminds us, "There is no odor so bad as that which arises from goodness tainted."

Consider how betrayal is observable on a larger scale, in the arena of international politics. The history of the world has been shaped by nations that cannot resolve their conflicts peacefully. Instead, they discredit other countries or ethnic groups by labeling them the enemy and portraying them in nonhuman, demeaning terms. It is easier to drop a bomb on the enemy if we can convince ourselves that they are malevolent or evil.[7] Once a public relations campaign has convinced us that this nation is indeed an evil empire or is led by a malevolent tyrant, there is ready support to destroy it. Similarly, a partner may be labeled bitchy, crazy, or abusive[8] in order to justify an unconscionable betrayal.

Wounded Trust

Most of us retain a wound of trust as a legacy of childhood. Even if our parents were well intentioned and semi-saintly, conventional child-rearing practices can inject a mild or heavy dose of shame and fear into our being. Even if shaming at home is minimal, it is overabundant in our schools and playgrounds. If we've been the object of repeated rejection or ridicule—or even unintentional humiliation—we find it difficult to trust and love. When love and acceptance have been dependent upon particular achievements or behaviors, we come to equate love with *doing* what is expected of us (or being perfect), rather than *being* our natural self.

When we've been hurt or broken, we may regard trust as a foreign concept. We are more prone to hostile outbursts and irritability in our adult lives when we've been neglected and betrayed as children. Rage and hostility are predictable reactions when our soul's longing to love and be loved is stymied. We then act out this tragic disconnection from our soul by hurting and betraying others, often unaware of the inner fragmentation that is really motivating us. Of course, our random ravings against the world for injuries sustained are self-destructive; they only dig us into a deeper hole of isolation and disconnection. And so the cycle of hurting and being hurt, betraying and being betrayed, continues.

As adults, our piled up rage might find a self-justified outlet in rejecting or betraying someone who is guilty of only minor insensitivities. Being poised to expect mistreatment, we may attribute darker motives to our partner or friend than actually exist. Even if today we are indeed taunted, misunderstood, or criticized, our current hurt may be amplified by former hurts and rejections, prompting a reaction far stronger than the current situation would seem to warrant. Unable to tolerate the hurt that accompanies small breaches of trust, we may betray our partner through emotional withdrawal or desertion.

Old Wounds Can Lead to Sexual Betrayal

Some people who grow up with self-doubt and insecurity try to compensate for years of neglect by seeking validation from new lovers. For example, wounded men may have multiple affairs to prove to themselves that they are powerful and desirable. Women may also seek extramarital sexual relations in order to gain the affection and approval they never received from their father, and are still not getting from their aloof spouse.

Their propensity toward secret affairs may stem from a long-standing condition of self-alienation. When their partner cannot satisfy their nagging sense of emptiness and unworthiness, they may try to fill this void through sexual liaisons. They may develop an entourage of sexual partners as a way to feel important and to ensure that they are never alone. "I was always searching for someone to fill up that hole in me—that emptiness," said Louise, a thirty-eight-year-old secretary. Unable to find her way to embrace her emptiness and aloneness, she used sex to feel temporarily whole, worthwhile, and alive. Jeff, a forty-one-year-old sales representative, expressed a similar sentiment in relation to his string of affairs: "It makes me feel good about myself. It makes me feel wanted and important."

Without a reservoir of self-trust and self-love, we may betray our partner in innumerable ways, rather than resolve conflicts in a responsible manner. We may embark upon a long journey of betraying one partner after another in a futile effort to make each of them into someone he or she is not and can never be, such as our parental caretaker. Or, however unwittingly, we may repeatedly invite betrayal until we develop some inner stability by building a greater bond of trust with ourselves, other people, and life itself.

UNREALISTIC COMMITMENTS

The anguish of betrayal and abandonment also results from the massive confusion regarding the meaning of commitment. Misguided commitments promote the very betrayal they purport to avoid.

Commitments are intended to help us enjoy greater trust and security in relationships. The commitment to marital permanence especially is intended to offer shelter and safety. But in reality, how much safer are we?

Why do people break the sacred vows they offer? Why is the divorce rate about 50 percent today? Perhaps less visibly, dissatisfaction among couples who stay together is reported to be rampant. Why is this so?[9]

For many centuries, the commitment to marital perma-nence safeguarded the well-being of society as a whole. If a father were to abandon his family, both mother and children would be thrown into a harsh struggle to survive. Similarly, if a woman took her children and left her husband, she would lose financial security. In current times, divorce may precipi-tate painful life changes, but the changes are often not as cataclysmic as in years past.

A marriage commitment means different things to differ-ent people. For many, it reflects steady devotion born of af-fection and good will. It expresses an honorable intention to love, nourish, and cherish another human being. It honors the mystery and miracle of life and procreation, and a deter-mination to nurture the well-being of the couple's children. It provides a container for the partnership so that quarrels occur in a context of relative safety.

But for some people, this commitment is guided more by fear than by love. For them, marriage offers protection from the terror of facing isolation and rejection. It offers the hope of creating the happy family they never had. It allays their fear of being a failure, and eases their anxiety over growing old alone. Most of us in our marriages are governed by some blend of love and fear.

However noble our motivations, we may make commit-ments without clearly comprehending their nature and mean-ing. What we call commitment may actually be a fear-based clinging or symbiosis. Rather than make sound commitments that nurture our aspirations for lifelong love, we may unwit-tingly make promises that add to our burden of disappoint-ment.

Naive Notions of Commitment

Most people have little idea what lies ahead when they commit themselves to a lifelong relationship. Through the intoxicating influence of romantic love, they may simply expect that harmony and happiness will—somehow—prevail. They may believe that a rewarding marriage is solely a function of finding the right partner, rather than doing the internal work that leads to personal and interpersonal fulfillment. Fixated on the goal of marriage, they may believe that a commitment to lifelong marriage is a prerequisite for finding the love they've always wanted.

Society offers enticing incentives for falling in love and getting married. However, our schools and social institutions provide little guidance in the art of maintaining and nourishing our partnerships so that harmony and happiness may indeed prevail. The government agency that offers the marriage license doesn't suggest ways of dealing with inevitable differences in our personal needs, wants, and visions. There is usually no one who voluntarily tells a young, unwary couple that sobering changes may lie ahead as they get to know each other and as life stresses trickle into the partnership. Even if someone tried to warn them, they would politely dismiss these exhortations in light of their hormonal reactions to each other, coupled with their romantic notions that promote a distorted vision of marriage.

The vow to stay together until "death do us part" has emotional appeal. It can be an expedient way to satisfy our needs for ongoing companionship and comfort. It can offer relief from the pain and disconnection experienced in childhood or in previous partnerships. We may persuade ourselves to believe that the broken trust and suffering endured in past relationships will never visit us again.

Seeking Protection from Life

Our most solemn vows do not safeguard us from life. We do not possess the power to anticipate the course of our future needs and wants, nor those of our partner. We cannot foretell whether one of us will refuse to grow in some fundamental way. We cannot know whether our personal visions and aspirations will remain compatible. There's good reason why separating couples often say, "We were just growing in different directions." We may feel betrayed when unanticipated differences or uncontrollable forces lead to broken promises.

It is humbling to entertain the idea that we have no ultimate mastery over the longevity of a partnership; it is unsettling to recognize that there are innumerable variables in relationships and forces in life over which we have little control. The part of the human ego that fears loss and disintegration will cling tightly to whatever security it has found and viciously attack when that security is threatened.

To the degree that we are governed by past deprivation, some portion of our traditional marriage vows may be based on a plea stemming from our unspoken fears and insecurity: the plea for total and complete care for the rest of our lives. We are only human in seeking and offering such reassurance, and there is certainly nothing wrong with wanting love and caring to endure. But can we guarantee that we can provide it under any and all circumstances? Even if we received the guaranteed companionship we seek, what would be the quality of that companionship? Can we know absolutely what the future holds for us, or do such presumptions reflect a lack of wisdom about the nature of relationships and how life works?

We fool ourselves if we expect our partner to provide something that we must learn to give ourselves. We unknowingly deceive each other, and possibly betray ourselves, if we serenely suppose that our vow to stay together will prove more powerful than any and all of the other forces that inevitably enter partnerships. Such forces—whether the death of a parent, the loss of a job, the conversion to a new religion, an attraction to another person, a new discovery about ourselves—might deepen our love and strengthen our bond if dealt with in a caring, mature manner. However, such challenges might also pose an unexpected threat to our identity and self-esteem, and that could precipitate a marital crisis.[10]

Or an unexpected clash in our beliefs, values, or lifestyle preferences might threaten our ability to stay together in a viable way.

Our myth-generating society does not encourage self-understanding. It betrays us by seducing us into romanticized images of marriage. Daphne Rose Kingma, a marriage and family counselor, points out that

> since we first embroidered this myth of "forever" on our hearts, our relationships have gone through innumerable transformations while our thinking about them has not. As a result, an incredible number of people are suffering through the trauma of ending their relationships with guilt, rage, self-flagellation and a profound loss of self-esteem as the only emotional hallmarks of parting.[11]

An important aspect of personal growth is to sort out the kinds of commitments that we as individuals are willing to make and are prepared to keep versus those that are promoted by social institutions and the media. Then, instead of placing our trust in the final product of marital longevity, we as a couple might redirect our trust and commitment to the more immediate, fundamental process of relating openly, fully, and forthrightly with each other. Our dedicated commitment to this *marital process,* rather than to *marital permanence,* may, paradoxically, provide our best chance for maintaining the enduring love we seek.

TOLERATING AMBIVALENCE AND LACK OF CONTROL

Why do we demand marital permanence? The commitment to permanence is designed partly to eradicate the possibility of betrayal. But an interesting paradox is that real trust cannot exist apart from this possibility. Psychologist James Hillman expresses it well:

> We must be clear that to live and love only . . . where there is security and containment, where one cannot be hurt or let down, where what is pledged in words is forever binding, means really to be out of harm's way and so to be out of real life. . . . If one can give oneself assured that one will come out intact, . . . then what has been given? If one leaps where there are always arms to take one up, there is no real leap. All risk of the ascent is annulled.[12]

Those who cannot tolerate the inherent ambivalence and unpredictability of life may try to coax and coerce others in order to enforce stability and certainty. However, it is only by taking an intelligent risk to trust—and then continually reaffirming that trust, rather than expecting guarantees—that a couple may be rewarded with ongoing intimacy, love, and well-being. Hillman observes that "this paranoid demand for a relationship without the possibility of betrayal cannot really be based on trust. Rather, it is a convention designed to exclude risk. As such it belongs less to love than to power. It is a retreat to a . . . relationship enforced by word, not held by love."[13] The more intent we are on getting others to swear their everlasting loyalty, the more we may actually be spoiling love and sowing seeds of disappointment, if not betrayal.

This is not to propose that we can never grow toward a soundly satisfying and mostly stable partnership, or that we can never rest in the warm knowledge that we are loved. It is merely to suggest that the sweet comfort and enduring tenderness we seek are more possible as we relinquish the fear-based tendency to control and manipulate a desired outcome. *The growth of trust and love is antithetical to our agendas of control.* Love and trust blossom as by-products of living life, being true to ourselves, and being genuine, sensitive, and responsive in relation to others.

The Commitment to Self

Our social institutions tout marital permanence as the ticket to a stable, happy life. However, vows are broken with such astonishing regularity that it leads one to wonder not so much about the integrity of those making these vows, as about whether there is something unsound about the vows themselves. Such commitments become a painfully regrettable hoax if they cannot provide the protection they promise, as our secular and religious establishments would have us believe.

If we are physically or emotionally abused by our partner, how long should we expect ourselves to hang in there patiently? If we discover that our spouse has been concealing an affair, do we have the right to at least consider leaving a relationship marred by such deceit? What if our partner decides to watch television all day, and remains emotionally unavailable and spiritually barren, and refuses to seek assistance for that condition of sterility? Such scenarios are less probable if both individuals are truly committed to their own growth. Yet the question remains: How long are we expected to remain loyal to someone who has become disloyal to his or her own well-being and personal development? At what point do we betray ourselves by remaining in a dysfunctional partnership? When does our commitment to self take precedence over our commitment to another?

The difficult decision to choose oneself was described touchingly by Sandra, who separated after three years of marriage. Although she appreciated the financial security, she never felt deeply connected to her husband. She initially felt his caring, but his own pressing needs were painfully eroding her freedom and autonomy: "My husband would pressure me not to see my friends. One by one I stopped seeing people who threatened him. And I stopped doing things that nurtured me in order to spend more time taking care of him. One day I kind of woke up and said to myself, 'I haven't been seeing my women friends, I haven't painted, I haven't danced, and I haven't been playing music.' I saw that doesn't work for me. I'm not being myself and I can't live like this. I'm living like a zombie. I'm half dead. I told my husband many times this isn't working, but he wouldn't listen. I felt like a pruned tree. I asked him many times if he was willing to work on stuff and he really wasn't interested, so I finally gave up. There was a lot of sadness. I actually had times when I would be in bed and these terribly negative thoughts would come to me. Or I'd be driving and have the image of hitting a tree and dying—like that would be the only way to get out of the situation! When I realized I was having those thoughts more frequently, I decided I had to get out of there."

Even those with the most heartfelt, positive intentions cannot realistically expect themselves to honor unconditional commitments. The commitment to stay together forever may set us up for eventual betrayal because one of us demands of the other—or of the marriage as a structure—the kind of refuge that can be found only within the self or in relation to life itself. We may both exhaust ourselves and each other in a futile battle to get the other to make us safe, whole, or happy.

We must consider, too, that people now live much longer than before. Not long ago, the average life expectancy was fifty years; today people can expect to live to age seventy-five or older. Remaining in an unsatisfying or destructive marriage for fifty years or more is a long sentence indeed!

Although I may hope and expect to be with you forever, I cannot know whether this will turn out to be in my best interest, or your best interest, or even the best interest of our future children. We cannot know that we will be as compatible in ten years as we feel today. Our differences may become insurmountable; our life paths may diverge. We may find one day that we still have love for each other but are no longer growing by staying together. In fact, we may be sorely unhappy.

We may be disconcerted by the realization that we do not have ultimate control over the evolution of our compatibility.

We may learn vital lessons through our partnership, but there may come a time when we must make the painful decision to move on. If we separate consciously, caringly, and with mutual consent, there is no betrayal. If our decision remains unilateral, there may be a betrayal that causes hurt. Yet this may be less morally reprehensible than the spiritual suicide of betraying ourselves.

Quite alternatively, we should not be shocked to find that our more clear-eyed and courageous approach to our marriage is liberating it, inspiring it, as it liberates both of us *within* the marriage. Perhaps our changing marriage is not dissolving; perhaps it is at some stage of becoming deeper and richer than we'd ever envisioned.

PROCESS COMMITMENT: AN ALTERNATIVE TO ROMANTIC PROMISES

What can we realistically offer one another? We can offer a somewhat less romantic, though more credible reassurance that arises out of a growing union of hearts, minds, and souls.

In our book *Being Intimate,* we proposed the notion that we look more closely at the nature and meaning of our commitments. We invited the reader to consider replacing unrealistic, conventional commitments with a more grounded "process commitment." This perspective may be initially upsetting or confusing for some of us until we grasp the subtle, yet powerful way that this commitment can nourish a vital and enduring connection.

The notion of being committed to the process, rather than the outcome, may at first evoke considerable fear: the fear of change, the fear of abandonment, the fear of being alone. These are among the deepest terrors we face as human beings; they reflect the existential issues that are at the heart of being human. They touch the core concerns of whether we are loved and lovable, whether we will find happiness, and

134

whether the universe is friendly. These issues have challenged humankind throughout the centuries.

Proclaiming our guarantee to maintain the same marital form in perpetuity may not be the wisest way to resolve these fears. The safety and stability we desire cannot be attained by attaching ourselves to a secure, parentlike presence outside ourselves. But to the degree that we can develop a stable, intimate relationship with ourselves, we may negotiate the process of relationship in a way that lends itself to lifelong love.

Being Committed to Conditions that Support Love

What does it mean to be committed to the process? A process commitment begins by shifting my focus from keeping my partner connected with me to staying connected with myself. It is by staying connected with my own living process that I create conditions under which love and intimacy are most likely to flourish. Then, rather than place my faith in a promise of permanence, I place my faith in creating conditions under which my partner is most likely to want to stay with me, and I with her.

How can I express this commitment to create such conditions? I can be committed to communicating my inner experience as clearly as I can glimpse it. I can be committed to divulging my real feelings in a direct, yet sensitive, nonblaming way. I can be committed to my own process of personal growth so that my words and actions flow more and more from the still, clear center of who I am. I can be committed to respecting my partner's feelings and wants and to stretching my awareness as I try to see things from her viewpoint. I can be committed to exploring the blind spots that lead to distance, distrust, and betrayal. I can be committed to using the partnership—and all it brings up—as a path to learn more about myself and life. I can be committed to tolerating periods of confusion, upset, and discomfort, getting through the tough times. The power of these process commitments should not be underestimated. They serve to deepen love and intimacy as nothing else can.

If I am committed to being honest with you, then my little discontents will be aired closer to the time that they arise—before they mushroom into the gigantic upset that might overburden our relationship. If I am committed to sharing my real feelings with you, then I'm less likely to surprise you later with an emotional explosion or an underhanded attack. If I am committed to listening closely to you rather than rehearsing a rebuttal or delivering a prepared retort, then I demonstrate a sincere openness to understand you. By being firmly committed to working through our differences as best we can, we face a greater likelihood that we will resolve conflicts as they arise. Through the commitment to be my genuine self, I give you the only self that is able to form a connection worthy of the term *intimacy*. Amidst our honesty and openness is an aliveness, a rich depth of connectedness that is continually renewed and revitalized.

The Commitment to Accommodate Conflict

Establishing vital relationships is more promising when we make it safe for others to experience and express the full range of their humanness—their seriousness and playfulness, their fears and longings, their joys and hurts. There are times in every partnership when we don't like what we see. But unless we encourage others to be themselves and avoid disparaging what they then reveal to us, we end up sabotaging our own desire for full-fledged love and intimacy.

Most fundamentally, a process commitment means being committed to facing conflicts that arise as the result of being ourselves (as best as we currently know how). This does not mean that we brace ourselves for difficulty or live in dreadful anticipation of the worst. It simply means that we recognize the potential for discord and differences within any relationship, and that we posture ourselves to accommodate clashing needs, wants, and viewpoints, rather than resist them.

Resisting conflict fuels conflict, or drives it underground, where it festers for a fiercer battle to come. Our best chance of keeping a relationship thriving is by allowing conflict to arise and dealing with it patiently, rather than pushing it away by withdrawing, raging, or imposing self-serving interpretations.

Andrew, who was in a ten-year marriage, frequently avoided his wife by playing tennis or cards several times a week. He wouldn't listen to her requests to spend more time together, insisting that he needed his freedom. One day she told him that another man was expressing interest in her and that she felt tempted to reciprocate. After blowing up upon hearing this, he agreed to couples counseling. Very gradually, they began talking about how they had felt hurt by each other in the past but had never really talked about it: his continuing attachment to a former partner he'd occasionally visited, her criticisms of him for not making enough money. Although it was painful to bring these volatile issues to the surface, Andrew slowly began feeling closer to his wife: "I used to fiercely resist looking at things and talking about things. But now that we've started to really talk about our problems I feel closer to my wife than ever before. I could never go back to the old ways of silent stewing and blaming each other." By stewing in his old hurts and being unwilling to talk about them, he'd become progressively more distant from his wife.

Our foundation of trust is weakened if I withhold the "unpleasant" truth because I fear that you might ridicule, reject, or abandon me, whether that truth is a past or current hurt, concern, feeling, or need. I may create my own worst fear of betrayal (as Andrew almost did), not because I divulged the unsettling truth, but because *I insulted you by hiding it for so long.* If I'm committed to the process of openness and honesty, then your dealings with me are based on reality. On the other hand, if I deceive or mislead you—or withdraw from you—you may later feel betrayed because I withheld the truth.

My taking refuge in the truth (as clearly as I can currently glimpse it) may appear to give me less control over the outcome of a relationship. In reality, the relationship is more likely to survive and thrive by my relinquishing my attempt at control and replacing it with a faith-filled commitment to follow the process wherever it may lead. This commitment to the process keeps a marriage, or any relationship, alive and viable.

Many of us might feel safer being ourselves once assured of a permanent marriage. We may then no longer have to struggle to please our partner or win his or her loyalty. However, the hope that we have finally "nailed down" a permanent marriage may prompt a new struggle (especially if we're not firmly committed to our growth)—the struggle to keep the partnership harmonious *at all costs.*

If the primary focus of our marriage is to keep it stable, we may avoid conflicts that could lead to its demise. If we equate conflict with potential abandonment, we may try to settle conflicts through our personal decrees—or by accepting the decrees issued by our partner (a policy of appeasement)— rather than allowing solutions to emerge from patient, open dialogue. We may try to make our partner into a carbon copy of ourselves, fearful that if he or she is manifestly different, that difference will spell doom for the marriage. We may avoid difficulties out of fear that addressing them might make the relationship even more precarious, keeping us trapped in a miserable marriage. We may then achieve only a pseudostability based on subtle collusions and avoidance, rather than a dynamic stability that comes from facing conflict and emerging a stronger couple.

Some people who bank on the permanent status of their marriage feel a greater permission to mistreat their partner, confident that no matter how abusive they become, their partner is bound by marital oath to tolerate their destructive presence. Then, if their battle-weary partner decides to no longer tolerate mistreatment, they can fight back with the self-righteous, manipulative, guilt-inducing statement "You're not committed to this marriage!"

A strong process commitment provides a solid, mature

base for discussing delicate issues that often get swept under the rug in security-based partnerships. For example, a process commitment may include a commitment to monogamy. However, we cannot promise that we will never be attracted to anyone else. We can agree not to act upon that attraction, but we might later have to deal with the inevitable infatuations and connections that arise during the process of living our lives.

Minimizing Little Betrayals

Being faithful to a process commitment is not easy. Then again, relationships are not easy; life is not easy. However, such a commitment is the best way I know to minimize the little betrayals that are part of every relationship. This choice requires practice and perseverance, the strength to acknowledge mistakes, and a willingness to learn from them.

A process commitment can begin the moment I meet someone I'd like to know better and can continue until the day I die. The commitment to know myself and share my real feelings and thoughts allows a prospective partner to decide if she wants to be with a guy like me. Through such openness and honesty, I avoid the betrayal of deceit and manipulation. The commitment to be respectful and responsive to her needs and sensibilities means that I avoid the betrayal of shaming or disdaining her. The ongoing commitment to be communicative with her about my wants, limits, preferences, dissatisfactions, and joys means that I "show up" in the relationship; I thereby avoid the betrayal of withdrawing and isolating myself from her. Such commitments increase the likelihood that I will really see and understand her, which will help our partnership grow on a sound basis. As we keep our eyes open and confront the little betrayals that, unattended, could lead to larger tremors in the relationship, we minimize the prospect of a more major betrayal. We slowly go deeper with each other.

THE PROCESS OF DEEPENING

Being committed to the process of relating openly and respectfully, we may attain a depth of love and intimacy that perhaps we had never imagined we might find. As we continue on a path of being ourselves, sharing ourselves, discovering each other, and respecting our differences, we enter new territory. Something fresh and alive is awakened in us through each other's presence. Persistent communication has forged deeper trust and understanding. We experience a consistent caring for the other's well-being, which derives from seeing that person's deeper essence and wanting to nurture that essence. We feel a sense of union, while being comfortable with our separateness.

If our relationship has a firm foundation, then I am likely to stay with you because I *want* to—it feels good to be *me* when I'm with *you.* I feel more connected with myself and life through our contact.

As I risk being myself with you again and again, I am touched by your acceptance and appreciation of who I am. As you risk being yourself again and again, I feel close to the essence of your being. My love and appreciation naturally extend to you. I yearn for your happiness. I want to do all I can to further your growth. These are compelling reasons to stay together.

A true marriage exists not merely on paper. It is an inner and outer union in which we *feel* married; that is, we feel connected with ourselves and our partner in some profound, mysterious way. We somehow open to the sacred vastness of life by being together. We feel a deep and tender resonance between us. Commitment then arises as an impulse to support the growth of our tender connection. It grows out of choice and freedom, not pressure or obligation. In short, it becomes a joy, not a duty, to be committed. This deeper surrender to our mutual journey becomes our natural next step.

Toward a New Commitment Vow

A new commitment vow might go something like this: "We feel such love and caring for each other. We really *like* each other, too. We're similar in ways that are important to us, and different in ways that are complementary. We have a track record of facing and working through difficulties. It continues to feel so good and so right to be together. We want to continue deepening our intimacy with ourselves, with each other, and with life. We feel so blessed and appreciative of being together that we're committed to working through whatever comes up during difficult times. We're committed to the process with each other. As mature people, we know that obstacles will periodically arise—our connection will not be continually felt. But we're committed to doing our best to resolve our problems, including asking for help if we need it."

Does this mean marriage forever after? Since our connection feels so big and so rich, we live and love as if we'll be together for the rest of our lives. Yet as mature people, we also recognize that this situation could change. Although our relationship may have the appearance of being a permanent partnership, it may turn out to be what psychologist Susan Campbell calls a "learning relationship,"[14] one that prepares us for a fuller and richer relationship to come.

Although a process commitment involves serious intent and a high degree of safety, it may not offer the foolproof protection desired by those wanting contracts of permanence. However, we more cruelly betray each other by making solemn commitments that are outside the scope of our power to honor. We may set ourselves up for betrayal by trusting each other's—and our own—alluring, yet questionable, promises.

Those who do not appreciate the serious nature of a process commitment might view it as a watered-down, insubstantial expression of good will and loyalty. They may see it as self-centered or selfish. They may interpret it as an inability to make a "real" commitment, or a fear of being "tied down."

Yet once we make a commitment to a particular form of being together, whether as live-in mates or as married partners, what can be a greater expression of our love and good will than being committed to the process that will best support our connection? This commitment to the process *requires a high degree of self-awareness and personal integrity.* It involves a serious application of our will and intelligence. It demonstrates healthy respect for the formidable potency of our emotional world. It recognizes that painstaking attention must be directed to that inner world so that the emotions and needs teeming within it are expressed in ways that nurture love, rather than unintentionally destroy it. There is no selfishness here. There is the sober recognition that we must overcome a complacency that might lead us to avoid a commitment to doing the inner and outer work necessary to create a fulfilling relationship.

Commitment to Accept and Understand Our Differences

An intimate partnership can provide one of the clearest illuminations of our personal blind spots and shortfalls. A process commitment demonstrates our willingness to face whatever is triggered in us through this partnership. This means summoning the courage to look at our inner life, even if the truths we discover are unsettling or painful. Without this kind of commitment, relationships can provide one of the most potent distractions from an authentic confrontation with ourselves. Once married, we may feel so safe that we enter a relaxed stupor. When we fall asleep at the wheel, our marriage eventually crashes.

Many individuals remain in relationships in which no real relating is going on. Partnerships that languish in disconnection and miscommunication, if not subtle deception and disrespect, are closer to bad roommate situations than to real marriages. Such a condition may endure because both people are too stubborn—or, more accurately, too wounded—to convert their verbal weapons into clear, open communication. They are too self-righteous—or, more accurately, too hurt—to really listen to the other person with an open heart and mind.

In other instances one partner may make a sincere, consistent attempt to reach out, but the other is unwilling to reciprocate or simply cannot find a self-affirming, nonblaming place from which to respond. As one discouraged woman described the latter stage of her marriage, "No matter what I did or said or no matter how well I said it, it was just another opportunity for him to invalidate me. He became so irrational. It was like talking to a drunk." Unless both people are ready for a mature commitment to resolving conflicts, the partnership will suffer or reach a breaking point for the more committed partner.

There have been recent suggestions that many exasperating conflicts are due to differences in men's and women's style of communicating. Deborah Tannen, a linguist and popular author, refers to these differences in dialect as "genderlect."[15] Some degree of miscommunication and conflict between the sexes is probably based on differing ways of viewing the world, whether due to biology or social conditioning. We may be able to resolve many of these differences if we are *both* firmly committed to getting to the truth and understanding each other.

A process commitment enables us to explore these differences—and to what degree they may be operating—without the blame and rancor that comes from insisting we are right, and our partner's feelings, needs, or ways of communicating are wrong (although we may mutually agree that some ways of communicating are more helpful than others). This requires that we make the effort to reach into each other's world. Without the firm intention to really understand each other, without the commitment and good will that is necessary to see each other clearly, we may break faith with our partner. We may lose the will to journey together. And, as a sad consequence, we may be left with the bitterness that fuels the war between the sexes.

Authors Aaron Kipnis and Elizabeth Hingston, who lead gender reconciliation workshops, encourage men and women to value their differing experiences and genuinely listen to each other in order to understand and appreciate the other's perspective: "Many of us fear that listening to the story of another will somehow weaken our own voice, our own initiative, even our own identity. The fear keeps us locked in adversarial thinking and patterns of blame and alienation. In this frightened absence of empathy, devaluation of the other sex grows."[16]

If I cling to cynical conclusions about the opposite sex, I actually betray myself. I give up on creating the deeper richness and connection that my deeper being still longs for.

Commitment and Responsible Freedom

I also betray myself by dallying in a particular partnership when I have soberly concluded that I am no longer growing in it, or worse, that it is actively harming me. I abandon the possibilities of further emotional and spiritual growth by remaining in a relationship that stifles my spirit and undermines my well-being. In effect, I then abandon my commitment to life.

By saddling myself with the obligation to stay with my partner, the part of me that craves freedom and growth may rebel against something that I experience as an externally imposed restraint. If I can release this pressure I feel toward our remaining together, then I can more freely explore the raw experience of our now *being* together: what I like, what I dislike, what gets in the way of feeling good about the relationship.

Many individuals have such a strong fear of losing their freedom that they never become involved in close relationships. They fear that once they enter a relationship, there will be no way out. This fear of entrapment prevents many people from giving relationships a fair chance. Such people might be relieved of self-imposed (or other-imposed) pressure by claiming their ultimate right to leave a relationship that proves unworkable. Within a context of responsible freedom, they may then feel more empowered to take reasonable risks.[17]

Again, this is not to suggest that we abandon people at the first sign of dissatisfaction, or that we "upgrade" to a new partner whenever someone more enticing drifts into our lives. Roaming from relationship to relationship may indicate that emotional blocks and shortsightedness are preventing us from achieving any relationship of depth. By switching to a fresh partner, we may only continue a pattern of glamorization and idealization slowly withering into disillusionment—and yet another separation from this latest partner.

Overcoming Blocks to Going Deeper

In every relationship there are times when we reach a point at which we feel bored and unchallenged. We may then incorrectly conclude that the partnership is the cause of our dissatisfaction. Misinterpreting our discontent, we resort to betrayal in our search for some overromanticized fantasy.

Rather than blame our partner or the relationship itself for our unhappiness, our real task may be to go within ourselves in a new, deeper way. Perhaps we are withholding some unpleasant truth, and that avoidance is deadening the relationship. Perhaps we are expecting our partner to furnish us with entertainment or vitality, and are not nurturing an aliveness and presence within ourselves. Instead of prematurely leaving our partner, we may need to "get a life" outside the partnership, whether by pursuing creative enterprises, personal growth disciplines, a career, volunteer work, or other meaningful friendships. Feeling more nourished in our lives, we have more to offer our partner; our sense of union may then be renewed. Being engaged in life, we become more engaging and interesting.

Some of us resort to betrayal when the relationship brings up feelings that are difficult to face and understand. One client, George, would become angry when his partner displayed "weaknesses," such as talking about work frustrations and being uncertain about her career. His explosive rage actually reflected his own shame of appearing weak and not knowing all the answers. Deep down, George felt *responsible* for her. He wanted to be able to take care of her, as a man "should." The swelling guilt and frustration of not knowing how to help led to self-contempt—and anger toward himself for not being "good enough" to solve her problem. In a curious way, getting angry enabled him to instantly obliterate any awareness of these excruciatingly painful feelings. The self-imposed pressure to be gallantly loving and protective (a pressure that's also generated by society as a whole) was only creating less love and care for everyone.

As George looked at what the relationship revealed about himself, he saw that he didn't give himself permission to sometimes feel vulnerable and uncertain, which created much stress and pain in his life. As he began allowing himself to accept this set of feelings, he could more easily grant his partner the right to have similar feelings without the compulsion to rescue her from them. This new approach required continual reminders to himself (and from his cooperative partner) to be caring and compassionate toward himself, to repeatedly identify and relinquish his efforts to solve and fix the problem. Recognizing the wisdom of accepting and embracing his more vulnerable feelings enabled the partnership to deepen. In short, George learned something truly profound, a core principle that both men and women need to apply to the conflicts that can destroy love and intimacy: *A couple must be willing to take responsibility to explore what arises within each of them as a result of what happens between them.*

George's new commitment to his inner life breathed fresh

life into his partnership. As he put it, "It's a tremendous relief to think I don't have to solve her problems or fix her in some way. I'm really liking the idea of just listening to her in a caring way without the compulsion or obligation to *do* anything about it. Instead of my energies going into figuring out solutions, I can put them into just being there. That's much more relaxing and freeing."

Process Commitment within Marriage

The principles of a process commitment are not antithetical to marriage; they are antithetical to guarantees of permanence; they are antithetical to efforts to find refuge in the marital form while neglecting the marital process. *Neglecting this marital process is perhaps the most severe betrayal of all because such inattentiveness underlies all other forms of betrayal.*

A process commitment within the context of marriage enables both individuals to use the relationship to explore blocks to intimacy and growth. For most people, marriage provides the safer setting for working through these personal and interpersonal obstacles.

A publicly voiced marriage vow can be an expression and celebration of love, reinforced by a process commitment. There may also be the intention and hope to maintain the marital form for a lifetime. Conflicts and issues may then be addressed without undue fear that our partner will abruptly leave us if unforeseen stress or discomfort seeps into the partnership.

Fulfilling Our Primary Covenant with Life

The evolution of the human spirit will always take precedence over those forms of commitment that are in the interest of convenience, expediency, or self-protection. There is a mysterious knowing presence inside us that propels us toward our fullest unfolding as a human being. This unfolding can accelerate through a partnership firmly rooted in mutual re-

spect, nonbrutal honesty, and the ongoing effort to understand each other. However, if conflicts or differences arise
that cannot be resolved through persistent, mature efforts
over the course of time, then we may need to part—on good
terms and with mutual respect (if we are wise and fortunate)—so that we are freed to fulfill our deeper obligation to
ourselves, our even more sacred covenant with life itself.

ACCESSING AND COMMUNICATING OUR INNER EXPERIENCE

Major betrayals often happen suddenly and unexpectedly, but
the stage for such betrayals is set long before they actually
occur. If we can gain an overview of the course of a partnership, we may observe more clearly how our glimmering hopes
turn to bitter disappointment.

During the early phase of many new relationships, we experience few problems. We are super-eager to please each other
and make a good impression. Sex is exciting and the companionship comforting. Conflicts are few. The gratification of
feeling close may even prompt us to live together or get married so that we can extract more delights from the relationship.

Gradually, almost imperceptibly, the inevitable happens.
We begin to see the less savory aspects of each other more
clearly. Our differences become more apparent. Many of our
hopes and expectations are exposed as unrealistic. Our romantic fantasies and sexual passions begin to fade. We fall out
of Eden.

Most partnerships pass through a critical trial in which
personal differences, which seemed insignificant during the
early romantic phase, surge into the foreground. For her,
going back to college or having children may become center-
stage concerns; for him, issues around the intrusive in-laws or
money may predominate. A messy kitchen may get on his

nerves more and more; she may resent his time away from home.

Some of these apparent differences represent power struggles rooted in the inevitable clash between personal preferences and our partner's needs and wants. Other differences represent discrepancies in our temperament and viewpoints, which can also lead to conflict.

Little betrayals begin to contaminate our partnership when mounting disappointment leads to hostile attacks and mistrustful accusations. Rather than look clearly at what is happening and communicating in good faith, we begin to lose respect for our partner, we begin to hold him or her in disdain. Increasingly, we feel justified in blaming and shaming our partner. As our hopes and aspirations are frustrated, we may attribute ill motives to our partner, who is seen more and more as an uncooperative "enemy." As we pin more and more negative labels on him or her (selfish, impossible, stubborn), we feel increasingly justified spewing venom without regard to its devastating impact. As our discontent and alienation grow, we may even find ourselves wanting to cause hurt. Carla, who was in a two-year partnership, put it this way: "I want to hurt him when he doesn't give me what I want. I use words to tear him apart. But he doesn't deserve that."

Over the course of time, other disillusionments may set in. A body once adored because of the sexual gratification it provided may now be seen as unattractive. Habits and mannerisms that we once thought were cute may now annoy us. He or she may upset us by snoring, talking on the telephone, spending too much money.

Our besieged or neglected partner may experience a growing desire to visit friends or pursue other interests, which might leave us feeling ever more empty and lonely. We may feel hurt to discover that we are not the only treasure in his or her life. We may not know how to deal with the discomforting discovery that our partner's needs, wants, or temperament differ from our own. As Carla expressed this sober discovery,

149

"It may sound strange, but I guess it's hard for me to realize that he's a different person than me. I don't really *get* that—especially when I want something from him. I sometimes see him as an extension of myself, not someone with a different personal history and a different set of needs."

The Earnest Commitment to Personal Awakening

Fortunately, conflicts and power struggles do not necessarily spell disaster for a relationship. As I have suggested, a consistent commitment to the process of being honest with ourselves and others is necessary to resolve the conflicts inherent in any partnership. When dealt with wisely and sensitively, these conflicts and differences can become a bridge to greater closeness and mutual understanding, rather than a trapdoor to betrayal and abandonment.

Safeguarding our relationships from the pain of betrayal requires that each partner be committed to a delicate process of personal growth. The vital love that once united us can be nourished and maintained only through a sober, earnest commitment to deeper self-understanding and understanding of others. There is nothing more central to building a healthy environment for ourselves and our children—fostering what has been called "family values"—than pursuing personal growth. Without it, we are condemned to repeat habits and patterns that create heartache and anguish for those we claim to love.

The term *personal growth* can become an old, tired phrase, its vital meaning lost to us. New expressions and fresh ways of looking at the process of maturation are necessary so that we may continually cast fresh eyes upon a fluid, changing reality. The terms *personal development, self-actualization, self-realization, individuation, achieving autonomy,* and *becoming whole* point to the same process of knowing ourselves more fully—expanding our capacity to embrace a full range of feelings as well as to experience well-being, joy, love, intimacy, humor, aliveness, and gratitude.

What must grow in order to achieve this is our *awareness*, our ability to direct attention to ever more subtle layers of our inner experience. We might call it "personal awakening"— becoming sensitized to all aspects of our being, as well as being responsive to the life outside us. This includes others' needs and today's social and environmental imperatives.

Awakening to Inner Experience

Whatever term we use to point toward an ever-greater wisdom, personal depth, and mature relatedness to others, and whatever path we choose to get there, at least one element is essential: the capacity to gain access to our inner experience. We do not become more wise and mature through "head knowledge" alone, although such knowledge certainly has its place. The growth of satisfying relationships requires a more subtle kind of intelligence—*awakening to the richly felt dimension of our inner experience.*

Such experience includes the sentient dimension of our humanness. The dictionary defines *sentience* as "the capacity for feeling . . . mere awareness or sensation that does not involve thought." In other words, instead of just living in our heads, we're connected to our body, our heart, and our soul. Reconnecting with these lost, neglected, and disowned parts of ourselves is the major challenge of personal growth.

We wreak havoc in our close relationships when we are unaware of the inner promptings that stir within us—our rich life of feelings, desires, and motivations. When we ignore the subtleties of what is happening within the innermost recesses of our being, we cannot communicate the full flavor of our interior world (our fears, hurts, hopes, and joys). Instead, we withdraw into an uneasy silence; we remain numb and non-communicative. Or we vent the first impulses and emotions that dart through us; we blurt out the first words that come to mind, rather than communicate from a deeper, more self-aware, self-contained place. As one client put it, "Whenever I run off at the mouth it just makes things worse."

151

If our awareness is limited to familiar beliefs, positions, and emotions, then we not only rob ourselves of a deeper self-knowing, but we deprive others of a clearer glimpse into our inner world—one that is necessary for trust and intimacy to blossom. A process commitment rests forever upon our willingness to be honest with ourselves, to ascertain our real feelings, needs, thoughts, and motivations, however unpleasant these self-revelations might be. The failure to contact and convey our inner experience lends itself to massive confusion and miscommunication between people, and in that gulf there will prevail a climate fertile for various forms of betrayal.

Dealing effectively with conflict requires first that we recognize when we are experiencing conflict, then that we turn our attention to how we are experiencing it. How does this conflict speak to us? What are the feelings associated with it? What do we really need or want? What hopes or goals are being thwarted? What is this conflict really about? Gaining access to our inner experiencing enables us to probe our deeper responses to these questions, ones that underlie our initial reactions and our pat interpretations that perpetuate everyone's pain. *Real communication is only possible to the degree that we can open to what is really happening inside us.*

Andrea, a forty-year-old teacher, thought of herself as happily married, yet she was troubled by a compelling attraction to a man with whom she was having a secret affair: "It's like I'm under his spell. I feel this intense pull toward him. I want to stay married to my husband, but I *need* this other man." As she explored what was missing in her marriage, she read from her journal: "I need him to look me in the eyes more. I need him to really listen to me. I need him to cuddle with me without always having sex." When I asked if she'd shared these needs with her husband, she said she didn't want to put demands on him; she wanted him to respond voluntarily. But when she looked more deeply, she came to a more poignant realization: "I'm afraid I'd be rejected if I told him the truth. I'm afraid he'd respond to me for a while, then stop. That would be so painful; it would make me feel *very* unimportant." Paralyzed by these hidden fears, Andrea had stopped trying to get anything from her partner. Instead, her need showed itself in her attraction to a man who was eager to give her the affection she craved. As she brought more awareness to her inner experience—her secret fears and slumbering needs—she became more willing to open a dialogue with her husband.

When our inner experience languishes in a remote, frozen wasteland, we are out of touch with ourselves. We are then exposed to impulses and inclinations that may propel us toward secret affairs, abrupt separation, or other types of betrayal. By casting a clearer light on our inner experience, we become less confused by the conflictual forces that whirl within us and without us. As we deal with conflict with greater awareness and wisdom, new depths of understanding and love become possible. As we create a stronger connection and firmer foundation to accommodate conflict, the chances of betrayal diminish.

None of us can be exquisitely attentive at all times to the subtle world of our inner experience, nor would we want to be. An excessive self-focus could become a narcissistic preoccupation, an obstacle to just letting go and living. In addition, the daily pressures of life create stress and anxiety that interfere with our openness and sensitivity. Nevertheless, a process commitment asks us to take a reasonable and necessary amount of time to attend to our inner world so that our important relationships do not wither through the force of neglect. Each individual and couple must discover the right balance that will work for them.

Since we cannot always be attentive to ourselves or others, we will inevitably hurt each other at times. But we have considerable control over how we deal with these smaller hurts and rejections so that they do not escalate into full-blown betrayal. The more safety nets we build into the relationship, the better our chances of recovering our balance when we slip.

Communicating from Inner Experience

Most interpersonal conflicts can be traced to a lack of awareness of our actual inner experience. Instead of communicating from within, we pronounce edicts and impose decrees from without. We live armored in our opinions. We interpret others' experience for them, instead of really listening. We tell them what to do, how to feel, and what to think. Dale, a forty-five-year-old computer technician, expressed it clearly: "The more I lose touch with myself, the more bossy I become. I lose sight of my real feelings, even though I *think* I'm expressing them."

What we believe to be an expression of our "feelings" are oftentimes judgments and concepts, not freshly felt experience. These judgments may be infused with emotion, but they fail to touch and convey the deeper fabric of our inner experience. Being emotional—the superficial venting of emotions—is far different from offering a soulful expression of our feelings. Being semihysterical or enraged involves more bluster and bravado than a heartfelt sharing of our deeper being. For example, Dale would often shout, "You're so arrogant and self-centered!" When he took a moment to look more deeply, he began to frame such comments as "I feel angry and hurt when you interrupt me. I really need you to hear me about a matter that's hard for me to express." This statement conveyed a clearer sense of how he was inwardly affected by his partner, as well as what he needed. Being less inflammatory and more self-revealing, he received a warmer response.

Until we open to the process of experiencing a fuller and richer range of our inner experience, we cannot really know ourselves, or be known by others. We may then communicate only our frenetic criticisms, explosive anger, or surface-level emotions. If we fail to contact our underlying feelings, then these remain hidden from our partner. If we do not express what we really want, our partner will not know how to satisfy

154

us. If we don't know our limits and boundaries and state them clearly, our partner will not be guided by knowledge of what hurts or overwhelms us.

Skimpy awareness of our expectations, hopes, and goals may also lead to conflict. If our expectations are excessive but we don't know that, we may make our partner's life miserable because no matter what he or she does, it will never be enough to satisfy us. But if we do not honor our legitimate hopes for happiness, we will be dissatisfied because we won't be availing ourselves of the many gifts available through a true partnership. If we are unaware of our goals or deny our right to pursue them, we will suppress our deeper aspirations. This may cause depression or leave us spinning in resentments that we display in furtive, destructive ways, such as by having an affair or spending money behind our partner's back.

There are times when people do not respond favorably to us because they are not willing or able to do so. However, it is a sadder situation when people reject or ignore us because we are not clearly portraying what is happening inside us. We may fail to value and unveil our inner world of feelings and needs in its fullness and subtlety. Or we may not trust that the personal truth contained within this world will serve us in any way. We may not trust that sharing our real experience will further our longing to feel connected, understood, and appreciated. By failing to get ourselves across to another person, we reduce our relationship to (at best) one of intimate strangers. "I never really knew my partner" is an all too common lament.

If we can begin to gain access to what is really happening inside us and convey the texture of our inner landscape, we can build an important bridge to another person's world. We then create a climate in which honest, deeply felt communication can replace betrayal as a means of dealing with conflict and frustration.

Honesty Informed by Self-Awareness

Many of us have a self-image of being honest and forth-right in our interpersonal dealings. However, it takes more than honesty to build a harmonious, trusting relationship. Honesty has little value if we are not simultaneously uncovering the deeper, more subtle layers of our inner experience.

We can be only as honest as we are self-aware. Superficial honesty is far different from an honesty informed by access to our quieter, second-tier level of experiencing—one that reveals its secrets as we create a gentle, caring attitude toward the hurt, scary, and tender places within us. This gentle turning inward not only enables us to reach within our own depths, but it can also set up an empathic resonance with those tender places in our partner. By being tender toward ourselves, we empower our partner to bring forth his or her own hidden tenderness.

Many people only go through the motions of honesty. For example, they freely vent anger or tell people what they dislike about them. They are eager to give their "honest" opinion, regardless of how it might affect others or how appropriate it might be for the situation. In such instances, what is called honesty is better characterized as brutality or disguised aggression. The term *honesty* is cheapened whenever it is used to justify cruel attacks on others. Such protestations are meant to legitimize the crude emotional satisfaction that's gained by blaming and berating people.

Mature honesty has a palpable quality of depth and requires a profound degree of personal responsibility and integrity. It involves turning our attention inside ourselves to ascertain our own inner experience, rather than turning on others and pronouncing what we think is wrong with them. Emotional honesty means sharing our deeper feelings and sentiments, rather than scorching others with our hastily formed opinions and rigidly held judgments. It is easier to perceive and proclaim the real or imagined faults of others than it is to disclose how we are inwardly affected by others' words and actions. It becomes easier to betray others when we have painted a dark and sinister picture of them.

Sensing Our Subtle Experience

Before we can reveal our inner experience, we must first feel and sense what is actually happening inside us. This means opening to our more vulnerable recesses—the vague fears, hurts, doubts, and insecurities that, in a split second, we instinctively evade when some person or event elicits those abhorred feelings. Honesty that contains depth requires that we soften into feelings that may frighten or embarrass us. As we feel safer uncovering these subtle, delicate feelings, we are better positioned to disclose them, first to ourselves, then to others.

Little hurts accumulate when we fail to plumb the deeper, more fundamental dimension of our inner experience, a dimension that might shed new light on old arguments. As conflict and hurt grind on without resolution, one partner may feel unable to take it anymore. A seemingly innocuous interaction or incident may then trigger a final blow to a fragile relationship. Although the discontent was building all along, the person being left might feel suddenly betrayed, while the betrayer might falsely believe that he or she had done all that was possible to save the relationship.

It is my experience that in many instances, those initiating separation have not been as clear and communicative as they suppose. There may have been vague statements of discontent or nonverbal indications of dissatisfaction, such as emotional withdrawal or sexual distancing. There may have been misdirected anger and hot-tempered hostility that did not touch the core meaning of the dissatisfaction. Despite these displays, there has been no clear warning that they've become so unhappy that it will take only one or two more straws of discontent to break the ever-weakening back of the relationship. Such people may be so preoccupied with a crushing press of emotions that they do not possess the calmness and clarity of mind to articulate what is really happening inside them. I often hear people say, "There was a lot that wasn't talked about; I felt too overwhelmed to sort it all out. We never got down to what was really going on."

Communicating Our Deeper Experience

Stable, growing relationships require that we become aware of our discontents and discover what these are about, and that we learn to express ourselves in responsible, non-blaming ways. Some readers might remark, "I know very well what I'm unhappy about and I tell my partner all the time!" I have repeatedly observed that most people do not communicate their deepest feelings. Instead, they are in touch only with their ideas about how things should be, or how their partner should be different. Instead of showing their hurt, they state over and over again the same ancient complaints. Whatever feelings are expressed are often couched in such a critical, attacking, and shaming manner that the message is overshadowed by its hostile manner of delivery.

Many of us vent our feelings rather than communicate them. We attack with anger when we are actually afraid. We become spiteful and insulting when we are hurt or jealous. We act out our feelings rather than express them responsibly. We speak in ways that undermine our partner's self-esteem. We elicit resistance and defensiveness rather than invite a receptive hearing to our legitimate hurts and concerns. Our lack of relatedness to what is really going on, coupled with incomplete communication, contributes immensely to the hurt and confusion that often lead to betrayal.

If, instead of trying to change others, we could change ourselves—to the extent of accessing how we really feel and showing these feelings to others—then we are doing our part to base our relationships on trust. By taking the risk to reveal our inner experience, we give trust and intimacy a chance to grow.

Discontent quietly festers when we minimize how upset we really are, or when we remain vague about what is really bothering us. Instead of dealing with these discontents as they're building, we may ignore them, or we may grimly conclude that our partner will never understand us. In reality, *we* may not know our own feelings and wants. As one insight-struck man put it, "How can I expect her to understand me when I don't even understand myself?"

When Judy asked to spend time with Jed, he'd often complain that he was too tired and would bury himself in the newspaper. He would sometimes shout angrily, "Would you quit bugging me! Just leave me alone! You're so needy!" When he looked deeper at his real feelings, he realized that his withdrawal from Judy served to protect him from potentially painful criticism. Like many men in our society, Jed was frequently critiqued and blamed as a child. He grew up with many pressures to perform well and "do things right." Spending quiet time with Judy was just one more thing that he might not do right, that he might get wrong. Indeed, there were times when Judy treated him abruptly and angrily, which reinforced his tendency to spend as little time with her as he could get away with.

Jed gradually realized that his tendency to withdraw from Judy stemmed from a deep-seated fear of being a failure, plus the shame of not being perfect: "I didn't realize how deep that went. I just thought I was somebody who needed a lot of independence, a lot of privacy. I didn't realize what was really driving me for all these years." Seeing his deeper fears, he understood more clearly his tendency to avoid communicating with Judy.

By sharing the old fears and hurts that led him to protect himself, he gave Judy a better understanding of his special sensitivity to criticism. As Judy put it, "I never realized how hurt he was feeling. All I ever saw was a brick wall. When he tells me his fears and hurts, it's a *lot* easier to hear him and be patient. It feels so much better being with him when I can trust that he's committed to understanding himself and telling me what's really going on inside him."

Just being able to talk about all this was an important step toward dismantling the distance and miscommunication that tragically blocked their love for each other. Jed's growing courage and willingness to have discussions like this, coupled with Judy's patience and understanding, went a long way toward rebuilding the closeness they both wanted.

Interpersonal conflicts assume a life of their own when we close off our awareness of what's really going on. Instead of peering within, we may decide awful things about each other and then live as if our cynical interpretations are correct, which promotes mutual mistreatment. We may insist that our partner change, without deeply looking at our own role in the conflict. *Learning to contact feelings and concerns at an earlier moment, then exploring those issues together, may avert a blind drift toward conflict and misunderstanding.*

Relationships can have an amazing capacity to bounce back from the edge of even a major betrayal when we take responsibility to connect with our inner experience and reveal that experience in an open, trusting way. The interpersonal wall of hurt and resentment can begin to crumble if one partner owns up to how he or she has contributed to a cold war of recrimination and emotional distancing. It is difficult to continue battling someone who has the humility to acknowledge his or her role in perpetuating a destructive impasse. Then, instead of continuing the power struggle, the other partner may be more willing to explore his or her part in the conflict. "Now that she's starting to be more real with me," said one client, "I'd be a jerk not to be real with her. Actually, it's a lot easier to let down my guard when I'm not feeling controlled and criticized."

Showing Others a More Authentic Self

Learning to gain access to our inner experience may sound mysterious, but it is a simple task. However, its being simple does not make it easy to undertake. We must first still the

160

incessant mental chatter that constitutes one line of defense (to be discussed in the next chapter). We must then feel good enough about ourselves to value our inner world of feelings. We must overcome our sense of inadequacy and chronic self-criticism so that we can hear the quieter music that echoes more softly within ourselves.[18]

The stage is then set to turn our attention in a patient, gentle way to the inner sensations and intimations that we generally refer to as feelings, or what I have been calling inner experience. As we begin to uncover and heed the more subtle feelings that pulse within us, we come to know ourselves in a deeper way. We can then share ourselves more completely with others. We can show them a more real, authentic, vulnerable self. If they accept our natural self and reciprocate by sharing their own inner experience, trust is likely to grow. If they remain distant and disconnected, then we may need to consider the option of directing our energies toward those who might appreciate who we are.

Contacting and sharing our inner experience takes time and patience—often a great deal of time and patience—plus a willingness to learn and grow from failure. Many people experiment with brief forays into this realm of personal growth, then become discouraged or give up when their accustomed methods of gaining control begin to slip away, with little faith that they can create a more effective replacement. In this journey of personal awakening, there is little of the instant gratification that our psyche has grown accustomed to in our sanitized, computer-assisted lives.

The lack of commitment to discovering what is really happening inside us, especially when coupled with the lack of motivation and skills to convey our inner experience effectively, is a major factor leading to the betrayal of others and ourselves. If we want to realize the promise of more satisfying relationships, we must call forth a steady commitment to patience, practice, and perseverance. Otherwise, we will likely retreat when things become confusing, difficult, or painful. Rather than work through the rough spots, we'll return to our familiar ways, even though they've led to unwanted pain and suffering time and time again. Like soldiers huddled in their bunkers long after the war has ended, we will cling to a peculiar comfort and safety rather than risk reaching for new possibilities.

NOTES

1. S. M. Campbell, *The Couples Journey* (San Luis Obispo, CA: Impact Publishers, 1980), 89.

2. Some people appear to be exquisitely sensitive to others' feelings, but their motivation may not be very pure. They may learn to "read" people in order to manipulate them better, or avoid conflict, or prove how caring they are so they can be loved in turn. Their sensitivity quickly fades in any situation in which acknowledging and respecting another's viewpoint or feelings might call for some change in their status or behavior—some loss of power over that other person, or some surrendering of the privileged position they've grown accustomed to.

3. D. W. Winnicott, *Playing and Reality* (London: Tavistock, 1968).

4. E. Erikson, *Childhood and Society* (New York: Norton, 1963).

5. See David E. Rosenbaum, *San Francisco Chronicle*, "Economy a Tricky Campaign Issue for Bush." 12 Sept. 1992.

6. The depth of emotional wounding inflicted by siblings is an area that is just beginning to receive the attention it deserves.

7. For more on this theme, see Sam Keen, *Faces of the Enemy* (New York: HarperCollins, 1986).

8. There are indeed times when we need to leave a relationship that is truly abusive. However, some people may use the term too loosely, such as when their own needs or wants aren't being met.

9. Even couples who see themselves as partners in honest, intimate relationships may be deceiving themselves. Susan Whitbourne, a University of Massachusetts psychologist, suggests that marital partners often paint rosy pictures of their relationship. See Kenneth R. Bazinet, *San Francisco Chronicle*, "Married Couples Fooling Themselves." 29 Jan., 1990. See also Susan Whitbourne and Joyce Ebmeyer, *Identity and Intimacy in Marriage: A Study of Couples* (New York: Springer-Verlag, 1989).

10. Scott Nelson, who interviewed seventy individuals who maintained or reestablished a friendship with former partners, found that some partnerships dissolved because one or both members had individual difficulties so great that the relationship could not be supported. One

woman, on being confronted with the death of her father, realized that she was carrying too much emotional baggage in relation to her father to continue being committed to her spouse. See Scott Nelson, *Lost Lovers, Found Friends* (New York: Simon & Schuster, 1991).

11. D. R. Kingma, *Coming Apart* (Berkeley, CA: Conari Press, 1987), 2.

12. J. Hillman, *Loose Ends: Primary Papers in Archetypal Psychology* (Dallas: Spring Publications, 1975), 67.

13. Ibid., 74.

14. S. M. Campbell, *Beyond the Power Struggle* (San Luis Obispo, CA: Impact Publishers, 1984), 140.

15. D. Tannen, *You Just Don't Understand* (New York: Ballantine Books, 1991).

16. A. Kipnis and E. Hingston, "Ending the Battle between the Sexes," *Utne Reader,* January/February 1993, 71. For more on this theme, see their book *Gender War/Gender Peace* (New York: Morrow, 1994).

17. Of course, there are ways to work with our fear of entrapment before evoking our ultimate right to leave a relationship, such as by affirming our right to take time alone within the relationship. This may free us to feel closer to our partner.

18. This is not easy to do alone. Seeking the assistance of a counselor or guide may be invaluable in helping us feel safer about opening to ourselves. The Guide to Resources at the end of the book provides suggestions for contacting counselors and helpers in various locations.

CHAPTER 6

Is There Life after Betrayal?

Experiencing a solitary state gives the individual the opportunity to draw upon untouched capacities and resources and to realize himself in an entirely unique manner. It can be a new experience. It may be an experience of exquisite pain, deep fear and terror, an utterly terrible experience, yet it brings into awareness new dimensions of self, new beauty, new power for human compassion, and a reverence for the precious nature of each breathing moment.

CLARK MOUSTAKAS[1]

Betrayal hurts. There are no magic formulas or surefire techniques for delivering us from the anguish and bitterness left in the wake of a major betrayal. However, as we move through our initial shock and disillusionment, there is a potentially promising sequel to betrayal. The weeks and months after betrayal afford an opportunity for understanding ourselves and life in a more deeply felt way. *Life's most liberating discoveries are often reserved for times when we feel most wounded or broken.*

The fresh perceptions and understandings that are culled from betrayal are unique for each of us. However, I have observed a pattern of discovery in those who have dealt with betrayal in a sober and wise fashion. Some of these lessons may seem obvious, but others may appear unrelated to our betrayal—perhaps because the lessons we most need to learn are those we most vigorously resist.

The aftermath of betrayal provides a fertile ground for new revelations, or for a renewed appreciation of realizations that need further integration into heart and soul. Such discoveries may include the recognition that there's a way in which we're alone in life, the need for supportive relationships outside our primary partnership, the need to acknowledge our possible role in the betrayal, and the need to improve communication and dialogue skills.

EMBRACING OUR ALONENESS

We point ourselves in the wrong direction when we tirelessly search for someone outside ourselves who will be our care-taker and savior. When our fantasy-desires of finding the per-fect lover-charmer, friend-companion, and parent-provider are consistently thwarted, we are thrown back upon our own resources. Perhaps it cannot be any other way. The frenetic search outside ourselves leads us back inside ourselves, though not without massive kicking and screaming. For those of us who live in denial of our basic aloneness, being betrayed can be a grim reminder of how utterly alone we are in the world.

When we are deserted by a partner, we are presented with the distasteful prospect that we must reface the aloneness that has always been ours. Many of us protest our betrayal by pronouncing a firm "No" to life at this juncture. We hide our open wound with cynical thoughts, reactive hostility, and sul-len withdrawal. We draw grim conclusions: "Relationships aren't for me." We denigrate the opposite sex: "Men can't handle intimacy" or "All women are controlling." We make fateful decisions: "I'll never let anyone get close to me again. Now I'll just take care of myself."

Others of us deal with our newfound aloneness by rushing

headlong into whirlwind relationships. We organize adventuresome romances that lead to familiar outcomes. We fill our social calendar so that we have no spare time to experience stark aloneness. We hurl ourselves into work or go on a shopping spree to distract ourselves from loneliness ("I shop, therefore I am"). We throw ourselves into activities that obliterate our nagging sense of separateness.

If we are to heal from betrayal, rather than distract ourselves from ourselves, we must learn to embrace our aloneness. Our postbetrayal time affords a unique opportunity to experience life and get to know ourselves apart from a relationship. Then, when we're ready to reopen ourselves to someone new, we have more of ourselves to bring to this new relationship. We have a greater awareness about what a partnership can and cannot provide, as well as how to nurture a loving, trusting relationship.

A year after being abruptly left, Joan expressed her need to be alone as follows: "I realize that I'm not really ready to open my heart to anyone new. It would just hurt too much to be abandoned again. I date occasionally, but I'm not emotionally available for a new partner. I feel my time is coming soon—when I'll be more healed. For now, I need to be with myself and learn whatever I need to learn so I don't go through this again."

If we want to establish sound, intimate relationships with others, we need to be intimate with ourselves. A new, stronger sense of self can emerge through the discoveries made during times of aloneness, which psychologist Clark Moustakas describes as "a point of intense and timeless awareness of the Self, a beginning which initiates totally new sensitivities and awareness."[2] Paradoxically, new possibilities for connection and intimacy arise as we face and embrace our separateness. *As we gradually learn to rest in aloneness, we come to reside in that still, pure center where intimacy happens.*

Embracing Solitude

Many people claim that they like being alone, but they do not really embrace their aloneness in the way I'm suggesting. They like being alone so that they can pursue hobbies, watch television, or enjoy a beer. In reality, embracing our aloneness means being with ourselves apart from doing things that entertain us or keep us busy. Most centrally, it means *embracing a positive, life-affirming sense of solitude.* Embracing solitude involves *being engaged in the creative process of being connected with ourselves apart from external distractions.*

Such solitude not only helps us connect with ourselves, it opens a doorway to richer connections with others. As writer Anne Morrow Lindbergh expresses it,

> When one is a stranger to oneself then one is estranged from others, too. If one is out of touch with oneself, then one cannot touch others. . . . Only when one is connected to one's own core is one connected to others, I am beginning to discover. And for me, the core, the inner spring, can best be refound through solitude.[3]

Learning to rest in our solitude is not something we do once or twice and then conclude that we have accepted our aloneness. There are ever-deeper levels at which we can experience it.

Although this task may seem stark and austere, we can connect with a precious new sense of ourselves by spending some of our postbetrayal time delighting in the embrace of our own company. I have encountered three paths on which to deepen our connection with ourselves and with life: the path of meditation, the path of self-inquiry, and the path of creative self-expression.

MEDITATION

The path of meditation is a simple, age-old way to befriend ourselves by bringing attention within ourselves in a consistent manner. Meditation is often misunderstood as some kind of esoteric technique. Actually, it's a natural human function that we all experience from time to time. Walking in the woods, gazing at our lover, looking fondly at our child, listening to an engaging song or concert—these experiences can open us to the beauty, mystery, and wonder of life. The world stops during these precious moments. Our mind becomes still. We are somehow carried into a wordless sense of presence with ourselves, others, or life itself.

To engage more formally in meditation, we may simply bring our attention to the sensation of our breathing. Doing so, we cultivate a calm, centered awareness that is less prone to mental distractions and sneak attacks from our shaming "inner critic." By resting in a tranquil sea of self-awareness, something strengthens in us. We become less preoccupied with the self-denigrating thoughts, hurtful impulses, and gnawing bitterness that may plague us after betrayal, or at any other time. As these external forces tug on us less, we come to rest more comfortably and wholeheartedly in the deeper source of our being—our soulful essence that survives and thrives despite whatever assaults it has sustained. Stuart, the man whose wife was having a secret affair, expressed its value as follows: "The meditation helped me find a safe place within myself—it gave me a way to connect with myself when I'm alone."

Meditation is not an escape from our life of feelings. As we relax internally, we gain greater access to important feelings that stir imperceptibly within us, ones that underlie our painfully familiar emotions and reactions. Therapist Wayne Muller expresses beautifully how meditation can help us embrace our deeper pain:

Simply sitting quietly with ourselves, we tend to feel our pain more acutely, we experience the depth and texture of our broken heart, we feel the poignant sting of tears yet to be shed. In stillness, without the distraction of being busy, we touch our inner landscape with excruciating intimacy, and we may feel for the first time the extent to which our tender feelings have been bruised. . . . perhaps our greatest healing comes when we listen quietly and carefully to ourselves and our sorrow. Maybe there is nothing for us to take out, nothing to fix, nothing to do but mindfully touch our heart and spirit with quiet, loving attention.[4]

Joseph Goldstein and Jack Kornfield, teachers of meditation, explain the merits of meditation as follows:

Meditation has to do with opening what is closed in us, balancing what is reactive, and investigating what is hidden. . . . We spend so much of our time lost in thought, in judgment, in fantasy, and in daydreams. . . . Meditation practice is neither holding on nor avoiding; it is a settling back into the moment, opening to what is there. And this balance of mind . . . makes possible a connection with a deep rhythm. . . . In order to find the rhythm, however, a great effort is needed. It's the effort to pay attention, to bring the mind into each moment.[5]

The physical and psychological benefits of meditation have been well documented and have been steadily gaining recognition in academic and scientific circles.[6] By regularly attending to ourselves in a calmly focused manner, we gain greater detachment from our restless ruminations and anxious brooding. As we descend into our depths, we become less frantic in our efforts to manipulate our environment to ensure that we're worthwhile. Through the consistent practice of meditation, we may find welcome relief from the self-blame, pain, and confusion we'd feared might be interminable. We may find a reservoir of peace and tranquility lying deep within our being, a calm sense of presence that may increasingly permeate our lives.

In the engrossing movie *My Dinner with André,* which explores a dinner conversation between two friends, André describes his globe-trotting search for a life with greater meaning, poignancy, and aliveness. At one point he explains:

> I had to put myself in a kind of training program just to learn how to be a human being. I mean, how did I feel about anything? I didn't know. What kind of things did I like? What kind of people did I really want to be with? . . . the only thing I could think of to find out was just to cut out all the noise and stop performing all the time and just listen to what was inside me. . . . I think a time comes when you need to do that. Now, maybe in order to do it you have to go to the Sahara, and maybe you can do it at home. But you need to cut out the noise.

Meditation is a primary way to quiet the internal noise and listen to ourselves.

By regularly touching a calm center of aliveness within ourselves—even for a few brief moments—we enjoy a refreshing respite from the clamor and drama of our lives. Gradually, we may learn to bask for longer periods of time in this reliable refuge that always exists within us. As our sense of well-being grows stronger, our trust in life may be restored. As we feel more connected with ourselves, we can see more clearly how we want to live our lives. As we feel more comfortable with ourselves, we are less inclined to betray ourselves or punish others, which bodes well for building satisfying relationships in the future.[7]

The ability to rest in our own depths provides the most potent antidote to the fear of abandonment. As discussed in Chapter 3, this fear can trigger rage when we feel betrayed (or when we're rejected or shunned). This fear of abandonment may also underlie our attempts to satisfy our needs by controlling and manipulating people, which can lead to an escalating cycle of conflict or betrayal.

The more we have ourselves, the less we fear being abandoned and alone. Of course, being betrayed or abandoned will still hurt, but it is far less devastating if we know how to be with ourselves. Also, we may come to focus less on what we can get from a partnership and more on what we can give, or we can learn to balance giving and receiving in a more harmonious way. The more we embrace our depths, the more of ourselves we have to offer.

In addition to helping us embrace solitude, the discipline of meditation can provide grounding for our sincere desire to make a process commitment to future relationships. As we find stillness within our being, we can more easily sense what is really happening inside us. As we touch deeper layers of ourselves, we have something more real and substantial to share with friends and loved ones: our genuine feelings, our aspirations, our true wants.

Perhaps most importantly, meditation is a central way to cultivate an authentic presence to share with others, a vibrant connection of soul to soul, being to being. Delighting in inner stillness—perhaps gently gazing at our friend or lover with soft eyes reflecting our tender heart—we may partake of a sumptuous soul nourishment. *This precious gift of mutual presence is a rare feast for the soul. It is a living experience of the deeper intimacy for which our essential being longs.* The only magic that's required is to quiet the turbulent torrents of thought, self-criticism, and analysis so that life's quieter beat may pulse through us and between us.

SELF-INQUIRY

The path of self-inquiry—moving toward what is loosely called self-understanding—involves gaining an ever-greater awareness of the feelings, thoughts, and impulses that flow through us and motivate us. Self-inquiry also involves getting clearer about our values, goals, and aspirations and finding creative ways to move toward their actualization. Are we aware of what we really want from life, or do we live mechanically and automatically? Have we lost touch with our life purpose and with our personal and spiritual values? How do we deal with obstacles that are placed on our path? Can we use them as stepping-stones to greater awareness and wisdom? How do we respond when things don't go our way?

Betrayal invites us to address fundamental questions about our lives in a fresh way. If we can learn to live with these questions, to inquire with a sincere heart and open mind, our spirit deepens, our heart opens.

The life-shattering impact of betrayal may prompt us to break faith with life. As our strength is sapped, we may abandon our quest for happiness, if not forsake the will to live. A mood of hopelessness, cynicism, or defiance may take over.

Releasing old outlooks about life and love can actually be a step forward. As our familiar ways yield to an unknown future, we experience a rawness, an openness that can allow new creativity and grace to enter. If we could gently welcome and embrace that rawness, a new, uncharted life would unfold before us, one that invites refreshing possibilities and surprises.

As we take time to feel and accept our vulnerability, we may notice the dawning of a new and deeper sensitivity—to ourselves, to others, to life itself. Our rawness keeps us connected to ourselves in a tender way. As one consequence, we become more available to be emotionally touched by others. Beth, who was left by her husband for a younger woman, was dealing with her loss in a constructive way. Several months after her betrayal, she was complimented by a friend: "You're more open now. It's easier for me to connect with you. There's a new softness in you that I like."

The desolation of betrayal can give rise to a newfound courage and durability. I have spoken with many people who have surprised themselves by discovering an untapped reservoir of inner strength and resiliency.

Helene, whose partner suddenly left her to live with another woman, was shaken to her core: "I suddenly lost everything. I didn't know who I was or what I believed in anymore. I wanted to die. But in the midst of it—when my heart was broken—I had deeper access to *me*. Inside that shell is the

172

meat—is me—the real me, no bullshit. When my heart was broken open, the 'no bullshit me' was there. I decided I might as well go for it and see what I'm made of. I now call it the 'severe opportunity.' It was really a gift to me because it shook the very core of me; I had to reevaluate who I was, to look at myself face to face in a much brighter light than I ever had before."

By spending time alone—taking long walks on the beach, writing in her journal, resting quietly at home—Helene discovered a new facet of herself: "I found a strength that I didn't know was there. Here I am. I'm strong. If anyone lets me down, I can always bank on myself now." Through persistent self-inquiry, Helene used betrayal as a rite of passage to a greater sturdiness, wisdom, and self-compassion.

If we can summon the strength and resiliency to spot a glimmer of light within the dark night of our soul—if we can muster even a *faint* resolve to move forward in life—then we can begin the process of replacing self-abnegation with self-exploration and self-affirmation. We move through disillusionment and begin to see what's really true. We enter a journey of learning and growing from our betrayal.

Our chosen method of self-inquiry is a matter of personal preference. For example, we might spend quiet time exploring personal issues within the privacy of our own thoughts. Or our exploration may be aided by joining a women's or men's support group, attending a personal growth workshop, reading relevant books, listening to educational tapes, or keeping a personal journal. These and other activities place us in reflective environments in which we may discover new hope and fresh directions in our lives. If we listen closely to the quiet stirrings within us, we will find our own best way to move forward.

If we are fortunate to have a trusted friend, someone who can listen to our hurt, our anger, and our fears without judging us, this may be an opportune time to avail ourselves of his or her precious companionship. If we lack supportive friendships, we might want to invest time in developing a small circle of kindhearted friends who are similarly committed to personal growth. Enlisting a counselor, minister, or educator might help us explore personal concerns and enhance self-understanding. This helping relationship might help us discover how the conditions of childhood have negatively affected our adult relationships. Or we might use this safe setting to uncover our deeper feelings, needs, and wants that we may have ignored or minimized.

A rude betrayal often highlights the fact that we did not know ourselves as well as we had imagined. It is also probable that we did not know our partner as well as we had supposed. A betrayal may raise questions about our judgment and choices in life. It may also provide an opportunity to look at our role in the demise of a relationship. We may find some measure of comfort in knowing that a thoroughgoing self-exploration is deepening our understanding so that we won't repeat prior mistakes.

CREATIVE EXPRESSION

Engaging in meaningful, creative pursuits is another way to reconnect with ourselves after betrayal. As we find refuge in creative solitude, we may discover assets and abilities that we never knew existed or embark on a path that we'd only considered in our wildest fantasies. Expressing our pain through writing, journal keeping, music, or art can transform heartache into creations of wisdom and compassion. By giving expression to our hurt, we move toward releasing it. The popular musician Sting reported in a "60 Minutes" interview that his best writing is born of pain. Some of the greatest works of art, music, and literature were created out of the anguish of those experiencing betrayal. Creative self-expression can introduce us to new dimensions of ourselves and reengage us with life.

Julia, a creative and courageous poet in Northern California, wrote the following verses in her journal, which expressed her pain a few weeks after being left by her partner: "I crumple to the ground. My legs can no longer hold my weight. . . . I scream from a place that goes beyond crying and tears. That deep gut place where secret wounds lay open and raw. That place I let *him* touch. That place where the scent of his soul still lingers, continuing its now uninvited way through the senses of my heart." Giving voice to her pain allowed her to touch its poignant depths. Courageously embracing her pain created a channel for its release, which enabled her to heal.

As we embrace periods of creative solitude, we feel more connected with ourselves. We find a center of strength and well-being within our very selves. By resting in our solitary depths, we become more available for the satisfying interpersonal contact we seek—not by *grasping* for closeness, but by *allowing* it to unfold. As we become more whole through befriending solitude, we connect more easily with those who are similarly growing toward wholeness and authenticity. As we cultivate a comfortable refuge within ourselves, we discover a closer connection with other people and with life itself.

THE NEED FOR SUPPORTIVE RELATIONSHIPS

Rather than embrace a healthy sense of solitude, some of us opt for self-imposed isolation. Ruled by interpersonal fears, we may seek solace by withdrawing from human contact. We may justify our isolation by believing that we like independence, or that we're loners, as did Jed in the previous chapter. In reality, our "independence" is often a reaction to our fear of rejection or our shame of failure, rather than healthy autonomy.

Isolation serves a protective function. It guards us against the dreaded possibility of facing the fear, humiliation, and hurt that might arise through interpersonal contact. Unfortunately, this protective function also prevents us from experiencing the very emotions that we must feel and integrate if we're ever to awaken to our genuine self. We betray ourselves when we allow parts of ourselves to remain isolated from the whole of who we are. Distancing ourselves from others deprives us of the interpersonal contact necessary to bringing forth parts of the self that remain dormant, beaten down, or constricted.

Men in our culture have a stronger tendency to isolate themselves from human contact when they're hurting. As men, we've been taught to "tough it out" and not appear weak. Peter, a middle-aged insurance broker who was left by his wife, conveys a common male sentiment: "This is just something I have to take care of myself. I should never expect anything from people, then I'll never be disappointed." This gallant bravado covered up a deeper hurt and vulnerability.

Many women also have difficulty allowing themselves to be vulnerable. Paula, a young woman who was left with a child when her husband abandoned her, put it this way: "I've let go of needing anything from people. I live my life one day at a time—my child and I will do just fine." I detected a coldness in Paula's voice and noticed an unwillingness to share—and perhaps face—her deeper pain. Similar to many men, I sensed a lingering hurt and bitterness that shaped itself into a rigid individualism and emotional distancing. Of course, reopening ourselves after such a hurtful betrayal takes time, but it also takes courage to share some part of our story with someone who displays caring.

By sweeping us away from an important source of caring contact and support, betrayal deposits us on a barren shore. Although at times we can benefit by being alone, we may also need the right kind of support. In fact, such crisis provides a unique opportunity *to see who our friends really are*—to see who responds to us with warmth and understanding when we're our most essential and vulnerable selves. During this critical period we may discover the curious paradox that life is a solitary journey that we cannot take alone.[8]

Finding Real Friends

We may be surprised to realize that some people we thought were our closest friends aren't really there for us during a time of crisis. They may not extend the kind of emotional support and nurturance we need when we are hurting. They may be uncomfortable as they witness our emotional display, perhaps because they are ill at ease with their own feelings. As a result, they may try to change the subject. They may attempt to cheer us up to distract us from our pain and vulnerability. They may repeat the same platitudes we've heard a thousand times before, or that we've been telling ourselves to no avail. Expressions like "You'll get over it" or "Time heals all wounds" might offer some meager support, but they do not reflect a depth of compassion and understanding that might help us heal and learn from our experience.

Other friends may flood us with "support" that is not truly supportive. They may encourage us to remain a pitiable victim, as Theresa remembered after separating from her husband. During their five-year marriage, he'd become angry with increasing frequency when she wanted emotional contact. According to her, he was "shut down emotionally." According to him, she was "demanding and overbearing." When she finally left him, she received much "support" from her friends, most of whom were not privy to the intricacies of their interactions. As she put it, "I got a lot of encouragement to wallow in victimhood. It's easier—but it's worse in the end. I didn't have to look at my part. I could just pity myself and get others to pity me. Friends would say, 'Oh that bastard, he wasn't good for you anyway. You were too good to him. He never appreciated you.' I got a lot of strokes by playing that game."

Theresa explained how her friend Dean offered her the greatest support: "I appreciated how Dean never took sides. He respected that I had to move through my stuff. At times when I was stuck in victimhood, others sided with me. They were protective of me. It would have been more helpful if they told me what they honestly saw, thought, and felt. I guess I could have *asked* for that kind of honesty from my other friends. Their feedback might have helped me become more self-aware—to see some patterns about myself—to help me see my contribution to the relationship, both negative and positive, and see my partner's contribution, both negative and positive. It feels good to have a certain amount of hand holding when it's first happening, but after a while it's just not useful."

By taking the risk to reach out in new ways, we may be delighted to discover deepening friendships with acquaintances never before approached in a true spirit of openness. If we're willing to risk sharing something real about ourselves with various people, we may find that some of them respond positively. They might recount a similar experience, thereby helping us feel less isolated. They might make a helpful comment that illuminates a cloudy aspect of the relationship. They might extend empathy in a way that enables us to get clearer about how we really feel. Most importantly, they might display a warm quality of compassion that touches our heart. Rather than employing strategies of control, they help us feel safe to let go. Rather than bolstering our defenses, they may reveal a more deeply held faith in us, *a trust that we're strong enough to heal and grow from our difficult and painful experience.*

Balancing Our Partnership with Friendships

When we first enter a heart-throbbing partnership, we may let other relationships languish. By designating our partner as lover, friend, and confidant, we build a sheltered nest apart from the world. We may become so enamored of this relationship that we have little desire to connect with anyone else. Our partner may lobby for further isolation by pressuring us to disconnect from our friends so that he or she can capture our complete attention.

It is understandable to want to spend exclusive time with our partner, especially during the early glow of romance. However, the danger is that by neglecting to nurture current friendships (including our friends who are still single), these sources of growth and support may shrivel. When we restrict our investment of time and energy to our partner, there may be little love and support coming our way if this partnership peters out. We may then need to repair old friendships as well as initiate new ones. But even more ominous, we may develop a narrow, limited view of the world by not availing ourselves of a fuller range of human contact. One man who found himself with no friends after a painful divorce explained, "I did the typical thing men do in our culture after getting married. Old friendships just kind of fade away and the woman takes care of the couple's new friendships."

The Limits of Friendship: Choosing a Helper

While friends can offer loyalty and companionship during a time of betrayal, their well-intended help may not be very helpful. It might even be destructive. In their eagerness to win our affection and appreciation, they might offer abundant advice and reassurance that diverts us from our deeper work. We sometimes need a firm hand to guide our attention toward discomforting feelings and perceptions if we are to arise from the cross of betrayal with heightened wisdom and greater compassion for ourselves and others. It often takes someone who is not too close to the daily drama of our lives to help us do this—someone who is not a friend, and therefore not dependent upon our friendship.

The consumer faces a confusing array of therapeutic and educational approaches to personal awakening, each with its own theoretical orientation and philosophical perspective. Some of these orientations complement and support each other; they focus on different parts of the overall process of growth toward autonomy and intimacy. Other approaches may divert us from our real goals and values. We need to choose wisely.

For example, some approaches to personal growth maintain that emotional and spiritual growth are inseparable. Other systems of psychology do not accommodate a worldview that recognizes the spiritual dimension of life. In fact, they may be antagonistic to such a perspective, viewing it as displaced sexuality or reducing it to a narcissistic quest to feel important. It is therefore crucial to choose an approach to growth that is consistent with your own philosophical inclination, unless you are willing to suspend or reexamine your orientation.

My own philosophical preference is aligned with approaches variously labeled as humanistic, transpersonal, experiential, and existential. These and similar approaches honor the primacy of each individual's personal experience and mainly focus on helping people gain access to this experience as a pathway to connect with self and others. These perspectives are suspicious of orientations that place excessive power and authority in the hands of the counselor or helper. While such authority may be readily projected onto any helper, it is minimized in the above approaches. By not fostering reliance on the helper for advice, by minimizing the interpretation of process, and by trusting individuals to gain access to their own experience and discover their own meanings, these approaches foster safe conditions under which people can discover that they are the authors of their own lives.

When interviewing prospective counselors, you might want to ask if they share any of the above perspectives. But even then, you need to use your intuition to sense whether this is a good match for you. Most crucially, it is the person rather than the stated orientation that creates a climate conducive to healing and growth.

ACKNOWLEDGING OUR ROLE
IN BETRAYAL

Betrayal deflates our hopes for a love-filled life. As explained earlier, our hurt is often converted to vindictive hostility and revenge to bolster self-esteem. The prospect of separation may produce such intense fright that we grasp all available weapons in an impotent offensive against our helplessness. Once these efforts prove futile, we may be tormented by internal dialogues and quietly seething ill-will. Even when the war is over and the divorce final, there may remain self-righteous justifications and biting resentment. We may be unwilling to suspend our testy viewpoints and positions and accept what *is*. A secret self-hatred may also prevail. Our sarcasm toward relationships and loss of faith in life may keep us bitter and unhappy for many years to come.

It is painful to be left. Even worse, the way we were left may have been shockingly insensitive or decidedly cruel. There may have been breaches of honesty and integrity that evidenced total lack of regard for our well-being.

Although we may have been the subject of emotional atrocities, it is rare for betrayal to happen without our own contributing role, however small. Eventually, life calls upon us to explore our part in the demise of a relationship. If we can overcome our shame of failing and our fear of being wrong and summon the courage to look and listen closely, we might discover how we actively or quietly conspired to design or perpetuate an unworkable relationship.

When examining our role in betrayal, *it is vital to create a climate of compassion and forgiveness toward ourselves.* Although we may have contributed to an atmosphere leading to betrayal, those contributions, subtle or overt, often originate from patterns learned in childhood and from values planted by society. The fears and defenses we developed to survive our youth get carried into our adult relationships. Despite our

181

sincere intentions, firmly planted romantic fantasies and beliefs may have disserved us. Due to a dearth of life skills
education and effective role modeling, we may never have
learned interpersonal skills to help us deal with little conflicts
that tend to lead to big betrayals. As Gene put it, "I never saw
my parents resolve their differences by talking about things.
They dealt with conflict by yelling at each other, or by giving
each other the silent treatment." We must not blame ourselves for these unfortunate legacies of our social upbringing.

The learnings we may gather from being betrayed are
unique for each of us. Perhaps we will recognize how we
participated in the creation of distrust and resentment. Maybe
our deeper fears caused us to be controlling—we may have
believed we were being assertive and powerful when we were
really being domineering. Or perhaps our partner voiced concerns that we didn't take seriously enough, whether relating to
our late work hours, a messy kitchen, or our emotional inac-
cessibility. As one client explained, "I kept telling my husband
that I needed more from him; he just didn't listen."

We may have dismissed our partner's concerns due to our
narcissistic viewpoint that they were trivial or invalid, or we
may have ignored our partner's complaints because we felt
that *our* wants were not being considered. We may have listened only halfheartedly because our attention was being
screened through a resentment-clogged filter. We may have
hardened into a position of being "right," while being convinced that our partner needed to do all the changing. One
man who had difficulty listening expressed it harshly to his
partner, "Look, leaving my dishes in the sink isn't the real
problem. Let me know when you figure out what's really
going on." Although deeper issues may certainly have been
present, invalidating the concern she voiced created more
distrust and distance.

Whatever the specific conflicts, there may have grown an
incremental dissatisfaction and distance. In the midst of the
mistrust and miscommunication, our partner may have decided that he or she couldn't take it anymore. Although we

may have felt abruptly betrayed, he or she may have felt more subtly betrayed because his or her wants and well-being were not being adequately considered. Perhaps neither of us was being honored and respected.

Extracting Meaning from Our Betrayal

However tragically our partnership may have ended—however callously and unfairly we feel we've been treated—the calamity is softened if we can extract some meaning from it. For example, we may discover that others' needs and wants must be taken seriously because these are important to them, even if we do not fully understand why. We may find that we can't always have what we want. We may learn that engaging in a tit-for-tat exchange is destructive to both partners, and that we need to find new, more constructive ways to express anger. Perhaps most significantly, we may realize that it is *our* responsibility to know when we're carrying unresolved resentments or underlying fears and hurts so that we can deal with them directly—so that they do not insidiously poison our relationships. In short, we may discover that the growth of satisfying, loving relationships is primarily a function of our overall self-awareness and personal awakening. We may see more lucidly that the best way to be committed to a partnership is to be committed to our own personal growth. These and other realizations are the gradual fruits of contemplating the right questions.

Unfortunately, the process of growing up often involves disillusionment and harrowing rites of passage. Perhaps it cannot be any other way. However, hard-won learnings can serve us capably in our next relationship, both in regard to the kind of partner we choose and how we conduct ourselves in the relationship.

Jerry, an engineer who learned a great deal through his pain, was dating a woman who was already involved in another partnership, although a seemingly troubled one. He naively (and perhaps egotistically) believed that she would leave her current partner to be with him. When she failed to do so, he experienced the bitter taste of betrayal. However, she never promised to leave her present partner, even though she spoke negatively about him.

Some observers might view Jerry as a victim of this woman's confusion and double messages. But more significantly, he was a victim of his own narcissism, self-deception, and poor communication. If he really wanted to know her intentions, he could have asked. If she assured him that she intended to leave this man and date him, then a breach of trust would follow if she reneged. But if she expressed ambivalence, then it was his choice to take his chances or not pursue the relationship.

For better or worse, life's richest learnings often come from ill-informed decisions. Jerry learned that he created much of his own pain by opening his heart to someone who was unavailable. He learned that bonds of attachment go deep, even in struggling partnerships: "Now I know that even if someone's relationship is a mess—at least in my view—they might still have something that's meaningful to them." He also learned that it is wiser not to become sexually involved with someone who is already involved in a partnership, since his heart and emotions become more attached through sexual union. He learned to gently ask more probing questions earlier in a relationship so that he could better assess someone's intentions and loyalties. If he hears discouraging words, he needs to embrace his disappointment and hurt, while feeling good about himself for demonstrating the courage to risk.

This series of realizations was very empowering for Jerry, even though disquieting. Rather than succumb to the thought that he was a failure, he learned something about himself and about people that he hadn't realized before. As a result, he derived important meaning from his pain, which alleviated much of its sting and accelerated his healing. Using his newfound wisdom, he became more discerning about his selection process and clearer about how to conduct himself in future relationships.

Sheila, a thirty-two-year-old consultant, sowed the seeds of her own betrayal by being consistently cold and irritable toward her spouse, Victor, who described himself as "walking on eggshells in this relationship." Whenever he tried to tell his wife that he felt angry, hurt, or controlled, she would snap back, "You're always angry," or "That's your responsibility," or "You have a weird imagination!" Although Victor's choice of words and ways of communicating were certainly less than ideal, there was nevertheless something important he was trying to say. Sadly, she wasn't able to hear him. As his frustration and discontent mounted, he announced one day that the marriage was over.

Sheila had been hurt in previous relationships and had also been hurt by Victor in the early part of their relationship when he was attracted to another woman. That experience reinforced her self-image of not being good enough. In some subtle way, she was punishing Victor for his lack of devotion and venting resentment toward the world for not having been loved in the way she wanted.

On some level, Sheila expected to be betrayed. She therefore had an exaggerated response to small things that didn't go her way. When she looked closely at the relationship, she appreciated many qualities about her partner. But she had acclimated to things not working out, partly due to past hurt and inflated romantic expectations, and partly because she had grown accustomed to conflict. As a result, she would become very serious, humorless, and critical. When she was angry and upset, she somehow felt more alive and enjoyed the illusion of being in control. She often felt out of control and bored when the partnership was going well.

After a lengthy self-exploration, she gained new insights: "I liked the drama that conflict engenders. I created pain because I wanted to feel alive. I'm finally getting it through my head that I can learn through joy as well as through pain." The courageous realization of how she contributed to alienating her partner served her well in future relationships.

Sheila also discovered that experiencing closeness and love

for any extended time raised the fear of losing her own identity. Creating conflict was a way to declare her psychological
separateness from her partner. On the positive side, this
helped her strengthen her sense of autonomy and independence, which had been undermined earlier in life. But by
using the relationship as her main way to forge an identity,
she was steadily alienating her partner—she was saying no to
intimacy.

By continually generating conflict, by attacking her partner
when his needs conflicted with hers, Sheila invited betrayal. In
order to move away from relationships characterized by excessive struggle, she needed to discover other ways to connect
with her inner source of strength, aliveness, and autonomy.
She began to spend more time alone doing artwork and silent
meditation. She renewed her commitment to a career that was
close to her heart, even though she had some fear of failing.
In addition, counseling helped her to set firmer boundaries
with others by communicating her needs clearly and directly
rather than acting them out by being critical and controlling.
As she put it, "I had so many of my own emotional problems
that I couldn't really be available for a healthy relationship. I
was manipulating, conning, dominating, and dishonest. I
used all kinds of tactics to try to get my needs met rather than
just communicating my needs."

Helped by a twelve step support group, Sheila gradually
began to embrace the hurt and helplessness that underlied
her efforts to control, and she began to communicate in a
more vulnerable way. She took courageous steps toward sharing these raw feelings rather than protecting herself with
anger and blame, through which she had unknowingly induced feelings of hurt and helplessness in others. As a result
of these measures, her autonomy strengthened; she became
less dependent upon a man for her sense of identity and
self-esteem. This newfound self-confidence formed a basis for
deeper intimacy with trusted people.

Empowerment through Self-Understanding

Both of the people discussed above found some initial satisfaction in blaming and attacking their betraying partner. However, they soon realized that they themselves played a leading role in their own betrayal. They discovered that their only real power and healthy control lay in exploring their own contribution to these unwanted outcomes (without crippling themselves with self-blame). Rather than trying to change others to satisfy their wants, they needed to find avenues of self-change, which requires both self-knowledge and self-acceptance.

Eric, the optometrist whose betraying partner falsely complained to her friends that he was abusing her, also learned important lessons as he replaced blame with responsibility: "I *did* choose to be with this person. I did hang in there far past when I should have, so I can't blame her for that. The whole experience made me a lot wiser. I'm more real. A part of me was in self-deception. I wanted the ideal image that this woman was projecting. I had to look at what was unreal about that."

Overcoming Self-Betrayal

As human beings, we are interdependent; we need contact, companionship, and support. Still, many people who have dealt with betrayal in a responsible way report a greater self-reliance, self-trust, and self-strengthening as an eventual legacy of their betrayal. But they first needed to patiently pass through their initial reactions. Beth, who dealt courageously with the pain of being replaced by a younger woman, expressed the growth possibilities colorfully, but succinctly: "If we could just get through the 'Poor me, I hate the fucker' phase and ask, 'Now what am I going to do with this experience; how am I going to use it?' Lots of people get stuck at that level of blame and self-pity and never get beyond it."

True self-empowerment requires that we become accountable for our experience, that we use the unwanted irritation to grow a pearl of wisdom and beauty.

Dorothy, who in Chapter 1 described betrayal as having the rug pulled out from under her, came to see betrayal as a major lesson in her life. "It made me rely more on myself and less on others," she said. "My tendency was to want *so much* from others. I put so much *over there*—expectation, accountability for things—and not enough *over here*. It was like I was going over there to get something and I never got it. I felt betrayed because I never got it. I don't need so much from others as I strengthen my own inner self."

Dorothy discovered that much of what she called betrayal was fueled by her own self-betrayal: "In all those instances it looked like somebody betrayed me, but actually I betrayed myself. I just didn't have the awareness to know better at the time. I kept looking for validation and self-worth by doing and being for others—getting the right job, the right man, the right car. If I could just line them all up at the same time then the whole package would look right and I would have made it. I can see how getting into recovery work would impact my experience of betrayal in the future. Now I'm developing a real sense of who I am instead of looking for value and esteem outside myself. The possibility of being betrayed is minimized as I make better choices based on my intuition. By listening to and following my inner-directed process, I seem to have found less opportunity to be betrayed by people. I'm less likely to enter a relationship that isn't appropriate, less likely to keep going through the same maze when there's no cheese!"

Sherry, the woman in Chapter 1 whose husband always told her what she wanted to hear, stayed in this painful marriage for eighteen years, until he died. Looking back, she gained a clearer perspective: "When I get really honest with myself, I see that he couldn't have betrayed me unless I was willing to betray myself. I was so willing to give up what I knew to be true to take on someone else's truth or opinion. When I really, really look into it, I can't continue to blame him because on some level I made a choice to betray myself. It's incredibly empowering to see that. I can be more true to myself now."

Sherry's courageous self-honesty was tempered by a self-compassion that is essential for working through hurt and pain: "I stayed with him because I thought divorce would be really hard—it would be incredible work, pain, sadness, heartache, and sense of failure, without any real sense of being able to succeed. What I didn't realize was that either way, it's very, very hard—either denying my truth or living it out. There was no easy route. I think staying in the marriage was actually harder in the long run because it ended up being a continual betrayal of myself. This double-edged betrayal—by both him *and* me—was very destructive and weakening; it was not sustaining of life."

There is indeed no easy route when we discover that our fondest hopes have crashed. Yet if we can discover some meaning through our disillusionment—such as how we may have betrayed ourselves and how that is no longer acceptable to us—then we may move through the rest of life a little wiser, a little stronger.

DIALOGUE SKILLS

As we grow, we are less prone to cast others in the role of being our caretaker. We're less likely to use our partner as a target upon whom we displace our scorn toward our parents or the world for having neglected our needs and wants. As we experience our own substance and durability more vividly, we can stand more confidently in our natural self.

Being more connected with ourselves and less ensnared by others' demands and opinions, we can relate to others from a stance of knowing ourselves and being ourselves. The more we know our own likes and dislikes, our needs and longings, our values and preferences, our feelings and opinions, the more we become aware of what we want in a relationship. Betrayal becomes a less likely scenario as we become clearer with ourselves and others about our wants and lifestyle preferences. As we replace the hidden agendas of our conditioned, false self with the increased clarity and honesty of our authentic, adult self, relationships are initiated on a more sound footing. The deception and confusion that so often lead to betrayal are minimized.

The growth of autonomy, self-awareness, and self-esteem provide a foundation for viable relationships. However, we need to nurture the additional skill of communication if we want to avoid the snares and pitfalls that accompany our ever-present tendency to relate to others through our narcissistically driven assumptions and expectations. In short, we need to speak clearly and listen well.

Many of us resist communicating openly and responsibly. As one client admitted, "I want my partner to take care of me and understand my every thought without having to speak it. I know that sounds absurd, but some part of me wants that!"

Our needs and wants may be so clear to us that we assume that they are glaringly obvious to others. Our feelings may be so strongly felt that we surmise that others can easily discern them. In truth, others may be so embroiled in the quiet storm of their own inner world that they are wholly unaware of our feelings and needs. Those occasions when we try to express ourselves may be rendered ineffective due to a lack of clarity or our half-hearted manner of self-expression. Or we may have vigorously verbalized our feelings, yet done so in such an acrimonious manner that we induced others to tune us out.

Much of our communication deficiency is a remnant of an upbringing in which our parents and teachers and their parents and teachers failed to model healthy communication. On a larger scale, our schools and society promote job skills while ignoring life skills. Most of us have not been taught the most basic self-awareness and communication skills that are necessary for revealing our real feelings, asserting our wants, and negotiating differences and conflicts that arise in relationships.

Some of us have achieved a considerable degree of self-awareness. We are fairly well connected to our feelings, wants, and aspirations. We know our likes and dislikes, as well as our strengths and limitations. But as well as we may know ourselves, we will not be known by others unless we let them see who we are. Communication connects us with our interpersonal world; it allows others to get to know us and understand us. Doing so takes commitment and repeated efforts.

If discontent grows without the outlet of communication, we may, out of frustration, hopelessness, or anger, prematurely abandon a relationship. Even if we are uncertain about what is bothering us, we may achieve greater clarity about our difficulty if we "just talk" about it. Likewise, hearing others' feelings can shed additional light on what's really going on.

Betrayal may batter us with the recognition that we played a contributing role by not communicating clearly, directly, and openly. Perhaps we expected others to correctly guess our wants and desires, a throwback to our romantic fantasies. Perhaps little discontents snowballed through the force of neglect. A hurtful betrayal may motivate us to develop conflict resolution skills and dialogue skills in order to resolve differences and increase closeness.

ESTABLISHING FLEXIBLE BOUNDARIES

Another lesson from betrayal may be a need to know our limits, to be clear with ourselves and others regarding what is acceptable and what is intolerable.

Without personal boundaries, we become enmeshed with others. Our reality merges with theirs; we lose sight of our own feelings, thoughts, wants, and values. Our world becomes part of other people's universe. They become more important, more substantial, more powerful than ourselves. We invest them with a lofty status of authority and validity, while minimizing our own experience, our own worth, our own viewpoints. With increased self-awareness, we can learn to modify our communication to reflect the boundaries that enable us to walk the razor's edge between being ourself and being part of a couple.

Boundaries allow for needed ventilation in our cherished partnerships. They give relationships the air they need to breathe. Without boundaries, there can be no healthy intimacy. We can only feel consciously connected when we can honor our separateness.

When we are unable to set clear boundaries that match our own universe of feelings, needs, and sensitivities, we're left with two choices: Either we acquiesce to our partner's preferences or we dominate our partner. Either we cave in to others' viewpoints and demands or we aggressively impose our own. We become a doormat or a door slammer.

The art of communicating our boundaries provides a middle path between submission and dominance. By uncovering the real source of the dissatisfactions and frustrations that lead to conflict, we have an opportunity to express them while they're building rather than after they've suffocated the relationship. We then let others know when their words or actions have hurt us. Of course, there's no guarantee that our partner will respond favorably to us. But if we're both committed to the process of communicating our feelings, wants, and limits—as well as committed to listening to each other, and embracing what arises inside us as a result of what happens between us—then there's a much greater likelihood that we'll respond positively to one another.

An Example of Setting Boundaries

There are many steps we can take to resolve conflicts and differences before the final decree of separation. By learning the art of setting clear boundaries, we take an important stride toward establishing trust in a relationship. The following example illustrates how we might walk that fine line between being ourselves and being responsive to our partner.

During a quiet moment, it may occur to us that we want to spend more time alone, pursuing our own creative interests.

Our sense of responsibility to both ourselves and our partner may prompt us to share this need openly. If we approach our partner in a flexible rather than rigid way, we might first ask if this is a good time to talk. If not, we can arrange another time.

It may seem strange to set a date with our partner just to talk. However, being sensitive to the timing of important discussions respects the boundaries of our partner, and ultimately serves us, too. If he or she is too tired or feels overstressed, then our conversation may only exacerbate our tensions. However, we can't wait forever. If he or she continually avoids topics that are meaningful to us, we may get the impression that there's never a good time to talk. We might then need to insist upon it.

Once we talk, we can continue to demonstrate flexible boundaries by being mindful of how our desire to spend time alone affects our partner. We're not imposing a firm decision in a unilateral way. We haven't made up our mind and that's it. We're engaged in a living process together. We stay open to changing as we hear how our preference affects our partner, who is important to us. We want to work something out that will be acceptable to both of us, if at all possible.

So we state our desire for solitude and describe what that's about for us. For instance, we might say, "I love to write and want more time to do that. I feel more connected to myself and more engaged with life when I'm writing. It's a creative way for me to respond to the pain I see in people's lives and in the world, as well as in my own life. I sense that I have something to offer and find a rich sense of meaning and aliveness by doing so." By providing our partner with a concise, clear picture of what our desire to write is all about, we increase our chances of being understood.

We may then ask how our partner feels about all this, and what the issue brings up for him or her. Perhaps she understands us and is supportive. If she loves us and wants the best for us, it would be difficult for her to refuse our request. Or she may love us yet have her own needs, too. Or, she may have

193

a fear of abandonment and need some reassurance, or she may simply have a preference to enjoy time together. Hopefully, we can honestly tell her that we love her and want to be with her. We may reassure her that if we spend less time together, we hope that the quality of our contact will be even more fulfilling. Perhaps we can set up some definite times to just "hang out."

Another possible outcome is that our partner clearly needs more time with us if we're to stay a couple. We'll then have to consider whether this will work for us. If we're excessively pulled away from something that helps us to be ourselves, then we'll resent ourselves for betraying ourselves, and resent our partner for holding us back. The delicate bond of love and closeness is likely to degenerate if we spend time together begrudgingly. Our sexual, erotic connection will likely diminish in a climate of obligation and pressure. This will serve neither of us. As we continue to talk, we might try to strike some compromise that arises from really listening to each other, then see if this works. If it doesn't and we continue being sorely unhappy, it may be wiser to separate sooner rather than later, and free each other to find partners better suited to our personal needs.

There may be other subtleties to be considered here. For example, if our desire to write is prompted by feeling distant from our partner, then our sense of integrity would hopefully prompt us to share that information. If we disclose our dissatisfaction, we can explore what's really going on and resolve the matter before it assumes a life of its own.

In another possible scenario, our desire to spend time alone may be accompanied by serious thoughts of separation. If so, we may want to reveal that we're having such fantasies, as well as express the dissatisfactions leading to such thoughts. This lets our partner know how seriously unhappy we are. The key to a satisfying outcome is to *remain open to the possibility that something might shift in the process of dialogue.* Perhaps we'll be touched in some new way as we extend ourselves into each other's world and see things from another viewpoint.

If nothing changes through such a dialogue and separation remains a possibility, we have at least included our partner in our decision-making process rather than coldly imposing our own will. Separation based on open dialogue is likely to be less painful than a decision to separate that excludes our partner. We are then sharing power. We're recognizing our basic equality. We're demonstrating respect and sensitivity, rather than trying to dominate or get even.

The Gradual Integration of Our Power and Sensitivity

The commitment to include our partner in our inner world of thinking and feeling reflects a great deal of personal growth. The all-too-common impulse is to detach ourselves from the effects we have on others. Having postponed taking care of ourselves, we now set boundaries with a vengeance. Having been overwhelmed by others' needs and desires, we now overwhelm others. Having been controlled by people, we now try to control them—victim becomes victimizer.

As we first learn to establish boundaries, we may be somewhat awkward, clumsy, and heartless in doing so. However, it is sometimes better to set rigid boundaries than to acknowledge no boundaries at all. We then give our emerging self the space it needs to become more self-directing, free-spoken, and strong-spirited. We begin to affirm our rights and feel our strength.

However, it may be prudent during a time of experimentation not to make major life decisions that might negatively affect us for years to come (if at all possible). For example, pursuing a child custody battle or suing for more spousal support is sometimes a necessary way to set boundaries with an ex-partner, but our overzealous pursuit may leave deep emotional scars. By taking time to consider what's really fair, we may save ourselves unnecessary pain and trauma.

195

As our right to be ourselves becomes more tangibly felt—as our self-esteem strengthens—we mature in a manner that enables us to be assertive *and* flexible, self-assured *and* sensitive. We become confident in our capacity to establish suitable boundaries as needed. We come to discover a new balance between our rights and responsibilities. By tolerating a certain amount of tension that results from allowing apparent opposites to exist side by side, we become more whole, more mature.

A truly strong self is a flexible self. A genuinely confident self involves an integration of our power and our sensitivity, which prevents us from being too rigid when setting boundaries. Unless we accept and embrace our bewilderment and vulnerability along with our power and competence, our power will race out of control, subduing and oppressing people. Real power doesn't bully people; it comes from a quiet sense of inner strength. *The essence of personal power is simple authenticity.*

When our power is tamed by our tenderness, we develop an agile, flexible self that pursues happiness while maintaining kindness and compassion toward others. Our boundary setting then supports the genuine needs of our real self, rather than seeks gratification by establishing dominance and aggrandizing ourselves. Pursuing the latter course would only ensure a continued sentence of isolation and separation.

Some recent trends in the personal growth and codependency movements unwittingly promote the rigidification of a self that isolates from others. Under the banner of "owning my power," "taking care of myself," or "setting boundaries," some people refine a preexisting tendency to coerce and control others. Those becoming "professional recoverers" (whether in recovery programs or less-than-productive therapies) may find familiar comfort by maintaining a contentious, combative, somber stance toward the world. However, such individuals are not any closer to enjoying the love and intimacy they want. By misusing the concept of boundaries, they may come to feel more powerful and alive by trampling others' sensibilities. As one disgruntled friend put it, "It's good to set boundaries as long as we don't become obnoxious about it."

Boundaries Affirm Our Dignity

Those who have endured personal abuse, political disempowerment, or social injustice need to reclaim their legitimate rights and powers. To avoid self-betrayal, it is crucial that we respect, honor, and care for ourselves. However, the best way to do so remains an open question. We do not exhibit self-care by developing a self-centered personality that overpowers, offends, and alienates people. It's true that we cannot avoid offending certain people at certain times, and we sometimes need to part from those who continually hurt us. This requires a steady will, courage, and determination. Nevertheless, the common expression "owning our power" may be better conceptualized as "affirming our dignity," although there certainly remains an element of power, if not occasional fierceness, in that dignity.

Personal boundaries protect our dignity by defining who we are and affirming ourselves, which doesn't necessarily require us to distance ourselves or hold ourselves apart from others. Personal dignity includes a sense of strength, vitality, and confidence but is free from the destructive inclination to hold power over people, or induce feelings of weakness in them as a way to feel worthwhile, if not superior. True dignity allows us to experience a kind of power that involves a natural grace and aliveness—simple, satisfying, self-contained yet not overly self-important, pompous, or haughty. *We have authentic dignity only when we can allow others to have theirs.*

As we grow toward genuine autonomy and dignity, there's an open pathway to our heart. We're strong enough to be tender and self-assured enough to remain emotionally accessible. The phrase "claiming my power" or "being a warrior" can be misused to ensure that others do not have the capacity to hurt us, get to us, or touch us in any way. Sadly, by remain-

197

ing impervious to the effects that others may have on us, we disenfranchise ourselves from the potential growth of intimacy. Fearful of "losing our power," we may remain solemnly vigilant and guarded, perpetually poised to attack or repel.

As we become more firmly rooted in ourselves, we develop strength that we can draw upon as necessary. We do not need to showcase our power. We can use our strength to repel abusive and denigrating treatment while maintaining a basic openness toward the world at large. Of course, attaining this dynamic balance takes time and patience—in fact, it involves a lifetime of refinements. But it's important to know where we're going, or where we *can* go, as we awaken to the larger realm of possibilities.

Examples of Flexible Boundaries

The following are examples of communicating in ways that reflect rigid boundaries as contrasted with flexible boundaries that enable us to have strength combined with sensitivity. They are offered to convey a sense of how boundaries can evolve over time. Keep in mind that rigid boundaries are not "bad." There are times when we need to be very firm and vigilant, such as when our partner displays repeated insensitivity toward us. We need not shame ourselves for setting rigorous boundaries when necessary. After all, a major purpose of setting them is to overcome the shame of feeling too inadequate to assert our rights.

RIGID BOUNDARY: "Don't tell me I'm selfish! I don't want to hear that."

FLEXIBLE BOUNDARY: "I feel hurt when you judge me as selfish. I'd rather hear what you're feeling."

The latter statement conveys the message that we do not want to be talked to in a critical manner. However, it leaves an opportunity for us to hear what is happening for the other person.

RIGID BOUNDARY: "I don't want to see you anymore. I've had it! Our relationship's over."

FLEXIBLE BOUNDARY: "I'm feeling unhappy in our relationship. It has to do with feeling distant from you. Nothing seems to change. I'm having thoughts that it might be best if we separate."

The latter statement gives our partner a chance to respond. We still have the option to separate, but something may change by conveying the depth of our dissatisfaction. We are then being ourselves by stating how we feel, while giving our partner a chance to respond. We are sharing power.

Forming flexible boundaries requires that we integrate qualities that may appear to be in opposition. As we combine assertiveness with receptivity, determination with adaptability, we develop a flexible strength that enables us to walk more gracefully in a world that can sometimes be hostile and hazardous. At appropriate times, we may need to call forth a resounding roar. In other instances, we can be playful and not so serious. As we become less rigid and more integrated, our boundary setting can proceed from a more balanced place within ourselves. As we learn to soften into our inner experience and communicate in a nonaccusatory way, we invite a friendlier response from others. We are then able to negotiate life's difficult junctures with greater ease.

MOVING ON

The ultimate boundary is one of total separation. If we have pursued open dialogue to no avail—if our best efforts have led to impasses time and time again—we may need to take the painful step of leaving the relationship. But rather than abandoning dialogue and shutting each other out of our hearts, we may want to set our sights on a different goal: *the mutual recognition of the wisdom of separating*. The purpose of continued dialogue would then be to arrive at a mutually shared conclusion, namely, that the relationship is no longer viable, that it is not serving the growth and well-being of either person. When the scales of pleasure and pain have been tipped for too long on the side of pain, it may be time to part company.

Arriving at a mutual decision to separate enables each of us to experience this important decision emanating from within ourselves, rather than being imposed by our partner. Although we may feel heartbroken to separate, we may spare each other additional anguish if we can find the emotional wherewithal to remain in communication until the wisdom of parting becomes a joint recognition. By sharing the power to decide, we avert the possibility of a far more agonizing betrayal, while increasing the prospect of maintaining a meaningful friendship.[9] As one man described his separation, "We didn't trash each other like most couples do. We both realized it was better to go our separate ways. We were hurt and angry at times, but we each took responsibility for our part. Our commitment to be honest and respectful enabled us to stay close friends."

Of course, we cannot expect ourselves to talk indefinitely until a reluctant partner accedes to our viewpoint. Our perspectives and needs may be too divergent to reach an amicable settlement. At some point, we may need to take care of ourselves by insisting on a separation, even if our partner accuses us of betrayal. Otherwise, we may perform the more grave disservice of betraying ourselves by prolonging our sojourn in an unsatisfying partnership. The poet Lord Byron offers an admonition to those who would endure an exasperating partnership year after year:

> Wait not, fond lover!
> Till years are over,
> And then recover
> As from a dream.
> While each bewailing
> The other's failing,
> With wrath and railing,
> All hideous seem—
> While first decreasing,
> Yet not quite ceasing,

200

Wait not til teasing
All passion blight:
If once diminished
Love's reign is finished—
Then part in friendship,—and bid goodnight.

Byron may go too far in suggesting that people part at the first sign of diminishing love. Such romantic fervor may only catapult disgruntled lovers from one relationship to another, without working through the power struggles and inflated expectations that will again greet them in their next partnership. Nevertheless, there is rare wisdom in Byron's words. A wise, timely recognition that a relationship is unworkable can spare much heartache, while increasing the chances of maintaining mutual love and respect. This possibility is often destroyed in an escalating cycle of mutual badgering and soul-mangling manipulations to change the other.

It is particularly painful to be left against our will. Our grief is deeper and our loss greater if we still want to stay together while our partner is determined to separate. We then have no option but to turn tenderly toward ourselves, embrace our hurt and our anger, and move on with our life.

In some instances of being the subject of unilateral separation, we may later recognize that parting was a blessing in disguise, even if it demoralized us at that time. We may realize in retrospect that we did not possess the vision or will to initiate the separation, but that it turned out to be in our best interest. Such an outcome may inspire us with a newly found faith that the hand of life sometimes nudges us toward a more fulfilling future than we would have otherwise planned. Beth, who fiercely resisted separating, expressed this well: "I realized there was a piece of work I needed to do on myself alone. To learn more how to love myself unconditionally—the way he loved me at times. He had a big, accepting heart. I grew a lot from that—but I was never touching into my own deeper self, my own inner voice. I needed that much pain, anger, and intensity of feeling to get in touch with myself. The discomfort awakened me to a deeper layer of myself. My inner voice was screaming so loudly that I had to listen to it. I can call forth loving energy for myself now. Knowing that I can just sit quietly for a couple of minutes and feel it—that's really shifted something in me. So the gifts I've gotten from all this are enormous."

A man in the helping professions expressed a similar sentiment when his partner left him. "Opening to all that pain really opened my heart," he acknowledged. "I'm grateful for that now. She touched something in me that I never let anyone touch before. That awakened me to a lot of pain stuck inside me from past rejections. I needed to feel that again so it could finally start to heal. Now I feel more ready for a good relationship."

OTHER SELF-DISCOVERIES

Other hard-won discoveries may emerge by going the extra step to uncover how we contributed to our own betrayal. Perhaps our own pressing need to be accepted may prompt us to believe people's false reassurances. We may soak up these expressions of apparent good will because we so desperately want to believe that we're loved, even though another part of us might be justifiably suspicious. Perhaps we surrendered to passion and pleasure before consulting with our good sense. In our urge to merge, we may fail to discern when others are trying to ingratiate themselves in order to win approval. For example, some people who flatter us or shower us with gifts may be secretly motivated by their own need for companionship, acceptance, or sex, or a subtle desire to control and manipulate.

Conversely, some of us are overly suspicious of others' kind words and actions. We may feel so badly about ourselves that we can't take in compliments or love. Deep down, we may feel that we don't deserve it, that if other people really knew us, they would not be so complimentary or benevolent.

202

As we grow in wisdom, we can better discern when it is reasonable to take what people say at face value and when it's sensible to look more deeply at their intentions. As a result, we become more perceptive, more streetwise. Such realism does not mean that we become wary or cynical. It means that we are awake enough to sense when it is relatively safe to be our trusting, spontaneous self, and when it's wiser to be cautious.

When unhealed hurts mutilate our innocence and openness, we don't take in the love that's there. We then leave others with the vague sense that they are not affecting us much, that they're not allowing us into their heart, that they're not making much of a difference in our lives. In short, they may sense or imagine that they are not important to us, which might prompt them to seek partnerships in which they feel more appreciated, more received, more connected.

Another possible discovery is that we must learn to identify our feelings closer to the time they are occurring. For instance, we may have the habit of withholding anger. Our hostility will then ooze out indirectly, such as by nagging, complaining, and judging, which creates an uncongenial, unsafe environment.

We may also have played a role in the demise of our relationship if being sexual was our only way to feel intimate. This one-dimensional intimacy may have left our partner painfully bereft of a deeper soul connection, a deeper sense of being loved. A once enlivening sexuality may have become boring because *we* became boring, which prompted our partner to seek an affair. We may have failed to pursue our own creative interests and meaningful friendships outside the partnership. When the flame of our own passion for life and love died down, so did our intimate connection with our partner.

Accepting the Limits of a Partnership

Another lesson that we may learn is that all of our wants and desires cannot be met through one relationship alone. Betrayal sometimes results from a failure to accept the limits life imposes. Those who drop one person after another must realize that they will probably never find someone who is a composite of all the best qualities that they have relished in each of their partners. For example, our partner may be a wonderful lover but may refuse to get a job. He or she may be artistically and intuitively inclined but may not attend to such details as doing the dishes or filing taxes. We may be drawn to his or her spontaneity and carefree attitude but may fail to realize that these benefits come with hidden disadvantages, such as losing the car keys every few days. Or we may be pleased that our partner provides a high standard of living but may complain that he or she is a workaholic. We may refuse to see that we can't have it both ways. The time and energy required for a high-salaried position may make it difficult to spend much time with us, or slow down enough to be in touch with feelings.

There is an amusing Sufi story that points to the need to overcome the narcissism of perfectionism. As the old tale goes, one day Nasrudin and a friend were sipping tea in a café. Their discussion turned to life and love.

"How come you never got married, Nasrudin?" asked his friend at one point.

"Well," said Nasrudin, "to tell you the truth, I spent my youth looking for the perfect woman. In Cairo, I met a beautiful and intelligent woman, with eyes like dark olives, but she was unkind. Then in Baghdad I met a woman who was a wonderful and generous soul, but we had no interests in common. One woman after another would seem just right, but there would always be something missing. Then one day, I met her. She was beautiful, intelligent, generous, and kind. We had everything in common. In fact, she was perfect."

"Well," said Nasrudin's friend, "what happened? Why didn't you marry her?"

Nasrudin sipped his tea reflectively. "Well," he replied, "it's a sad thing. Seems she was looking for the perfect man."[10]

Each person has strengths and limitations. There will always be disadvantages to the advantages we enjoy. For example, if we want a woman who is exquisitely attractive and dynamic, we may have to deal with jealousy when desirous men are attracted to her. If we want a man who is assertive and self-confident, he may slip into arrogance at times. If we are waiting to find the perfectly balanced and well-integrated person, we may be waiting a long time—indeed, the rest of our lives. Instead, we need to be clear about whether we can accept the limitations involved in a particular partnership; that acceptance can then free us to enjoy what is there. If we're each committed to our personal development, we might help each other (in a non-codependent way) to become more authentic, whole, and happy.

NOTES

1. C. Moustakas, *Loneliness* (Englewood Cliffs, NJ: Prentice-Hall, 1961), 7.

2. Ibid. I have taken the liberty of changing Moustakas's description of loneliness to that of aloneness.

3. A. Morrow Lindbergh, *A Gift from the Sea* (New York: Vintage Books, 1991), 44.

4. W. Muller, *Legacy of the Heart: The Spiritual Advantages of a Painful Childhood* (New York: Simon & Schuster, 1992), 105–106.

5. J. Goldstein and J. Kornfield, *Seeking the Heart of Wisdom* (Boston: Shambhala, 1987), 15–20.

6. See D. H. Shapiro and R. Walsh, eds., *Meditation: Classic and Contemporary Perspectives* (New York: Aldine, 1984) and M. Murphy and S. Donovan, *The Physical and Psychological Effects of Meditation* (San Rafael, CA: Esalen Institute, 1989).

7. For a descriptive account of the various types of meditation practices, see Daniel Goleman, *The Meditative Mind* (Los Angeles: J.P. Tarcher, 1988).

8. A participant in Ira Progoff's journal workshop once wrote in her journal: "This solitary work, we cannot do alone." From I. Progoff, *At a Journal Workshop* (Los Angeles: Tarcher, 1992).

9. In some situations, total separation is often best. In others, a period of separation may be necessary before attempting to be friends. See *Lost Lovers, Found Friends* by Scott Nelson (New York: Simon & Schuster,

1991) for more about the possibility of maintaining a meaningful friendship.

10. Quoted in R. Fields, with P. Taylor, R. Weyler, and R. Ingrasci, *Chop Wood, Carry Water* (Los Angeles: Tarcher, 1984), 35.

CHAPTER 7

Toward Compassion and Forgiveness

> "Oh, argh, forgiveness? you say? Anything but that? But you know in your heart that someday, sometime, it will come to that. It may not come until the death-bed time, but it will come . . . The important part of forgiveness is to *begin and to continue*. The finishing of it all is a life work."
>
> CLARISSA PINKOLA ESTES[1]

I F we approach the experience of betrayal with the open-eyed intention to learn more about ourselves and life, we may become not only wiser but more compassionate as well. *Compassion* is from the Latin *com,* meaning "together," and *pati,* meaning "to suffer." *Compassion* is defined in the dictionary as "sorrow for the sufferings or trouble of another, accompanied by the urge to help." However hurtful betrayal may be, we can find meaning in it by transforming pain into compassion.

Some readers may wonder why they would want to develop compassion as the result of being betrayed. Why would they want to experience sorrow for the suffering of others? After all, they're the ones who are suffering.

Some people cite moral and ethical grounds for developing compassion, but a more compelling reason is that compassion enriches us. We are filled with a warm feeling when we experience compassion. Lending our compassionate attention to others brings us into a place inside ourselves that harbors our joy and peace, as well as our openness to life and to love.

If we have been suffering through a painful betrayal, I am not proposing that we quickly cultivate compassion toward the one who has treated us with contempt or cruelty; that would be asking too much of ourselves. But I am suggesting that during the latter stage of healthy grieving we may discover a compassion that shines within and without. If a gut-wrenching betrayal makes it too difficult to feel compassion toward an ex-partner, we may more realistically feel this gentle impulse toward those who are struggling or hurting in some way—in short, the bulk of humanity.

Experiencing compassion toward others begins by cultivating a climate of compassion within ourselves. Doing so is difficult, for it requires that our awareness expand to embrace many aspects of who we are. The impulse toward self-compassion grows as we gradually integrate our wisdom, our strength, and our vulnerability. As we overcome childhood shame and fear, our self-esteem, love, and autonomy begin to meld with one another. As we learn the art of shifting attention from self-critical and repetitive thoughts to the quieter emotions and sensations that flow through our bodies—perhaps with the help of experiential approaches, such as meditation and Focusing—we grow more in touch with the deeper strata of the self.

Self-compassion grows as we become wise enough to know that we deserve love and joy in our lives, yet humble enough to recognize that we are not superior to others. As we grow stronger, we may drop our efforts to fashion an image that pleases, impresses, or controls others. We may then more readily embrace a certain quality of helplessness and woundedness shared by all of humanity. Gradually, we may rise to become a "wounded healer," one whose depth of compassion flows from having tasted the pain in life.

Our own pain is the prime ingredient in the growth of

compassion. To feel compassion for others means that we recognize their physical, emotional, or spiritual suffering. Until we have embraced our own hurts and losses, we cannot perceive and embrace the pain of others. If our steadfast agenda is to avoid pain, then we will distance ourselves from others' pain, while assisting them to do the same. To be touched by others' suffering means that we know from the inside how it feels to hurt. True compassion unfolds as we are touched by others' concerns and hurts without losing our own connection with ourselves.

Stuart, whose wife had a secret three-year affair, described how he felt a deeper compassion as a result of opening to his pain: "It brings up my own pain when someone else talks about their pain. It resonates with mine. It just makes me that much more sympathetic when somebody else is hurting."

Some people try to be caring and compassionate because they believe it is the "right" thing to do. They put aside personal needs in order to respond to others' concerns. This surely involves some elements of caring. But without a *bodily felt knowledge of pain,* our caring lacks a quality of depth, which is required for true compassion. A strong connection with our soulful depths is necessary for such compassion; in it, we feel carried along with another's pain but do not become lost in it, and we find ourselves spontaneously offering love and support.

People we identify as compassionate usually have experienced much pain. Buddha, who was known for his infinite compassion, began his spiritual quest as a search for the meaning of suffering. As he continued observing the anguish of others and learning to embrace his own pain through the practice of meditation, his love and compassion grew. Mahatma Gandhi, a proponent of the path of love and nonviolence, was jailed several times and endured many painful trials during his lifetime. Socrates, Jesus, and others were betrayed and persecuted for their radical viewpoints that upset the social order.

This is not to suggest that we become another Buddha or

Gandhi. However, their lives may inspire the hopeful possibility that we, too, may find deeper meaning, love, and fulfillment by learning to transform tragedy into triumph. As one man found after a painful betrayal, "It expanded my capacity to love and respond to people's pain. It humbled me. I felt the pain of the world more intensely."

EMBRACING PAIN

Compassion does not automatically visit those who absorb the required dose of suffering. Many people endure great pain and hardship but never grow from it. They somehow attract unpleasant experiences time and time again. They migrate from one dissatisfying relationship to another. As discussed earlier, some people even gain perverse gratification in seeing themselves as wounded victims of life.

We develop compassion by learning the elusive art of embracing our pain in a caring way. One reason this is so difficult is the pervasive tendency to try to change the other person or manipulate the situation in order to relieve our hurt. Embracing pain begins by *accepting what we cannot change*. However, this does not mean that we passively endure hardship or resign ourselves to suffering. Once we accept a given situation, we can engage in an active process of noticing and embracing whatever feelings of pain, hurt, and sorrow may be present. This delicate process of befriending our vulnerability is easier said than done. Our challenge is to discover the *right kind of relationship to our pain*, an enterprise that involves creative struggle and frustration but that can ultimately lead to a triumph of the human spirit.

Carl Jung has stated that all neurosis is a substitute for legitimate suffering. Psychotherapy may be seen, in part, as an exercise to coax clients into experiencing their natural pain. Abraham Maslow expresses it well:

> We protect ourselves and our ideal image of ourselves by repression and similar defenses, which are essentially techniques

by which we avoid becoming conscious of unpleasant or dangerous truths. And in psychotherapy the maneuvers by which we continue avoiding this consciousness of painful truth, the ways in which we fight the efforts of the therapist to help us see the truth, we call 'resistance.' All the techniques of the therapist are in one way or another truth-revealing, or are ways of strengthening the patient so he can bear the truth.[2]

THE MOVEMENT FROM BLAME
TO COMPASSION

As we work with the pain of betrayal in the ways I've been describing in this book, we may find ourselves moving gradually from pain and blame to compassion for ourselves and others. When we've just been deserted by a partner, we may react in a predictable way. We may conclude that we've been wronged and abused. We may feel outraged and resentful: "What kind of human being would do this to me? How could anyone be so cruel and insensitive?" We may find some satisfaction by recounting a long list of our partner's negative traits. We may derive some gratification by grumbling about him or her to our friends. This initial phase of blaming and belittling our ex-partner helps release some pain. But only temporarily.

Before long, we must reluctantly admit that holding on to our resentments and judgments does not help us feel better. Even if we're right, our rightness does not bring us peace. It only creates agitation through the grinding replay of our now familiar judgments and opinions. However, suspending our resentments and viewpoints is unsettling when we have nothing to replace them with.

Our strident stance of attacking and demeaning our ex-partner is shadowed by a less visible posture of self-blame and self-criticism. We may dig at ourselves with such thoughts as "Was I that undesirable? What did she find wrong with me? Why did I waste so much time and energy on this relationship?

211

Why didn't I see his flaws sooner? Will I ever find a decent relationship?" Fueling such questions is a gnawing sense of shame that we're somehow defective, along with the fear that we will never love again.

These redundant waves of shame-driven thoughts begin to subside as we inch our way toward affirming ourselves. As we create a friendly inner climate for our real feelings, we may glimpse more clearly an underlying loneliness, sadness, or hurt. As we accept and love ourselves while experiencing these feelings, we may notice a quality of sadness that is far richer and deeper than our previous pain and tearfulness, which were colored by overwhelming shame and self-condemnation. Somehow we feel better as we touch the deeper pulse of our feeling life.

As we gradually feel more connected with ourselves, we may discover a new appreciation for the rewarding aspects of the relationship. Rather than stay stuck in our all negative rendition of our ex-partner, we may recognize that the partnership contained some blend of negative and positive features. We may feel a sadness related to losing the good parts of the partnership, the warmth and tenderness that were present, the support and nurturance we received when we were afraid or discouraged, the various ways we grew. As we make a perceptual shift that reflects a more accurate, balanced view of the relationship, we experience a movement toward compassion. We feel a new warmth toward ourselves and a clearer recognition of the human struggle we face in relationship.

As we feel our painful loss over the course of time, we may feel closer to the vulnerability that our former partner may be feeling during his or her own quiet moments of solitude. She may be experiencing a similar loss. He may be touched by nagging self-doubts, disappointment, and the fear of being alone (unless he's entered the arms of someone new). As we feel closer to our own vulnerable core, we feel closer to the core of our former partner. We may even feel some tenderness toward him or her, a warm compassion simmering in our heart. We are touched by a somewhat painful, somewhat joyful sensitivity toward him or her as we recognize the human predicament we share.

Such warm feelings do not come quickly. It may take many months or even years before we can find such compassion toward an ex-partner. Also, such feelings do not mean that we want to get back together. Whatever led to our separation might very well happen again if we were to reunite as partners. But a new form of friendship (or at least mutual caring) might emerge if we are both healing in similar ways. However, the possibility of a revived friendship will depend upon such factors as how vicious or mature we were during the process of separation, how much we still have in common, and how much we are still feeling nurtured by the relationship.

As we reflect further, we might understand more clearly the human predicament shared by all of us—the desire to be seen and appreciated, the longing to be loved, wanted, and cherished. We might be struck by the poignant recognition that deep down, we both wanted the same thing, but that somehow we just weren't able to meet. We weren't able to see beyond our anger, judgments, and acrimony to the deeper essence of each other's being. We couldn't get to the core of what was really happening within our varied worlds and communicate this with the right balance of clarity, assertiveness, and sensitivity. As a result, we weren't able to remove the obstacles to actualizing our hopes and dreams. Sadly, the obstacles may have been too big to be removed.

As we reflect further on our broken partnership, we may make other discoveries. Perhaps our mutual resentment and hurt were too deep and too prolonged to perceive and respond to each other's deeper essence. Perhaps the wounds from our own childhoods—the shame of being ourselves, the fear of being genuine and direct, the deep-seated expectancy of failure—led to the re-creation of our worst fears. Perhaps we didn't know how to ask for the help we needed to work through the childhood legacies that we dragged into the partnership.

A brief glimpse of our partner's deeply held, unexpressed

pain might open our heart enough to soften our blame and contempt, as Henry Wadsworth Longfellow explains: "If we could read the secret history of our enemies, we would find in each man's life a sorrow and a suffering enough to disarm all hostility."

Getting Beyond Self-Blame and Other-Blame

Is there anyone to blame for our shared human predicament? Can we blame our parents for instilling fear in us, instead of drawing out our real feelings and wants? Or did our parents basically do their best, according to what they learned from their own imperfect role models? Should we give the school system a failing grade for not teaching us the self-awareness and communication skills that we now lack as an adult? Or were our teachers unaware of these skills? Or were we betrayed by a board of education who conceded to parental fears that courses in sex education or interpersonal skills might lead to unbridled sexuality? Perhaps we should focus the brunt of our blame on our former partner. Or is our partner, like ourselves, a troubled victim of the myriad forces that have thwarted a ripening of the self-esteem and autonomy necessary for real and lasting intimacy?

There is no doubt that others played their part in creating our current pain; they bear some responsibility in the matter. But responsibility is different from blame, which involves a hostile reproach and denigration. Unless we stop looking to blame others as a way to liberate ourselves from our current sorrow and loneliness, we will never graduate to the work of true healing. While assigning blame may temporarily appease our searching mind by offering *explanations,* it cannot offer the *transformation* we really seek. Blame keeps us stuck in the role of a child. By taking responsibility to heal, learn, and grow, we move forward in life.

By gently embracing our pain, we become disentangled from subtle defenses designed to shield us from the hurts of life. As these defenses subside, we can see our situation more

214

vividly, including our former partner's shortcomings. But more importantly, we may see where we could have been more conscious and sensitive (though without punitively blaming ourselves). Perhaps we can remember situations in which we weren't aware of how we really felt or what we really wanted. Instead, we complained about peripheral issues, which probably confused and alienated our partner. Perhaps we were accusatory and critical, which was easier than revealing the depth of our fears and the breadth of our hurts. We may see times when we took more than we gave, while remembering other times when we gave too much for too long without getting enough back. Our incapacity to take care of ourselves during these critical periods may have created resentments and distance, which harmed the relationship.

Another possible discovery is that our occasionally callous treatment of our partner stemmed from a failure to love and accept him or her as is. We may have tried to shape our partner into the kind of person who could satisfy our idiosyncratic tastes. Instead of seeing him for who he really was, did we perceive him as who we wanted him to be? For example, did we neglect to recognize the career pressures he felt in his life? Did we really listen to her? Were we emotionally available to meet her needs, or were we narcissistically preoccupied with our own? Did we fail to walk the fine line of validating our wants and responding to hers?

This is not to suggest we berate ourselves for having needs and preferences. The relevant questions here are: Did we choose a wise path for meeting our needs for love, respect, and affection? Or did we cajole or pressure our partner to give these gifts to us? Did we distrust that our partner would come our way in the process of letting him or her see us in our vulnerability? Did we love and respect ourselves adequately? Or did we stridently demand of our partner something that we could not give to ourselves? Did we expect our partner to be our caretaker? Or did we neglect to be our own caregiver?

These questions are best asked in a spirit of self-compassion. The partnership didn't go our way. There is hurt, fear, and sadness. Can we accept these feelings? Can we affirm that we did our best, that we conducted ourselves according to what we knew at the time? Now we know more. In retrospect, we may wish we'd done some things differently. Hopefully, we can do better next time to offer understanding, communicate clearly, and extend ourselves into our partner's world. Perhaps we would also benefit by spending more time in solitude or meditation so that we can remember who we are apart from any relationship.

We aren't well served by dwelling on blaming ourselves or condemning our partner. Whenever we are revisited by hurt or sorrow, we can do our best to embrace it in a gentle, caring way until it is ready to pass—until we are delivered back to a more nearly whole sense of ourselves.

Seeing Our Ex-Partner and Ourselves More Clearly

Within a comforting climate of self-understanding, we can come to accept whatever limits may have constrained us during the course of the partnership: perhaps our limited self-knowledge, our capacity for self-expression, our ability to accept, understand, and love our partner. As we become reconciled to these personal limitations, we can more readily accept similar flaws that existed in our partner. As we feel more compassion for our own shortcomings, we can better appreciate that we both partake of the same human frailties.

That sick feeling that sometimes arises in the pit of our stomach—the tension that stems from our resentment and shame—subsides as we recognize that we shared foibles in common. Although we periodically experience hurt in relation to our ex-partner, we may begin to perceive his or her goodness beneath the coldness and insensitivity that was shown us.

As our wisdom and understanding grow, we may feel compassion even if our partner left us to be with someone else. Our hurt is likely to be more intense if we were discarded in favor of another man or woman. In such instances, we may need more time to find it in our heart to forgive, especially if the relationship was secretive. But to continue carrying a grudge only eats away at *us*. Swirling in unremitting thoughts that he or she is bad or evil creates a corresponding tension in our own gut; it constricts our own life energy. The willingness to move toward forgiveness relieves us of a gnawing resentment and malice that corrodes our own well-being and creates hidden anguish. In addition, what does it say about us if we chose to be with someone whom we now characterize as vile? *We denigrate ourselves by denigrating our partner.*

As we find greater peace with our hurt and pain, we somehow experience a shift of attitude toward our partner. Our longing to get something from him or her diminishes. As we no longer desire to be with our partner, we can see his or her positive and negative traits with greater impartiality. Our ex-love is neither a demon nor a saint, but just a human being who is similar to us in many ways and different in others.

While being betrayed may have had something to do with our own imperfections, we may discern that it also had much to do with our partner's shortcomings—his lapses of clarity and honesty, her tendency to belittle us, his unrealistic demands, her failure to express appreciation to us. But perhaps most significantly, there may have been too many differences between us. Our worldviews, personal visions, temperaments, and needs may simply have been too diverse and incompatible, through no fault of our own.

For example, we may now see that our partner needed more reassurance than we were able or willing to give. We may perceive our partner's fears more clearly—the fear of rejection, the fear of isolation, the fear of being wrong. We may notice the hidden pain beneath his seemingly confident appearance. We may sense how her hurts or fears made it difficult to be honest with us about issues that really mattered.

We are less inclined to fault others as we recognize similar faults (or different shortcomings) in ourselves, even if ours seem less obvious. As an ancient Sufi saying aptly warns, "Those condemning a person for a sin will not themselves die before committing it."

Discerning our partner's weaknesses and inconsistencies may give us some modicum of comfort during weak moments, such as when we blame ourselves for the betrayal. However, this exploration has severe limits. Without hearing our partner's side, our scrutinizing thoughts are a blend of fantasy and reality. When taken too far, they become a defense against embracing our feelings and being responsible for our own shortcomings. It is often more gratifying to blame our ex-partner for our continuing dissatisfaction with life than to chart a new course for ourselves. It's easier to weave tales about how our ex-partner conducts his or her life than to get on with our own life.

For example, we might feel exasperated to imagine that our straying partner migrates from one relationship to another without achieving a connection of depth. But even if this perception is correct, it is he or she who must struggle with that condition. We are not being asked for our armchair analysis. More important is what *we feel*, perhaps fear or sadness. More important is what *we want*, perhaps a deep, fulfilling partnership. By restricting our focus to the boundaries of our own reality, we move a little closer to knowing what it will take for us to create a satisfying relationship.

Meanwhile, we may notice and relinquish our own sabotaging, self-critical thoughts, as well as other people's discordant opinions, viewpoints, and advice. We may cherish the companionship of caring, safe friends. We may open ourselves to new people we encounter and let our inner light be seen by those we recognize as kindred spirits.

Important lessons rarely come easily. Suffering is more tragic if instead of finding meaning in it, we remain a sorry victim of circumstances. All is not lost if we can learn something from both the partnership and the betrayal that can deepen our wisdom and compassion, thereby serving us in future relationships. Pain that helps us fathom and befriend our core fears, hurts, and aspirations brings us closer to the heart of humanity.

FINDING PEACE WITH OURSELVES THROUGH FORGIVENESS

Forgiveness is the ultimate act of revenge. Living a happy life is the best way to get back at our ex-partner. This is a cute way of saying that it is only by letting go and forgiving that we finally undo our own tangled feelings. The satisfaction we seek through hurtful actions can be attained through this ultimate act of heart and compassion.

Achieving forgiveness is perhaps our most effective way of disengaging ourselves from another person's continued power to affect us negatively. The inner changes ushered in through the gradual process of forgiveness make us psychologically less susceptible to another's intentional or unintentional harm. As we move toward forgiveness, we slowly relinquish our resentment and attachment. We gain some measure of protection and safety as we disentangle ourselves from the continuing drama of giving and receiving pain.

Forgiveness means that we feel less emotionally reactive in relation to someone who has hurt us. It slowly incubates in an inner climate of compassion and forgiveness toward ourselves. Through self-love, we focus on our own life; we do our best to overcome betrayal without further betraying ourselves. The more in a state of love, compassion, and forgiveness we are, the more rapid and enduring our recovery will be from betrayal.

Being betrayed raises this vital question: What is an intelligent response to betrayal? The desire to inflict harm is one common response, deriving from such causes as injured pride and self-esteem ("You had an affair, so now I'll have one"). International and ethnic wars are larger reflections of the bitter battles we wage with each other in an attempt to resolve differences and reclaim dignity. However, we cannot retrieve dignity by acting in an undignified manner. Although destructive impulses may be unavoidable, we are presented with the choice of either acting on these inclinations (which perpetuates a cycle of hurting and being hurt) or finding constructive ways to deal with life's insults.

Forgiveness as a Value

An increasing chorus of voices in the psychological community are suggesting that forgiveness is a crucial component in resolving feelings of pain, bitterness, and disappointment. Some psychotherapists, notably those with a humanistic, transpersonal, and object-relations bent,[3] are suggesting that forgiveness is a final, necessary step in psychotherapy, whether such forgiveness is directed toward a spouse, lover, friend, or parent.[4] Forgiving those who have betrayed us reflects a mature perception of their limitations, a recognition of their inability to appreciate the legacy of emotional carnage they may have left in their wake, whether intentionally or not.

While some psychotherapists are just beginning to recognize the psychological significance of forgiveness, spiritual teachers have long espoused its value. In Western society, Jesus represents a model for transforming the crucifixion of betrayal into the resurrection of forgiveness. He has come to symbolize the promise that we, too, can do the inner work necessary to release our resentments toward those who have injured us. Suffering the worst kind of abuse, Jesus asked God to forgive those who persecuted him, "for they know not what they do." Rather than respond with hatred and bitterness, he found compassion and love in his heart.

But even Jesus had moments of doubt and rage, such as when he shouted despairingly, "My God, my God, why have you forsaken me?" Presumably, even Jesus had to work through a painful emotional process before he could arrive at a genuine forgiveness. Still, an important step is to hold forgiveness as a value—as something worth working toward because it serves ourselves, as well as others. Then, even if we cannot feel genuine forgiveness right now, we can gradually move in that direction. And we can do our best to avoid impulsive actions or words that might add to our own or others' misery, thereby making forgiveness more difficult.

Stan was betrayed by his friend Steve, who became sexually involved with his girlfriend. For many years, he bristled at the thought of forgiving him: "I used to say to myself, 'Why forgive that bastard! I'll never do that!' I was so outraged. But when I got some space from it after not seeing him for many years, I realized I was carrying a jammed-up hurt inside of me. Carrying that hurt wasn't helping me grow or be peaceful. So I told myself, 'You've indulged yourself enough here. It's time to move on. Let's get over this one, guy.' "

For Stan, moving toward forgiveness began by recognizing it as a value—that it would be valuable for his own growth and development to let go of his hurt and resentment. But wanting to forgive Steve didn't mean that Steve was suddenly forgiven. It did mean that when Stan noticed resentment, hurt, or other feelings coming up in relation to Steve, he made the conscious effort to accept and embrace these feelings, rather than turn them into blame and ill-will. As he entered this forgiveness process, he began to release his "jammed-up" hurt. And he began to understand things more clearly.

THE ART OF LETTING GO

Forgiveness that is genuinely felt, rather than restricted to our good intentions, requires that we pass through a process of letting go that varies for each individual. *Forgiveness is a process, not a decree.* We must begin by acknowledging and accepting whatever initial emotions may be present, however unsavory we may judge them to be. Forgiveness is one of the final fruits of our painful confrontation with injury or loss.

To forgive is defined in the dictionary as "to give up resentment against or the desire to punish." Before we can give up our anger and resentment, we must first allow ourselves to experience these feelings. All too frequently, we short-circuit the process of forgiveness by leaping over emotions that we find distasteful, or antithetical to our "nice guy" or "good girl" self-image. This mindless flight into forgiveness is a dodging of our authentic feelings. We thereby prolong our pain and postpone the final triumph of forgiveness.

The common phenomenon of "process-skipping"[5]—the attempt to bypass our real feelings, or obliterate them by declaration—was described by Dorothy, the woman in Chapter 2 whose partner broke off their engagement. Dorothy had attended many personal growth workshops where forgiveness was a theme. At each subsequent workshop, her unresolved feelings betrayed the fact that she hadn't really forgiven him. She put it rather wryly: "But I forgave him at the last workshop! How can I still be trying to forgive this man fifteen years later?" Apparently, her approach to forgiveness skimmed over her deeper feelings that needed attention in order to release the pain and resentment that disabled her from truly letting go and moving on with her life. As she observed, "The emotional work hadn't been done, so the feelings kept coming back. I could *say* I would forgive, I could *intend* to forgive, I could go through the rational process of forgiveness, but none of the emotional stuff around forgiveness had been done, such as experiencing the pain of the loss."

Stan took a more "feeling" approach to forgiveness. He described the process of forgiving Steve as follows: "Forgiving him began by deciding that's what I wanted to do. Being willing to forgive him meant that I was willing to face it. So I spent time in meditation sitting with my feelings about it— facing my pain, hurt, and resentment, rather than steering away from these feelings. Gradually, I stopped blaming him and began seeing him as a human being who's doing the best he can to meet his own needs. He didn't have malevolent intentions toward me. He wasn't intentionally trying to hurt me." Getting to a place where Stan could see Steve as a struggling human being—like the rest of us—helped him release his resentment.

The road toward healing and forgiveness is full of twists and turns. At times during this journey we may feel forgiving, at other times our resentment returns. This is a natural part of the overall movement toward letting go. Since forgiveness is a process, it takes time to dissolve our resentment and move on with our lives.

The Beginning Stage of Letting Go

We begin to experience considerable relief by simply opening to the energy of whatever feelings are bristling within us. We may go a step further by understanding the meaning of these emotions. Our pain may be more readily released as we sense a meaningful linkage between our feelings and what they are all about. For example, if the betrayal was amplified by intentional brutality, we may feel tormented by the recognition that someone with whom we felt so intimate would now try to devastate our lives. If our partner wants to be with someone else, we may take this to mean that we are unworthy. If we were abruptly left, we might be frightened by the sudden life changes that lie ahead, or we may simply be sad to have lost a companion. Dorothy expressed her loss as follows: "The most painful part was his presenting the possibility of marriage and then taking it away. It's like hearing, 'You're someone special. I want to create a future with you.' To have become so excited about that possibility—and then to have it taken away. That *really* hurt."

By identifying the different aspects of our loss—not in a cold, analytical way, but rather in a poignantly felt way—our pain becomes more vividly defined. As a result, we take a step toward letting it go.

When we are busily denying the depth of our loss and minimizing the scope of the personal life changes that have been foisted upon us, we are far from forgiveness. We cannot simply "forgive and forget" through some kind of mental acrobatics. In order to forgive, we must deal directly with what has happened to us. We must open ourselves to the emotional reality that has entered uninvited into our lives. It is only by welcoming the unwelcome that we can move toward a genuine release of the anger, pain, and bitterness that accompany betrayal. Forgiveness involves healing from these affronts to our being—finding peace and tranquility in relation to them, not trying to forget about them.

The Fruits of Grieving

What does it look like as we approach this place of peace and equanimity? What are some signs that our process of grieving has progressed to the point at which we may be on the verge of forgiveness? If betrayal has led to separation, our healing progresses to the degree that we are no longer mentally or emotionally preoccupied with our former partner. One client put it simply, "I no longer get worked up about it." Whatever thoughts or images arise are not tainted with self-blame or the desire to hurt. In addition, we are no longer plagued with a longing to reignite the relationship. We're more at peace with *what is*. However, our emotions are not repressed or muted; they are calm and unagitated in relation to the betrayer, as when a storm has passed.

When we truly accept the major impact of a betrayal, we are largely free of bitterness, blame, pain, and regret. Some traces of these emotions may be awakened from time to time, perhaps triggered by external events, such as an anniversary, a birthday, or an unexpected encounter. Apart from these occasional memories of our pain, perhaps coupled with a sweet sense of the good times, we basically accept what has happened. As our grieving progresses, we may rediscover some of our lost innocence, an innocence now informed by increased wisdom and self-understanding. As a result, we once again become available to give and receive caring and affection without undue hesitation or self-consciousness. We learn to love again.

Moving toward forgiveness is often more difficult when a

common tie to the children requires an ongoing involvement with each other. Still, we can minimize contact if doing so will promote our healing, which, in turn, will serve our children. For example, we can drop off the kids at our ex-partner's home without getting out of the car. Gradually, we may be able to have a more amicable relationship.

The Challenge of Letting Go

The possibility of forgiving people presents the challenge of opening our heart wide enough to free them to live a happy life apart from us. Lois, who had a tumultuous breakup with a partner with whom she'd been very attached for two years, called him a year later to apologize for her role. Their conversation was very touching: "I told him that when I was in a relationship with him I wasn't able to meet his needs or take care of myself. I was pretty dysfunctional. I forgave him for the ways he hurt me and I apologized for my behavior. And I saw in that moment of apology that by holding resentment against him, I had this grip on his life. Only a small degree in the larger scope of things, but I had some kind of negative control over him because I hated him. When someone holds a grievance against you, it can negatively impact your way of life. So when I let him know I forgave him and asked forgiveness for me, it was like he was in a cage and I opened the door and said, 'You can fly out of the cage—you're free.' "

This generosity of spirit to free her ex-partner did not come easily. It meant really accepting and honoring the fact that he could be happy without her: "There was a moment in our conversation when I saw the joy that was present for him. I saw how I was freeing him, and I thought how I wanted it back. I don't want him to be that free because he's gonna take all that joy and freedom to go be with another woman! I regretted it for a moment. I wanted him for *me* because he was free now. But then I thought, 'No, I've got to free this man and let go of that grip I've had on his life.' "

Freeing others is the flip side of being free. Releasing others is the final product of releasing the hurts within our own heart. The grief that flows from gently embracing our hurt repurifies our heart. Holding on to resentment and ill-will contaminates our tenderheartedness and our happiness. As Lois explained it, "Forgiveness is really about both of us. Forgiving him also freed me because I don't have energy tied up in punishing him, getting even with him, making him wrong, or trying to control him."

What Are We Forgiving?

Forgiveness relates not so much to accepting the event of betrayal, as to accepting and embracing the painful emotions and sudden life changes that have ensued. We do not necessarily forgive people for what has happened, but rather for how they unknowingly contributed to our hurt.[6] Or we forgive them for having been so disconnected from themselves and from the marrow of life that they intentionally tried to harm us.

Forgiveness involves accepting our mutual humanness, our mutual shortcomings. We recognize that we did our best in the relationship, and we entertain the likelihood that the other person did his or her best, even if their best wasn't very good in our "humble" opinion. Nevertheless, our forgiveness involves the recognition that even those who have hurt us have the capacity to grow and change and to conduct themselves with greater integrity in their next relationship, just as we grant ourselves the possibility of bringing greater awareness and love into our next partnership.

The most deeply felt forgiveness and compassion arise from a clear and loving glimpse into the heart of the human condition. Springing from our personal passion for life, love, and happiness, our compassion extends toward the struggles and anguish of others, as well as ourselves.

Forgiving from a Distance

Forgiving people for their shortcomings does not necessarily mean that we become good buddies again. As one client put it, "Forgiveness in the sense that everything is okay again is not real." We may forgive people while simultaneously deciding that we want no contact, or want minimal contact. We can forgive while maintaining a prudent distance. As one woman put it, "The best way to love him is to leave him alone for a while." She was able to forgive him while deciding not to invest the substantial time and energy that would be required to repair the fragile fabric of trust that was torn: "I can't just have a casual conversation with him because we haven't addressed the real issues. Unless they get addressed fully I can't be at ease talking with him." Another client expressed similar sentiments: "I still have all these feelings for her and they have nowhere to go. So it's best that I don't see her at all—at least not for a long time."

Honoring Our Deeper Soul Connection

Genuine forgiveness allows the possibility of maintaining an openness to the betrayer so that if we have a shared child, or must discuss business matters, or if either party desires to talk with the other, we can do so without ill-will or hardheartedness. After all, we were once close. We shared many intimate moments, perhaps profoundly rich and touching ones. Forgiveness lends itself to the formation of flexible boundaries so that we may protect ourselves as necessary, while honoring the deeper connection that may still exist on some level.

Some people (including many therapists) discount the possibility of ever achieving genuine forgiveness toward someone who has hurt them. They dismiss it as being too idealistic and Pollyannaish. They have a constricted, glum view of their human potential, a view they steadfastly refer to as "realistic." They may believe that the best they can hope for is some stoic acceptance of a grim reality. Failing to recognize how they can take an active role in their healing and growth, they believe that only time and distance have the power to heal.

Of course, emotional healing and forgiveness take time in any case—sometimes many years, depending upon the nature and scope of the betrayal, and the depth of our past and present wounds. Some forms of betrayal are so heinous that we should not expect to reopen our heart to that person (although doing so may be easier if he or she expresses genuine remorse). But even if we cannot reopen our heart to that particular person, we serve ourselves by overcoming our resentment so that we might open our heart to new or current friends. As one betrayed man put it, "If I don't forgive her, then I have to hold on to something that I don't want to hold on to—my anger. I don't want to have a connection with her on that level of intensity. I need to be free from it so I can love others."

Our personal values, philosophy, and attitude toward life—what we believe is possible and achievable—play a crucial role in determining how we approach painful experiences such as betrayal. Those who have an openness to a deeper dimension of healing, if not reconciliation, can use the experience of betrayal to become wiser and more compassionate. For such individuals, betrayal can become a stepping-stone toward the dimension of life that has been termed spirituality.

Although the meaning of spirituality varies from person to person, there may be at least one element common to any sound approach to spiritual growth: the capacity to experience an authentic forgiveness and compassion toward people, eventually including those who have hurt us. If spirituality involves a journey toward oneness with life—an orientation of love, caring, and compassion for all that lives and breathes—then we cannot be fully genuine in that quest if we permanently and bitterly close off our heart to any part of that life, including our former partner.

The Possibility of Remaining Friends

When compassion, love, and forgiveness become deeply held values, then a betrayal may yield to a meaningful friendship. This assumes that both parties are willing to be committed to the process of being open and honest with each other while doing the inner work necessary to heal our hearts.

Greg and his new partner were vacationing in Guatemala when she suddenly deserted him during an argument. Although her abrupt departure left him deeply hurt, he remained committed to the process of communicating with her about it after returning home, even if they weren't to remain partners: "My feeling is that if I lose the couple connection, I don't want to lose the connection. I want to find something else. Some people go from being lovers to nothing—and they're better off with that. *I* want to go from being lovers to being friends. That makes more sense to me, especially as I get older. A part of our connection might end, but my love doesn't end. My soul connection to her doesn't end. It doesn't mean that some of her behavior isn't impossible for me, or that some of my behavior isn't impossible for her. But that still doesn't invalidate our soul connection. Love for me isn't just what we can *get* from each other. Love also has to do with what we can *give* to each other."

Remaining friends isn't for everybody. But in situations where it is possible or desired, we must first be willing to forgive each other and ourselves.

FORGIVING OURSELVES

We take a sound step toward forgiving others as we forgive ourselves for our own shortcomings, as we accept the fact that, just like our betraying partner, we may have been unresponsive to his or her legitimate needs and grievances, even if we were far less hurtful. We may have displayed defective reasoning, self-serving argumentation, faulty priorities, and insensitivity. We may have betrayed our partner in subtle or overt ways. The pressures of work, family life, or financial worries may have been so consuming that we had little time and energy remaining for self-reflection or for attending to the emotional intricacies of the relationship. In addition, lack of experience in relationships may have led to some regrettable blunders. For some, this might include the blunder of staying in the relationship too long. As one woman said: "Why did I keep trying to get feelings from this man when they just weren't available?" Forgiving ourselves for personal deficiencies, as well as for the limits that life itself has imposed upon us, can move us closer to forgiving others.

Forgiving ourselves and forgiving others are two sides of the same coin of compassion. When we are harsh, unforgiving, or even violent toward ourselves, we are not inclined to forgive others. When we scold and abuse ourselves, our heart cannot soften into forgiveness. Likewise, when our hardened, wounded heart exudes ill-will and hostility toward others, we perpetuate a state of inner agitation that precludes the experience of self-love and self-forgiveness.

We move toward forgiving others as we learn to rest gently in ourselves, which is the deeper meaning of self-love. Whether we are the betrayed or the betrayer, creative change and growth occur in a climate of self-acceptance and self-love. Carl Rogers, a founder of humanistic psychology, expressed this tenet clearly: "When I accept myself as I am, then I change. . . . I have learned this from my clients as well as within my own experience—that we cannot change, we cannot move away from what we are, until we thoroughly accept what we are. Then change seems to come about almost unnoticed."[7]

The movement from bitterness to openness, from blame to forgiveness, from coldness to compassion does not just happen at our command. Lasting change is the fruit of our steady willingness to confront courageously what is really happening within us. It requires an ongoing commitment to our emotional and spiritual growth. This includes giving ourselves the time we need for gentle reflection and healing.

Months after separating from her husband, Theresa, who felt she had given up too much of herself in the marriage, described the atmosphere in which she embraced her on-going process of grieving, and emerged with forgiveness and love toward her husband: "Late at night or home alone when it's quiet, I'd just look. I'd notice all the woulda's, coulda's, shoulda's and pass through those. At times I'd feel gut-wrenching sorrow, at other times I'd be pounding the pillows, and at other times I'd just have these quiet little realizations. As I accept and move through my fears, reactivity, and upset, reality just starts softly coming out—so this is how it is—without all the trappings, emotional attachments, and psy-choanalyzing. Just little truths coming through quietly—like how he served my growth, how I still feel love for him, how it's best that we don't remain a couple. Then I tell myself, 'You did the best you could. You'll heal. Life goes on, hopefully a little wiser.' I then send him love and wish the best for him. I feel forgiving."

It took many such evenings for Theresa to grow toward a more stable place of letting go of resentments and healing her pain: "I'd go back and forth between longing, hurt, being okay and not okay—major mood swings. I'd often think every-thing was fine, then something would trigger me to cry again; all of a sudden I'd just start crying. I can't tell you how many times I thought I was over it—and then bam!"

For a few of us, embracing our inner process comes natu-rally. But most of us have to pay special attention to our subtle life of feelings. We must deliberately train our attention to rest comfortably within ourselves. This is why the regular practice of self-awareness disciplines, such as meditation and Focus-ing, can be so helpful. We need the leverage provided by persistent attention to our most subtly real experience in order to overcome the destructive thoughts and behaviors that lead to hurting ourselves and others. Gradually, a loving sense of self-presence comes more naturally.

By cultivating our attention in this way, we can more readily embrace our pain and pleasure, our sorrow and joy, our fear and strength. As a result, we become a more integrated, more whole person. We become less afraid of life, and thereby less hostile and reactive when things don't go our way. In addition, we're less likely to seek external sources of relief and gratification. We're less inclined to resort to the various addictions and distractions that have proven to be so destructive to human relationships. We find an inner source of love and nurturance.

Until we have a direct experience of the extraordinary sense of well-being, calm confidence, and inner freedom that accompanies the tender embracing of ourselves as we are, we will flail around in that jumbled state of mind that Thoreau called "quiet desperation." We will minimize our pain and stifle our hurt. We'll subtly dominate others. We'll continue to hold others responsible for our wounds and dissatisfactions. We'll try to look good by making others look bad. We'll try to feel good by making others feel bad. We'll be secretly angry at the world.

As we consistently practice being with ourselves and being "in" ourselves, we discover our private refuge. Rather than searching far and wide for salvation or happiness, we find what we need quietly stirring within our own inner depths, only awaiting the right conditions for it to announce itself. But we must take the time to search and struggle, while embracing the rhythms of triumph and failure, if we are eventually to find a more stable wellspring of love and compassion sparkling within us.

OUR ROLE AS BETRAYER

Forgiveness is one of the most delicate and difficult of human achievements. It becomes especially arduous when the betrayer refuses to be accountable for his or her role in hurting someone. James Hillman expresses this clearly:

The wider context within which the tragedy occurred would seem to call for parallel feelings from both parties. They are still both in a relationship, now as betrayer and betrayed. If only the betrayed senses a wrong, while the other passes it over with rationalizations, then the betrayal is still going on—even increased. This dodging of what has really happened is, of all the sores, the most galling to the betrayed. Forgiveness comes harder; resentments grow because the betrayer is not carrying his guilt.[8]

Without cooperation from the betrayer, we must rely solely on our own inner resources to become reconciled with our emotions and our new situation. When Helene's partner suddenly became involved with another woman, she was left to deal with it on her own: "The ideal would be talking about our issues and feelings together. But since I'm not going to get that, I have to get my own closure. I have to go through my own completion process."

By betraying others, we threaten their sense of safety and security in life. We restimulate their fear of being abandoned or replaced and the shame of being inadequate. When we betray others, we may impel them to marshal defenses to cope with overwhelming fear and hurt. We may incite their resentment and aggression, if not toward us, then toward their next partner or toward innocent others upon whom they displace their contempt. As a result, we contribute to the battle between the sexes—one that hurts us all.

Hillman points to the dangers of not acknowledging our role as betrayer:

If I am unable to admit that I have betrayed someone, or I try to forget it, I remain stuck in unconscious brutality. Then the wider context of love . . . is missed. Not only do I go on wronging the other, but I wrong myself, for I have cut myself off from self-forgiveness. I can become no wiser, nor have I anything with which to become reconciled. . . . [However], by bowing before the shame of my inability to keep my word, I am forced to admit humbly both my own personal weakness and the reality of impersonal powers.[9]

Owning Instructive Guilt as Betrayer

The point is not to shame ourselves as the betrayer, but to recognize that we have hurt someone. Even if we are guilty of intentionally hurting a person, we must eventually forgive ourselves for our past cruelty and self-centeredness and do our best to correct the situation. Rather than suffer silently (or not so silently) in guilt, we must hear the message contained in our guilt if we are to rediscover our integrity.

Guilt comes in various forms. *Destructive guilt* deluges us when we feel overly responsible, such as when we are physically or verbally abused and believe that we must have done something wrong. But another type of guilt is useful and healthy. *Instructive guilt* enables us to recognize when we have hurt a fellow human being, when we have disrespectfully violated another's dignity, rights, and boundaries.

Many counselors and therapists mistakenly believe that all guilt is toxic and try to relieve their clients of any and all forms of guilt. While their intentions are good—to alleviate suffering—they may actually betray their clients by annihilating a feeling that contains a hidden wisdom, a vital message.

Lewis Andrews, a thoughtful writer on the relationship between spiritual values and emotional health, states that we often ignore the "correctional imperative" of our guilt. This is not to suggest that we endure self-blame, suffering, and depression, as if doing so will atone for our misdeeds. Andrews advises us that "no amount of self-blaming depression can quell the real intuitive message of our guilt, which is not that we must *suffer* for our past misdeeds, but that we must take steps to *rectify* the damage we've created, insofar as this is reasonably possible."[10] He further suggests that our "intuitive pangs of conscience, reflecting our deeper wisdom," are best relieved by doing our best to give the other what he or she needs. If we can embrace instructive guilt with a light touch, rather than with a paralyzing self-blame, then we can act constructively to alleviate some of the pain we've caused another person.

Making Amends as the Betrayer

Moved by instructive guilt or heartfelt caring, we may want to find greater peace in relation to a major betrayal, even if it happened years ago. Through time, we may bring greater perspective to our past. During a moment of clarity and compassion, we may want to make amends in order to relieve ourselves of residual guilt and incompleteness, while easing the burden our ex-partner may still be carrying.

It may be easier for our former partner to release his or her pain if we, the betrayer, acknowledge our role in the betrayal, as well as the hurt we've generated. Rather than remain distant or make up excuses, we may offer a heartfelt apology, share our feelings of sorrow or guilt, or simply ask for forgiveness. We might even acknowledge that a deep heart-level connection continues to exist. By lowering our defenses, revealing our true feelings, and seeking some sort of healing, we courageously demonstrate a renewed respect for the betrayed, a generosity of spirit that reflects our caring for each other even though the shape of our relationship has changed. By accepting our fair share of responsibility and extending respect and esteem to our partner, we allow him or her to realize more clearly that the betrayal was not his or her fault, that he or she is indeed a good person. We may each enjoy a deeper reconciliation with ourselves and with life by recognizing the ways we caused hurt, or hurt each other.

If we wish to remain a couple following sexual betrayal, a heartfelt acknowledgment of the pain we have caused may lead to a deeper reconciliation. As a spirit of remorse softens the anger between us, we may pursue an ongoing discussion of what the betrayal was all about. By exploring the motives and factors leading to sexual betrayal, we may uncover hidden dissatisfactions, whether in the partnership or in our personal life.

Such was the case in the partnership between Frank and Joanne. When Frank learned that she had been having an affair, he was understandably angry and hurt. Not unusually, he entertained thoughts of leaving her. By maintaining his commitment to himself and the partnership, he stayed with the process: "I was surprised that my self-esteem remained so strong. That was a key. I didn't have to play a lot of games; I didn't have to retaliate. It helped that she felt badly about it; she saw how much it hurt me. This helped me to really listen to what prompted her to do this—what she was acting out by having the affair. Her getting clear about what was missing for her in the relationship—and my seeing how strongly it was obviously affecting her—led to a new understanding and closeness. I was surprised at how better things got after that."

By simply acknowledging the humanness of those we have hurt or betrayed—their heartbreak, their grief, their struggle—some residual pain may ease. Their self-esteem may strengthen, and their bitterness and resentment may subside. It is more difficult for them to hold on to their hostility if we feel badly about what has happened.[11] Perhaps most importantly, some trust may be revived and a sacred trust in life may be renewed.

However horrified we may be to glimpse the vile or unconscious ways we treated a partner or friend, we can make some meaningful amends by expressing our genuine regrets and remorse, whether verbally or through a letter (the latter is often better, as it gives the person time to mull things over without needing to respond immediately). We might take another courageous step forward by asking if there is anything further we can do to make amends.

This is not to suggest that we offer unfounded hopes of a reconciliation if we have parted ways, but that we simply consider honoring the person we have betrayed by soberly acknowledging our role. Supreme strength is required to reopen ourselves in this way to someone we have hurt. Great courage is necessary to admit that we were wrong, cruel, or limited in some way.

As the betrayer, we may stay isolated from the betrayed, perhaps due to our shame, self-righteousness, or fear of admitting a mistake. We may then further burden the betrayed with the painstaking task of working toward forgiveness without the benefit of a clear expression of our remorse. However, we must be careful not to restimulate an ex-partner's hurt by making contact before there has been sufficient time to heal (especially if we are with a new partner and he or she is not). We might also open our own wound if we reach out before we are ready, or if we are unclear about what is motivating us (such as a secret desire to get back together). It is important here to listen carefully to our clearest sense of what will be most helpful.

It is sometimes not so easy to distinguish the betrayer from the betrayed. A series of little betrayals by one or both partners may have precipitated a big betrayal by one partner. Whoever first finds the strength to acknowledge their unseemly role may want to reach out in some appropriate way. Extending themselves in a spirit of compassion and kindness may hasten healing, while helping to restore a sense of faith in humanity and faith in life.

NOTES

1. C. P. Estes, *Women Who Run with the Wolves* (New York: Ballantine Books, 1992), 369.

2. A. Maslow, *Toward a Psychology of Being* (Princeton, NJ: Van Nostrand, 1962), 57.

3. For a brief discussion of forgiveness from an object-relations perspective, see S. Cashdan, *Object Relations Therapy* (New York: Norton, 1988), 140. See also S. M. Johnson, *Characterological Transformation: The Hard Work Miracle* (New York, Norton, 1985), 298.

4. It should be noted that for those who have survived incest or physical abuse, forgiveness is too ambitious a goal in the early years of recovery. However, forgiveness in the sense of letting go of resentment can emerge as the work of healing progresses.

5. See E. McMahon, *Beyond the Myth of Dominance* (Kansas City, MO: Sheed & Ward, 1993), chapter 8.

6. I borrowed this helpful idea from Sheldon Cashdan, author of *Object Relations Therapy* (New York: Norton, 1988).

7. C. Rogers, *On Becoming a Person* (Boston: Houghton Mifflin, 1961), 17.

8. J. Hillman, *Loose Ends: Primary Papers in Archetypal Psychology* (Dallas: Spring Publications, 1975), 79.

9. Ibid., 80.

10. L. Andrews, *To Thine Own Self Be True* (New York: Doubleday, 1987), 41.

11. However, it is not impossible. Those who persistently maintain a hardness and resentment toward us are likely to be carrying unresolved hurts from previous betrayals in life.

CHAPTER 8

Resting in
Trust

> At the heart of love there is a deep but simple secret:
> the lover lets the beloved be free. What he would like
> to possess totally, he must allow to have a life separate
> from, although shared with, his. This is the gift which
> lovers work at giving to each other all through their
> lives. . . . A great deal of dying goes into this gift;
> indeed, it is in the measure that we accept this dying
> that we begin to grasp the meaning of life that is
> hidden from all but true lovers.
>
> EUGENE KENNEDY[1]

A PRIMARY question for those who have experienced betrayal is this: How can we build safe, trusting relationships?

We human beings have limited wisdom. Although we may not intend to mislead people, we often say things that are not wholly true because we do not know ourselves. We give false reassurances because we do not want to hurt others, and perhaps, more commonly, because we wish to protect ourselves from potential conflict and rejection. We convey inaccurate impressions of who we are. In short, *we fail to build a framework of trust.*

Our perceptions of others are colored by our unmet needs, coupled with resentments, hurts, and fears that linger from our past. The phenomenon known as transference, which happens between counselor and client, is operative in every significant relationship. Because of a selective perception shaped by personal longings, we conjure up qualities in others that may not really exist. We perceive people according to how we want them to be and what they have to offer us. When our views of others are based on our own pressing needs and wants, others become unknowing objects of our personal inclinations and wishful thinking.

The possibility of satisfying relationships depends largely on our ability to see people clearly, as well as on our effort to allow ourselves to be seen clearly. Real intimacy and love can arise only between individuals who perceive each other with a fair degree of accuracy. Closeness and trust grow as two people experience a mutual understanding that is brightened by an open window into each other's ordinarily hidden worlds.

A FRAMEWORK FOR TRUST

The word *trust* is often applied loosely, without appreciating its full meaning. Interpersonal trust emerges as we gain entrance to the microcosm of our real feelings, needs, and vulnerabilities, then selectively allow others entrance into that tender inner world.

The willingness to let ourselves be seen as we really are contains an implicit hope—an openness to promising possibilities. Hope differs from wishful thinking in that genuine hope can be softly felt as a life-affirming, energizing pulse within our being. Hope differs from expectation in that the latter makes others responsible when we're disappointed; it makes our well-being dependent upon how others respond to us. Also, genuine hope is open-ended. If we are unwilling to embrace the unknown, hope can quickly degenerate into a search for security, certainty, and predictability.

Hope says, in effect, "I am open to life, I am willing to risk showing myself as I really am. I may be disappointed, but if so, I am willing to embrace my sorrow. I have a sense of faith—

sometimes weak, sometimes strong—that I will ultimately rest in the greater love and connection that I seek."

How do we carry this hope forward as we meet potential friends and lovers? When our spirit is buoyed by the prospect of a potential heart-mate, it's as if our soul is saying: "In order to let you see who I am, I hope you will not intentionally hurt me. I hope you'll want to understand me so you're less likely to hurt me unintentionally. To feel safe extending tender affection, I hope you'll receive me gracefully, rather than respond in a way that makes me feel self-conscious or rejected. In sharing my fears and hurts, I hope I can be vulnerable without worrying about negative consequences—that I won't be shamed for being "weak," that I'll be appreciated for the *quiet strength required to share my humanness.* To let you feel my energetic strength, I hope you're strong enough to let me be sturdy and assertive without being threatened by my self-confidence and power. I hope we both grow in ways in which we feel good enough about ourselves so that we don't get stuck in being competitive or controlling, and that we welcome our becoming equals in a way that supports our growth and creativity." Trust grows as these and other hopes become progressively actualized.

A major challenge in building trusting relationships is to take repeated, though intelligent, risks to be honest and open. If we have been punished for feeling angry or hurt, we find it scary to affirm ourselves when we perceive such feelings rising within us or within others. If we have been ridiculed or rejected for speaking our minds, we may have concluded that it is safer to remain quiet and reserved. If we have been denigrated for disagreeing, we may have decided to go along with others' beliefs and viewpoints. As a result, we disengage from real contact with others. We go into hiding.

Once we have calculated that we cannot get what we want by being our authentic, natural self, we lose faith in ourselves and in others; we lose the hope that inspires the will to live openly. Our natural openness is then replaced by cynical methods of control and manipulation cleverly designed to secure others' companionship or favors. Or we become competitive as a way to feel better than others, which keeps us distant and aloof.

When we lose hope that love will find us—when we lose the will to share ourselves genuinely—we forfeit the promise of trust-based relationships. "I just kind of closed down inside," said one middle-aged woman. "I lost all hope of finding love." A man who experienced painful rejections stated, "I only let people get so close now, and that's it. I've been hurt too many times."

Giving up hope may actually be a positive step if what we were hoping for is mere fantasy, such as finding someone to be the all-giving caretaker or the perfect mirror for us. If we've been driven by naive hope and optimism, we may need to disengage from any relationship for a time so we may reconfigure the shape of our hope and our direction in life. If we stay committed to the process of personal awakening, surrendering false hope can lead to the newfound richness of building real trust.

Healthy, growing relationships are based on trust, not legal contracts or the money back guarantee of a secure future. The nature of trust is that it can be built only upon the firm foundation of *what is real*. It cannot grow if we are hiding our true feelings and remaining emotionally unavailable. It cannot develop if we're overeager to please, or determined to displease in an attempt to assert our independence. Trust doesn't grow in a climate of subtle or not-so-subtle deception. It can develop only through our courageous commitment to remaining awake to our real self and sharing this with selected others.

FASHIONING A FALSE SELF:
THE LOSS OF TRUST

Many people who have lost hope and trust attempt to build a relationship based on the perfection of their false self. Sadly, they try to actualize an image of who they believe they must be in order to gain acceptance and love. This image is fashioned according to the model provided by parents or society. For instance, individuals might try to be funny. They might wear Italian suits and be big spenders. They might be sweet and accommodating, even when mistreated. Or they might rebel by constructing a self in opposition to parental and societal dictates. Gradually, the inward life that quietly calls to them is crowded out by the outer life they scrupulously design. The private self becomes dominated by the public self. The natural self is replaced by a fabricated self. They struggle to attain what Fritz Perls, the originator of Gestalt Therapy, calls "self-image actualization," rather than genuine self-actualization. Offering a religious parallel, such individuals have fallen from grace—the grace of being connected to self, life, and love. The construction of these false self-images constitutes our original self-betrayal—the betrayal of who we really are.

Most of us have at least some tendency to identify with an image that we show others. It's scary to be stripped bare of the defenses that have protected our weather-beaten, vulnerable self. We fear that if we stray from the false self to which we have entrusted our well-being, we may expose ourselves to foreign forces that have proven so often to be unfriendly and wounding. However, by continuing to suppress and withhold our real self, we set ourselves up for betrayal.

As children who may have been repeatedly shamed or abused, we needed the protection of a false self. However, many of us continue to seek a dubious refuge by protecting our natural self behind inflexible defense mechanisms. We do not show who we really are. We hide our hurt by displaying anger; we conceal our fear through emotional withdrawal. Our partner may experience us as fierce and hardened, rather than as the tender, shy person that deep down we know ourselves to be. Or our friends might experience us as being quiet and withdrawn, when in reality there is a rich world of feelings and aspirations within us. Others may have a hunch that there is a softhearted or sturdy soul beneath what we display. However, if we scrupulously protect ourselves, we deprive ourselves of the deeper connection our soul longs for.

The contact that our partner needs is with our authentic self. He or she can't live long on the false calories offered by our fabricated self. If we keep our vulnerable essence hidden, our partner will eventually feel distant from us and may become bored, disinterested, and numb in the relationship. Our partner might even abandon us. However, the "us" that would be forsaken isn't the real us but rather the false us. It is the meager offering of a scared or insipid self that our partner would be abandoning, which is the only self we've shown. Since a relationship of trust has never developed with our authentic self, our partner may not experience betraying us, but simply believe that he or she is leaving a relationship with someone who's frequently superficial, closed-down, or upset. Our partner may experience himself or herself as simply parting from a bad relationship.

If we rarely reveal our hurt to our partner—our weak points, our sensitivities, our humanity—she may have a meager understanding of our real self. He may have little idea of what he really means to us, especially if we rarely tell him. She may have no clear sense of how she contributes to our well-being. He may misunderstand us because we don't allow him to know us.

Our vulnerability may be so benumbed, our trust so weak, that even as our partner walks out the door, we may still not reveal our hurt, but instead, display the same sarcasm and aloofness that have been instrumental in prodding him to leave us. We may refuse to let ourselves be experienced as a man who hurts, as someone who longs to be embraced and loved. Or, due to false pride or a hidden resentment that says "I'm not going to let him know how he's affecting me," we hide our hurt, as we've been doing all along, and which now, more than ever, reflects an unwillingness to let ourselves be seen as we really are.

Even as our partner walks out the door, we may not bring

ourselves to express these delicate feelings. We cannot, or perhaps more accurately, *will* not let down and allow ourselves to be seen as someone who is afraid of being alone, as someone who is horribly sad that our potential together is disintegrating, as someone whose hope-filled dreams are crumbling.

Since we haven't risked revealing the progressive layers of our true self, we haven't nurtured a relationship in which trust might flourish. Instead, our blame and criticism have introduced shame and fear into the partnership. Our reticence has isolated us and kept us strangers. We may now accuse our partner of betraying us, but have we not betrayed our partner, as well as ourselves?

It is painful to acknowledge our role in a troubled or dying relationship. During a moment of quiet honesty, we might muse, "I wish I knew more about how to build trust. I wish that at those critical junctures when I could have either succumbed to my usual defenses or divulged my deeper fears and hurts, that I'd had the courage and skills to disclose my real feelings and hear those of my partner. I wish I'd had the presence of mind to respect my partner's viewpoints and honor her wisdom and feelings, rather than quickly promote my opinions and impose my solutions. I wish I'd reached out for help. I wish I'd given trust a chance to grow, rather than used my misguided intelligence to control my partner's behavior and coerce her into changing."

GIVING TRUST A CHANCE

The tragedy of relationships is not so much that we're rejected for being ourselves. It's that *we so often hide our real self, thereby never giving trust an opportunity to unite us*. In order to build trust, we must draw upon our wisdom and courage to practice what authors Gay and Kathryn Hendricks call "telling the microscopic truth"[2]—that is, discerning the more subtle feelings, thoughts, and wants that often go unnoticed.

For some of us, revealing the microscopic truth means uncovering the fears and hurts that are regularly dismissed, such as the fear of being deserted or the hurt of not being understood. For others, it means exposing secret resentments that are coated over with "niceness" or deceitful wiles, such as stating that we feel angry when criticized in public. For still others, it means revealing the shrouded hopes and wants that we so easily dismiss, such as wanting more hikes in the woods, time alone, or relaxed evenings to share affection. By divulging these truths and sensing their being accepted and understood, we begin to feel safer being ourselves with others.

Many people fear that their partnership cannot withstand too much truth. They stifle their wants, conceal resentments, and fail to admit their unhappiness, even to themselves. They make a diabolical pact to exchange the truth for an enduring partnership. However, a relationship that so endures may become a test of endurance rather than a source of enduring nurturance and intimacy.

It is one thing to recognize the value of sharing our feelings; it is far more challenging to put our good intentions into practice. It takes an act of courage to affirm our feelings and wants, then share them in an honest, nonblaming way. The feelings we are most reluctant to reveal are often those we most need to share if we want to develop trusting, intimate relationships.

We often hold back because we're afraid we won't be loved if we expose our true self. But I've seen again and again that when committed couples enter into a good faith agreement to be genuine with themselves and each other, their risks to be real are rewarded with increased closeness. For example, Patrick, who was in an eight-year marriage, became angry whenever his partner wanted to discuss their lack of emotional and sexual closeness. Looking deeper, he noticed an emotional paralysis beneath his anger. He recognized a fear of being yelled at and criticized—the way his mother would humiliate him as a child. Acknowledging this deeper sensitivity to being shamed and rejected was a revelation for a man who had the self-image of being strong and tough. As he softened into his fear of being criticized, rejected, and abandoned, he noticed an even deeper hurt and sadness. Sharing these tender feelings with his partner didn't push her away, as he'd feared. Quite the contrary; it was an important step toward bringing her closer to him. As he put it, "It was quite a revelation that it's actually okay to let those feelings be there. At first, I found them repulsive. But the more I do it, the more comfortable I am with showing my feelings. It was a pleasant shock that she *wants* me to express feelings that I thought I was supposed to hide." Patrick's new commitment to truthful, heartful communication helped slowly reignite the emotional and sexual attraction that was nearly extinct.

We often live as if people will find our natural, unrehearsed self repulsive. Author Ken Keyes suggests that "deeper honesty requires you to trust that you are naturally lovable when you are being yourself."[3] As people become more emotionally healthy, they appreciate seeing our real, unguarded self. As they find greater peace with their own genuine self, they naturally feel appreciation and affection for those walking a similar path.

Individuals who are committed to embracing their vulnerability often feel isolated and lonely in a world that rewards aggressiveness and dominance. These determined, yet gentle souls are often eager to connect with those who are likewise becoming emotionally accessible, both to themselves and to others. As we drop our own pretensions and performances, such individuals feel safer revealing their own true essence to us. If we want to find people who are authentic, tender, and open with us, then we need to display those qualities ourselves. As Gandhi said, *we* need to be the change we want to see in others.

This is not to suggest that we spill our feelings onto everyone we encounter all in the name of trust building and openness. As discussed earlier, we must discern when and with whom it is relatively safe to reveal something personal. If we are received in a sensitive and respectful manner—if we're heard and understood—then we may enjoy a growing sense of trust with this person. As we feel safer sharing our peripheral feelings, needs, and concerns, we may become increasingly willing to divulge feelings and needs that are closer to our core. Therapists Herbert Gravitz and Julie Bowden call this "share-check-share."[4] We share a little of ourselves and check to see how we are received. If we feel respected, accepted, and understood, we may want to reveal a little more.

Moving toward deeper sharing in a partnership requires that we build a safe container that can withstand honest communication. We often avoid the truth because it can bring up conflict and pain. If we each trust that we're both committed to the process, honesty feels less risky, less hazardous.

TRUSTING OURSELVES

Trusting others feels especially precarious when we fail to trust ourselves adequately. Letting another person touch our vulnerable core is too scary or disorienting if we cannot peacefully inhabit that tender core. If we are unable or unwilling to embrace and care for ourselves, we will not feel safe allowing another to get close to us or care for us. Instead, we will put up roadblocks, create conflict, or find other ways of keeping our partner from getting too close. If we cannot rest in our own stable center, our relationships will remain unstable and confusing.

Gloria had often accused her deserting partner of not being caring and understanding during their volatile relationship. After separating, she took time off from relationships, getting to know herself better and pursuing personal interests she had long postponed. Soon thereafter, she had a touching, tender conversation with him, telling him how painful the separation was for her. Having taken time to embrace her hurt and grief and coming to affirm herself more, she was able to talk without the blame and accusations that contributed to the wrenching separation. Contrary to her expectations, he was caringly attentive to her hurt: "When I expressed my deeper pain without attacking him, he *was* there for me! I wish I'd done that more while we were together. Now that I can be there more for myself, it's easier to allow others to be there for me."

As we find the inner strength to rest more comfortably within our own deeper essence, we become less reserved about revealing ourselves to others. As we feel more self-assured that we can find a safe haven within our own being, there is less to risk and little to lose. *Relationships then feel less scary, less dangerous.* If we're rejected, we know that we can embrace our hurt rather than be consumed by it. The more we have ourselves and trust ourselves, the freer we feel to be open with others. Opportunities for connecting then multiply. The gateway to love and intimacy opens more widely.

The growth of self-trust is a gradual, developmental process. The more wounded we've been in childhood, the more work that is necessary to heal and rebuild a basic faith in ourselves. Developing a resilient sense of self that is not subject to despondency or bitterness in the face of rejection, abandonment, or betrayal is the deeper nature of personal growth work.

Trust in Our Ability to Embrace Life's Hurts

Lasting inner peace and contentment rest upon that elusive quality known as self-confidence. The word *confidence* comes from the Latin *confidere* meaning "to trust."

We cannot trust ourselves if we are busily avoiding and denying the human feelings that are part of who we are. Having confidence in ourselves means trusting our ability to deal with the feelings that arise as a result of life's disappointments. Rather than disempowering ourselves through self-blame or by blaming others, we have increasing faith that we possess the strength to embrace the hurts of life without being debilitated by them. Through experience, we come to trust that these emotions pass when they are accepted, rather than linger as a result of our resisting them. As this truth gradually seeps into our core, we enjoy ever-greater confidence in being ourselves. As we develop a more trusting, comfortable relationship with the feelings that arise within, we know that we're finding a safe refuge that has always existed within us. More and more we come to rest in self-trust.

Self-Affirmation

The cognitive aspect of building self-trust involves a continuing practice of self-affirmation and self-validation, which are rooted in a growing awareness of who we are. Self-confidence grows as we discover our positive traits and appreciate ourselves for them. For example, we may value our integrity, honesty, or basic goodness. As we build a base of acknowledging and appreciating our current strengths and abilities, self-trust grows. If others later reject us, criticize us, or treat us poorly, we are then served by a self that can deal with unpleasant encounters. We can bring our own locus of self-evaluation to bear on the situation.

No matter how low our self-esteem may get, we can always find something we like about ourselves in order to counter the deeply ingrained human fear that we are worthless or inadequate. For example, I might affirm myself in the following way: "I appreciate myself for the values that I hold dear, such as world peace, a clean environment, and caring about people. I appreciate myself for the kinship I feel with the animal kingdom and for respecting the rights of other living creatures. I appreciate myself for eating semi-healthily, exercising fairly regularly, and having a good, though admittedly strange, sense of humor. I also feel good about the friends I've drawn into my life. Finally, I'm grateful that I have chosen a path of personal growth in a world where so many people feel hopeless and beaten. Rather than joining them in cynicism, suspicion, and self-deception, I feel good knowing that I am attempting to live more honestly and openly, that I'm doing my best to develop creative, rewarding relationships based on trust and mutual respect."

Remembering some of the things we like about ourselves helps us to be gentler toward ourselves, an attitude that is easily lost when we feel mistreated by the world. Gradually, we may value ourselves simply by affirming that *"I am"*—regardless of personal qualities or achievements. Interestingly, this growth toward unconditional acceptance and love of self has been a major theme of the great spiritual traditions throughout the ages.

Growing to like and trust ourselves also requires that we have a realistic sense of our limits and that we accept these. If we demand too much from ourselves or have inflated expectations, we continually undermine our self-esteem.

At the same time, we cannot grow unless we trust our ability to stretch beyond our current limitations in order to move toward what we want in life. Courageously going beyond our limits means that we'll be disappointed or hurt occasionally, if not frequently. We must therefore accept that we'll sometimes fall on our face. However, that won't mean that we are a failure. We can pick ourselves up, learn a painful or embarrassing lesson, and move forward a tad wiser than before. We can trust ourselves to be a bit more perceptive next time—a little more cautious, or perhaps less cautious and more spontaneous.

Trust in ourselves also increases as we trust our ability and determination to set appropriate boundaries. It is we who choose to let people in or keep them distant. When we know how to set boundaries, we are not a victim of others' mistreatment or abuse. We can allow ourselves to get closer when we feel sufficient trust. We can express anger or outrage to those who treat us disrespectfully. We have the right to leave a relationship that is harming us. We feel safer in the world as we establish our boundaries to protect our vulnerable core without isolating ourselves from those we want to welcome as part of our family or community.

TRUSTING LIFE

It is easier to risk trusting others when we have some faith or trust in the life process itself. If we are single and want an intimate relationship, we are well served by having faith that there is someone out there for us, someone who will like and appreciate us. Until we find someone, we may trust that this is a time for our soul to deepen by nurturing ourselves in solitude. If we have a partner, we are served by having faith that we can resolve difficulties by confronting them in a spirit of goodwill and mutual respect.

If we can trust that life accepts us as we are, it becomes more okay to be ourselves with others. It's easier to be daring and honest when we're a trusting participant in what mythologist Joseph Campbell calls "the hero's journey." We then trust that our faltering efforts to move forward in life are never wasted, and that in some mysterious way, life supports us when we are sincere in our desire to love and be loved.

TRUSTING OTHERS

There are no guarantees in relationships. People change. Needs change. An interpersonal trust based on self-awareness, self-affirmation, and self-trust is our most formidable antidote to betrayal.

When a common thread of trust unites us, we are less inclined to resort to deceit and trickery to get our way. When we trust that our partner is genuinely concerned about us, changing needs and wants can be negotiated in a climate of mutual respect and caring. We are less likely to badger and bully our partner if we trust that our concerns are taken seriously, that our partner will do his or her best to give us what we want. Being committed to nurturing trust and intimacy creates a safer container for the partnership.

The more we trust that our partner is there for us, the less we'll be tempted to resort to the manipulative, combative tactics that leave our partner wounded and confused. The closer we live to the vulnerable core of our partner, the less likely we will be to speak or act in ways that might harm our tender connection. The more we trust that our partner is responsive to us, the less likely we will be to judge him or her or exert pressure for change. Being confident that we will be handled with care, we feel freer to discern our fragile feelings and share them uninhibitedly. The more we trust, the more revealing we can be without fearing negative consequences. *Nurturing a positive trust cycle is our best insurance against betrayal.*

Building interpersonal trust must be informed by the awareness that there are limits regarding what our partner can provide us. No one can offer continual care and attention. In addition, our partner may have wants and interests that conflict with our own.

Trusting Our Partner to Know His or Her Limits

Another aspect of trust building is to trust our partner to know his or her limits and communicate them clearly. Trusting that our partner can take care of himself or herself leaves us freer to ask for what we want without being unduly inhibited, overprotective, or guilty. If our partner has the self-awareness and determination to set appropriate boundaries, then we needn't be preoccupied with second-guessing what his or her limits and needs are. We have enough difficulty figuring out our own!

Maria wanted more sexual contact than her partner, Gary, but she hesitated to ask for more. On the one hand, she felt guilty to be so "demanding," and on the other, she wanted to be free to assert her needs and wants. Discussing this matter together, Gary realized that he often went along with her desires even when he didn't want to, which would lead to angry accusations: "You're too needy and demanding!" Such attacks left her feeling crippled in guilt, fear, and inadequacy. As a result, she withdrew from making any requests of him.

A surprising step toward resolution emerged when Gary realized that he had a right to say no to her requests for sex. He had been feeling guilty about saying no, while also being afraid she would leave him if he failed to please her. So his resentment would build and then explode, which pushed her farther away and left him feeling even more guilty. His willingness to take more responsibility to say, "I don't feel like being sexual right now," freed her to reach out for sexual affection without feeling guilty about it—without feeling like a nuisance.

Trust finds fertile ground when two people are free to ask for what they want while respecting each other's limitations. Over time, we become familiar with these limits. If we cannot accept them, then this may not be the right relationship for us.

Within the context of a trusting relationship, we can be calmly assertive without being demanding. There is little need to communicate combatively when we have faith that our requests will be carefully considered.

Trust Helps Us Be More Flexible

The more we enjoy a growing love stemming from trust, the more inclined we are to keep our agreements and be reliable. We are unlikely to make agreements we can't keep because we know that breaking our word may hurt our partner and jeopardize our hard-won trust. If we want to break or change an agreement, we can feel more comfortable doing so if the relationship is enveloped in trust (as long as the agreement we break does not strike at the heart of our bond). For example, if we're late for a dinner date, our partner is less likely to imagine the worst if trust is strong. Suspicious thoughts, such as "He doesn't care about me" or "I'm not that important to him," are replaced by more realistic speculations, such as

"Traffic must be slow" or "He must be running late for some good reason."

Although there may be inconvenience or mild annoyance as a result of our being late, our partner is less likely to feel hurt or resentful if trust is firm. When we finally arrive, we can offer an explanation, which is likely to resolve the matter. When healthy trust and communication exist, understanding is not far away.

If a relationship is riddled with distrust, then there is likely to be upset fueled by the unfounded suspicion that we do not care. Persistent suspicions stemming from former hurts and rejections can quickly undermine trust in our current relationships.

The more we trust, the more flexible we can be with each other. The freer we feel to be ourselves, the more we're walking on solid ground rather than on eggshells. As understanding and trust replace suspicion and fear, we reinforce a positive pattern with our partner. We can then give each other more slack to be ourselves and make mistakes.

If we trust our partner's intentions and integrity but still feel resentful or insecure, we may distrust ourselves more than our partner. Perhaps we do not trust that we are worthwhile or desirable, or we may distrust that we really can be happy. Cindy, who was forty years old and twice divorced, was in a new, promising marriage, but she began having fears that she would push her husband away like she did with her other partners: "Just when things start going well I pick a fight. I can't let go and trust. When we fight, I know he's there. When we're not fighting, things get nebulous for me. It's harder to feel connected."

Fighting was a familiar theme in Cindy's original family. It was a way to feel heard and connected. But this connection was prompted by fear and forged through rage, not based on trust. To stop fighting and allow herself to trust meant allowing feelings to surface that were thoroughly suppressed in order to survive in an unsafe home for many years. As she

struggled with letting go of control and opening to her vulnerable feelings, especially hurt, fear, shame, and loneliness,
these feelings began to loosen their grip on her. As she trusted
herself to accept and embrace these feelings, she softened.
She could then slowly let in her husband's love. Their improv-
ing emotional, sexual, and spiritual connection was the rich
reward of their ongoing commitment and patience.

PARTING IN TRUST AND
UNDERSTANDING

The various concerns that bring people to my counseling
office often have their underpinnings in deeper issues of trust
and intimacy. Relationship difficulties are often traceable to
an absence of understanding and connection. As our self-
awareness and communication become more refined—as we
become stronger, wiser, and more sensitive—the major reason for separation subsides. When we do our part to
strengthen the underpinnings of self-trust and interpersonal
trust, the dissatisfactions that are based on distrust and disconnection subside. The prospect of betrayal diminishes.

The extraordinary blessing known as trust increases the
likelihood of a lifetime connection. *When a presumption of trust
guides our approach to quarrels and differences, we operate in a
climate that is conducive to positive outcomes.*

Mutual trust that's based on a history of resolving conflicts
and continually renewing our commitment to mutual understanding is a rare and precious gift. We're unlikely to abandon
such a relationship unless some major difference or incom-
patibility surfaces.

Nevertheless, even though trust may be strong, unanticipated differences can lead to irreconcilable conflicts. We
may discover significant differences in our emotional needs
that we have long overlooked but that have nevertheless been
a continuing source of irritation. As one woman discovered
after struggling with differing values and worldviews for fif-

teen years, "It wasn't appropriate for us to spend our lives together. We were operating on different wavelengths. There's no one to blame; it was just a miss. It's not that my way was right and his was wrong. We were just headed in different directions on different paths."

A bond of trust softens the rough edges in a sober discussion of our differences so that both of us may come to recognize the wisdom of separation. Love itself is not enough to keep a partnership thriving. But if love for our partner can somehow triumph over our fear of abandonment and isolation, we may find our way to supporting our partner's preference to take a different path in life. Of course, there will be disappointment and sorrow, but we will be spared the bitter heartbreak of betrayal.

A base of trust enables us to address the possibility of separation in good faith. A major life decision that would drastically alter our partner's future would not be undertaken without carefully considering how it might affect him or her. If trust is present, we would surely include our partner in our decision-making process, not just declare our decision to leave. Instead of shutting out our partner, we would listen to his or her feelings and wants. Through loving intentions and sensitive dialogue, we might even discover some creative breakthrough. Or we may both agree that separation is the wisest choice.

The differences that can lead to a mutual decision to separate vary for each individual and each couple. I have observed the following variations and differences to be among the more common reasons for separating:

- Differences in our emotional, sexual, or spiritual needs, wants, temperament.
- Differing communication needs or styles. For example, one person wants more interpersonal dialogue, while the other isn't willing or able to participate.
- Differences in lifestyle preferences, such as where we want to live, our relationship to money (how and when to spend it), our relations with family members.

- Differing desires for children.
- Differing values or vision.
- Differences in sexual preferences. One person wants to be monogamous, the other doesn't.

Of course, some of these differences may be resolved through a committed dialogue. But when they cannot be settled over the course of time, separating may become the least painful choice.

When parting becomes a joint decision governed by understanding and acceptance of each other's different needs or wants, there is no betrayal. Separation may then proceed without the usual rancor and bitterness. If trust and love remain alive, the relationship may even continue to be satisfying and enduring as the nature of the relationship transforms. Although we may want some temporary distance in order to disentangle ourselves from our partner, we might find that a rewarding friendship can emerge as we cease trying to get something from each other that's unattainable.[5]

PARTING IN TRUST:
A SCENARIO

Since the human need for love and closeness is so strong, our emotional reaction to loss and separation is predictably intense. But this does not condemn us to a knee-jerk reaction to events. We are human beings, not automatons, and have the capacity to bring our wisdom and understanding to bear on life events. This radically alters our experience of and our response to them. We learn and grow as our mind and emotions work harmoniously together.

Our understanding of our experiences—the way we perceive and relate to them—is colored by our level of trust in ourselves, others, and life itself. The experience of abandonment or betrayal can befall a wise person and a not-so-wise person (such wisdom being based on experience and the depth of learning culled from that experience). Each of their responses will be totally different, based on their depth of trust and self-understanding.

As we bring greater wisdom to the painful events in our adult lives, our response is determined more by the inner resources that meet those events than by the events themselves. We then grieve the losses of life more gracefully. We emerge with continued trust in ourselves and faith in life. Our heart remains open.

The following scenario explores different ways of dealing with loss, based on the phases of growth I've observed in clients, friends, and myself.

I'm dating a woman I really like. She possesses many qualities I appreciate. I'm attracted to her. She seems to like me, too. Our communication is pretty good. I have relished the time we have spent together over the past few months. Then the unexpected happens. She tells me that she's met someone else whom she wants to see. My heart sinks as she mouths the painfully familiar words "I just want to be friends."

I immediately feel angry. I accuse her of leading me on. I attack her for deceiving me. I grill her with questions: "How long have you known him? Why didn't you tell me sooner? What do you find in him that you don't find in me?" I express my suspicions about whether she ever really liked me, and I proclaim that there's no way I'd want to be friends with her.

At another time in my life, my reaction would have been different, but also dysfunctional. I would have stifled my anger and upset. I wouldn't have shown my real feelings. I would have shriveled up inside and kept my hurt in a privately painful way. I would have cut myself off from her, remaining secretly resentful, and perhaps deciding that women are sly and untrustworthy. It would have been a long time before I trusted again.

Now let's assume that I'm a bit wiser as a result of learning from my experiences. My greater self-understanding will now prompt a response that is vastly different from my past reactions of attack, accusation, or retreat.

I now realize that my hostility and withdrawal had more to do with *me* than with anything my partner did to me. More specifically, my impulsive reactions were fueled by unresolved grief from previous relationships. I had grown accustomed to being abandoned by girlfriends, as well as by elders and teachers who weren't really there for me when I needed their support and understanding. My tendency to withdraw stemmed from feeling badly about myself when things didn't work out. I thought there was something wrong with me, that I was fatally flawed in some way.

In recent years, I have been blessed with good friends who understand and appreciate me. I enjoy creative pursuits and feel good about my values. Gradually, I have come to appreciate my worth. I feel better just being me. My self-esteem now derives more from how I feel and think about myself than from how others value me or treat me.

As a result of my new self-affirmation and self-trust, I'm less apt to get angry and more likely to accept what I cannot change. I realize how I used anger as a defense to protect me from the deeper wounding that resulted from past humiliations and rejections. I feel sad to recognize how difficult it was for me to allow myself to touch my deeper fears and hurts, or allow others to see me in pain. When people came close to touching this pain, I scorched them with my anger, as if to say, "There's no way I'm going to let you get close to my vulnerability."

This deeper hurt was especially apt to bubble up when I was on the verge of receiving caring and love. I was carrying too much pain and bitterness to let love in. Instead of softening into the pain so that it might find an avenue of release, I clamped down against it and reclaimed my defensive stance toward the world. I took refuge in my coldness and emotional distance. No wonder people had a hard time being in relationship with me!

I can now forgive myself for my lack of awareness and wisdom. I just wasn't prepared to experience the pain and grief of my previous losses. Instead, I found protection through my anger and emotional distancing. As I have found greater peace with my pain, I no longer need the defenses that shielded me from it, while simultaneously hardening my heart against the tender love I wanted. As I've found the outer support and inner strength to embrace the pain and grief that accompany loss, I can see the current situation more clearly and respond accordingly.

Now when my woman friend informs me that she's interested in another man, I check in more closely with my experience. I feel a vague inclination to fly into rage and criticism, as I was once prone to do. But my self-esteem has become more resilient as my awareness and self-trust have grown. I feel some anger, but I'm now strong enough to allow myself to feel the hurt beneath my anger. I like this woman and believed that there was good potential between us. I feel sad to abandon the hope of actualizing this potential.

After spending some quiet time with this sadness, I realize that my first impressions of people have often been distorted. I've frequently chosen partners who turned out to have vastly different needs, values, and orientations toward the world than I'd suspected. I've stayed in touch with some of these former partners and have observed our divergent paths in life. As a result, I now feel thankful that we parted, although at the time I fiercely resisted it. As I have come to know them better, I realize that we had too many differences to be partners. As I feel the sadness and tenderness that accompany this recognition, I have the budding awareness that my current situation may also turn out for the best.

I know there will be periodic waves of sadness connected to my current loss. I'm likely to experience rounds of fear and pain as a result of being alone again. I cannot talk myself out of these feelings. I will need time to heal. But I am already beginning to glimpse this situation with some perspective.

Now, when she tells me that she wants to see someone else, I don't accuse her of misleading me. I don't attack her for deceiving me. These suspicions resulted from my own negative self-image. In reality, I have no reason to suspect that she never liked me. I know from personal experience that it is possible to like more than one person. I remember how painful and confusing that can be.

Although I hate to admit it, I've also felt justified in switching partners when someone "enticing" has come along. So I can't really fault her for wanting someone who is a better fit for her, someone who is more appealing for whatever reason. And after all, we're not married. She never made any promises about the future. I never asked for any. I feel hurt and abandoned, but not betrayed, as my hurt "inner child" might have claimed in the past. She never broke any agreements with me. In fact, she is honoring an agreement by being honest. I appreciate her for telling me the truth, rather than being with this man secretly, which would have felt like a crushing betrayal when I finally found out.

Although I feel hurt, I know that she is brave to clarify her position now, rather than later, as people often do when they're afraid of hurting my feelings or evoking my disapproval. I even experience a sense of gratefulness that she's telling the truth. If there is something disagreeable she finds about me, I prefer to know it now. We can then either resolve it or move on, rather than be shocked later when we're married and have children dependent on us.

From my experience with relationships, I'm aware that she may merely be infatuated with this man, and that they may part before long, as people often do. I know that I have the option to keep tabs on her, and, if they separate, to make myself available if I am so inclined. I may accept her offer to be friends for now, or for as long as that serves me and serves us. Perhaps we still have love and caring available for each other, even if it's not expressed in the way I'd prefer. Or our being friends may be too difficult. It may connect me with an intense pain that relates to wanting more than I can have. I can then decide not to be friends, at least not right now.

As I have grown, I've developed the humility to recognize that I'm not the best possible catch for every woman on the planet. I feel hurt that she prefers another man, but I know that she's entitled to choose someone who is more matched to her own felt needs and preferences. I realize that there are other men out there who might be better suited to her temperament and tastes. I respect her right to pursue what she wants in life—a liberty that I also take for myself.

Rather than blame myself or blame her for our separation, I understand that there are many possible reasons for it. We may discuss this at greater length if I want to know her reasons. Perhaps she's disheartened because I'm not enthusiastic about having children. Maybe I don't earn enough money to meet her financial requirements. Perhaps she doesn't find us sexually compatible.

If she's leaving me for any of these reasons, I'd probably feel hurt. I might even wonder if these are sufficient grounds for separating. But I recognize that this isn't for me to judge. I can't control her likes and dislikes. She has a right to set her own standards—she's the one who must live with them. Most importantly, *I remind myself that her dissatisfactions are no measure of my self-worth and value.* We may simply want different things from life. Or there may just not be the right kind of chemistry between us. That's not anyone's fault.

Another option is to listen closely to whatever feedback she offers. Perhaps it's consistent with other feedback I've received, such as a suggestion that I communicate in blaming ways or that I don't extend myself far enough into my partner's world. If I'm willing to do some soul searching, the separation may provide a key to understanding how I might grow in order to be with someone in a more fulfilling way in the future.

I'm free to question her if I suspect that she may be withholding her real reasons for distancing from me. Some new understanding might emerge as a result of an honest, courageous discussion. She might even feel closer to me and decide to give our relationship another chance. But if I get drawn into analyzing and evaluating her reasons for leaving me, I may become hopelessly lost in the labyrinth of my mind. Also, if I violate her boundaries through cunning criticism, I'll only succeed in making her feel "wrong," thereby distancing her further. If I approach her with a blend of gentle inquiry, respect, and a recognition of my ultimate helplessness to change her, I may feel satisfied knowing that I did my best to communicate with integrity.

Another possible scenario is that this woman has a habit of leaving men with whom she begins to feel emotionally close. She may want intimacy but also dread it. She may abruptly leave men before they decide to leave her. Or she may be attached to the excitement that comes from being in a new relationship. If any of these are true, I can't help her with that. I can't change her.

The outcome might be different if she wanted to be with me but has some fears of being close. We might then talk about ways we could feel safer being together. But I'd rather not persuade her to stay with me. What if she said yes? I might have a bigger problem on my hands later. I might have to abandon her at some point if her continuing ambivalence or fears of intimacy are more than I can handle. Or we might separate in a more painful way in the future if the traits she dislikes about me become even more unacceptable.

As I ponder all this, I know there are other people out there who are eager to have a healthy relationship. I may not be the most enlightened, dashing, dynamic man in the world, but I know that I do possess many desirable qualities. I have faith that there is someone else out there for me, and that I'll meet a woman who is a better match. In the meantime, I may need to learn things that come only from being alone. I may need to nurture friendships for friendships' sake. I may need to be less fixated on finding "The Relationship." I may need to nurture within myself the love that I'm seeking "out there." I may need to become the kind of partner I'm looking for.

Such reflections are not meant to suggest that there is a "right" way to deal with separation or rejection, but rather that we can learn to respond with greater wisdom and compassion when parting is inevitable or preferable. As we find greater trust in ourselves and the life process, we will cling less tightly to those who do not want to be partners with us, or who do not really love us. We will have greater faith that life has something else in store for us, as the hopeful words of Ralph Waldo Emerson echo:

> Though thou loved her as thyself,
> As a self of purer clay,
> Though her parting dims the day,
> Stealing grace from all alive;
> Heartily know,
> When half-gods go,
> The gods arrive.

Separation is never pleasant. But the combination of embracing the full spectrum of our feeling life and bringing our wisdom to bear on painful events provides a supportive environment for healing and growth. Moving forward in this manner is a gradual process. There are likely to be periods of terror and turmoil alternating with periods of relative calm. At times, we will feel overwhelmed and hopeless; at other times, we will reemerge with clarity and perspective. The important thing is that we trust the process and remain committed to it, that we remain true to ourselves, even if family, friends, or others misunderstand us[6] or try to distract us from our healing and growth. Gradually, we learn to ride the waves of change without drowning in them.

BUILDING TRUST THROUGH INTEGRITY

Trust is similar to what Christian spirituality refers to as grace. It is not something we can design through willpower. However, we can nurture a climate in which trust is more likely to grow. Just as we can care for a flower bed, we can give our relationships what they need to flourish. We cannot coax the flowers to grow by yanking at their stems, yelling at them, or criticizing them. They bud in their own time and their own unique way.

Trust grows between two individuals living with a high degree of integrity. The dictionary defines *integrity* as "the quality or state of being complete; wholeness." We move toward wholeness as we take the initiative to look honestly at ourselves and come to know ourselves as we really are. We become more whole as we gain access to our feelings, our wants, and our truth. Our relationships become more satisfying and complete as we find the generosity of spirit that leads us to communicate in clearer, more sensitive, nonblaming ways.

Living with integrity prompts us to make only those agreements that we are fairly certain we can keep, rather than say what is expedient to avoid disagreements or get the results we want. Living with integrity also means maintaining the flexibility to renegotiate agreements in order to preserve our more primary commitment of being true to ourselves. If we must make the difficult choice of breaking or changing an agreement, our integrity may move us to offer a heartfelt apology for the pain we may cause, as well as doing what we can to make amends. We may then reassess our needs, limits, and capacities so that we don't continue hurting people, and consequently, harm ourselves.

Integrity refers to a life orientation in which we are committed to becoming more self-aware and appropriately responsive to others. Rather than blaming others or holding them responsible for our unwise choices, we trade in our role of victim for the role of self-responsible adult who culls the learnings inherent in all life experiences, however unpleasant they may be.

We break our trust with life itself when our integrity yields to cynicism, ill-will, and self-pity. We become unpleasant company when we lose faith in the process of life and growth. When we betray life, people are prone to betray us.

Living Our Values/Holding Our Beliefs Lightly

We live with integrity by discovering the values that are dear to us and periodically asking ourselves if we're living according to those values as best we can. For example, we may value honesty, truth, and love, but are we being forthright in our relationships? Do we look courageously at what is really going on during a conflict or argument? Are we being loving? Or do we subtly betray people through deception, denial, and disrespect?

A life of integrity also asks us to question our beliefs and viewpoints. There is nothing that so thoroughly hardens our heart—nothing that ages us so rapidly—as our taut, unquestioned beliefs. There is no more potent way to isolate and disconnect from our fellow human beings than to hold our beliefs as definitive and indisputable. For example, we may believe that assertive women are unfeminine bitches (while simultaneously holding the contradictory belief that they are weak if they let themselves be taken advantage of). Or we may believe that soft-spoken men are wimps (while simultaneously complaining that men are too aggressive and arrogant).

In reality, our views may be shaped and distorted by the social stereotypes that become rigidly etched in our minds. Or we may have formed early opinions based on others' compelling arguments, ones we now take for granted unless we consult carefully with our actual experience. For example, during the sexual revolution of the sixties and seventies, many of us were persuaded to believe that having sex early in a relationship was a good way to get to know somebody. Since then, the personal experiences of many people have shown that it may be wiser to get acquainted in nonsexual ways before allowing the powerful energies of sexuality to come into play in the relationship. Quickly acting on our sexual feelings can overpower other ways of being intimate.

By periodically reevaluating our beliefs, we stay alive and fresh with whatever is dear to us, rather than become rigidly

dogmatic or self-righteous. Ancient Taoist teachings suggest
that the wiser we become, the less opinionated we are. An old
Sufi saying maintains that *whatever perspective we may arrive at,
there's always one beyond it.* Growing in wisdom means including an ever-widening perspective that keeps incorporating
unexplored viewpoints.

Bowing before the gods of Reason and Certainty, many
people feel ashamed and embarrassed if they don't hold solid
beliefs or know where they stand on every topic. Candidates
who do not espouse confident viewpoints on social and political issues are branded as wafflers. Personally, I have greater
trust in people who are strong enough to give up the pretense
of knowing, who can admit that they must give a matter more
thought or consult with others about it, or that the topic is so
complex that they're not sure what is best. Oftentimes, a
"waffler" is someone who possesses the intelligence and integrity to view an issue from many different angles before
making a decision that will affect the lives of so many for so
long. The writer F. Scott Fitzgerald reminds us that "the test
of a first-rate intelligence is the ability to hold two opposed
ideas in the mind at the same time, and still retain the ability
to function."

Integrity comes from the Latin word meaning "whole" or
"entire." We grow toward integrity as we integrate diverse
feelings, experiences, and perspectives into a more whole,
more expansive sense of self. We embody integrity as we make
choices that are well integrated with our beliefs, wants, and
values—as clearly as we can currently glimpse them.

In one way or another, we have each caused pain to ourselves and others as a result of not being true to ourselves. The
following is one man's chronicle of events that unfolded from
not living in a fully authentic way.

"I want a partnership but am not inclined to want children.
I find a woman I want to be with. As we grow closer over time,
we consider marriage. She raises the topic of children. I know
that I love her and sense that I could be happy with her, but
I'm not sure that I want a child. I'm afraid that she'll be

critical of me if I don't want children. I fear being alone again if she leaves me for this reason.

"Deep down, I don't want children, at least not now. I want to take some years to build our connection first. Also, I don't feel settled enough in my career. I don't feel ready for the responsibilities of parenthood. Some people tell me confidently that I may *never* feel ready, that I should just do it and things will somehow work out. My partner broadcasts the same reassurance. It begins to sound reasonable. I slowly reassure myself that it would be good to have a child. I tell her it's fine. We get married and have a child soon thereafter.

"Before long, my worst fears materialize. The child takes most of my partner's time. She is tired much of the time. She doesn't have the same quality of attention and energy for me. We don't have sex as often as we used to. Between our work and parenting schedules, there is little time to just hang out.

"I feel abandoned. I react by being resentful and withdrawn. I spend more time with other friends to get my needs met. I work longer hours to pay our ever-growing bills. I am also half-consciously aware that I vent some of my resentment by working late hours. My wife accuses me of not helping out enough. She feels betrayed. The more I feel attacked, the less responsive I become. Our relationship continues on a downward spiral.

"Although we have many arguments, there are also good moments. There are times with the family that are joyful and fulfilling. There are moments I feel deeply moved when I look into my child's eyes and know that through some miracle of life, a part of me has been passed on. But if I'm honest with myself—if I dare admit to the microscopic truth—I wish that I had listened to the still, small voice that told me not to have a child, or at least to wait. My life feels too overwhelming now. This isn't the way I wanted to live my life. I feel angry with myself for having betrayed myself. And I feel some resentment toward my partner for pressuring me to have a child, even though I agreed to it.

"By agreeing to have a child, I abandoned my own vision

of how I wanted my life to be. I caved in to the pressure I felt from my partner. In truth, I betrayed myself to avoid being alone and experiencing the pain of losing someone I cared about. Now I feel more abandoned and alone than I felt when I lived alone. I wish I had had the integrity and wisdom to listen to myself and had been willing to face the consequences. Doing so would have best served me. And it would have best served my partner, who must now raise a child with a less-than-willing spouse.

"I trust myself to make the best of the situation. I trust that by communicating honestly and openly, we can work through our respective feelings of resentment and abandonment and grow closer again. I even trust that I can learn something through this process and perhaps grow closer to my family in some new way. If this does not happen, if she or I (or both of us) want to separate, I trust that our lives will still move forward, although not without further pain for each of us.

"Still, I wonder how my life would have been different if I had trusted my earlier sense of truth. Did I need this pain to grow in some way, perhaps to become more generous and less self-centered? Or is the lesson simply to trust myself more, rather than be swayed by others' wants and demands? Perhaps there is some truth to both perspectives. But the main thing now is to maintain my integrity by acknowledging my dissatisfaction and dealing with the situation as best I can."

THE POTENTIAL TO LOVE

Painful events can open new windows to self-discovery. Whether we are the betrayer or the betrayed, we can use the experience of betrayal to learn more about ourselves. But in order to learn anything, we must first be *committed* to learning and growing from the unpleasant circumstances that befall us, or that we help create.

When our self-esteem is shaky, we may protect ourselves by insisting that calamitous events are strictly the other person's fault. If we believe that we are "bad" for being shortsighted or imperfect, we will want no part of the responsibility. If we think that a failed relationship means that we are a failure, then we will not possess the calm, nonjudgmental presence of mind to learn from our mistakes so that we can move forward with dignity and grace.

Wisdom goes hand in hand with accountability for our choices, though without the added burden of self-blame. As we find the strength to gently embrace our hurt, our fear, and our shame, we can come to understand where we became lost so that we don't repeat past errors. It is a remarkable victory of human awareness and courage to negotiate our way through the biologically programmed fight or flight response in the face of conflict or betrayal. That is, our immediate instinct is to vent blame or absorb blame, to attack or withdraw, to fight life or give up on life rather than soberly investigate our role in the matter so that we may bring greater understanding to our relationships.

Have We Betrayed Anyone Lately?

When exploring our role as betrayer, we may behold the appalling vision of how we have intentionally injured others. We may suddenly see how we've hardened our heart while shutting off any concern for others' well-being. We may be alarmed to recognize that we have cultivated a passion to dominate rather than to love. As a result, we are likely to feel appropriate guilt and need to make some kind of amends in order to find peace within ourselves.

We might also bring attention to our unintentional betrayals that have wounded others. To the degree that we lack self-awareness, and to the extent that we are governed by our own pressing needs, we will tend to overlook the negative ways we affect people close to us. Given the prevalence of these unintended betrayals, we might do well to regularly ask ourselves: "Who have I betrayed lately?"

A growing number of people are venturing to embody

caring and compassion in a world filled with deceit and betrayal. Doing so involves casting a gentle light on the betrayals shared by all of humanity—the everyday failures to look, listen, and respond to the fears and cares of our friends, family, and people whose lives we touch. Such individuals are accepting life's ultimate challenge to love well and to love wisely. Fulfilling an unspoken, sacred pact with life, they are realizing their potential to be fully alive and to extend their authentic self to others. They are committed to building trust in their relationships—and in the world.

By being committed to this direction, we not only serve others, we also replenish ourselves. We further our own journey toward expanded love, dignity, joy, and creativity. We contribute to a world that becomes a bit safer and more satisfying for all of us—one that mirrors back the trust and love we have nurtured.

NOTES

1. E. Kennedy, *The Heart of Loving* (Niles, IL: Argus Communications, 1973), 131–132.

2. G. Hendricks and K. Hendricks, *Conscious Loving: The Journey to Co-Commitment* (New York: Bantam Books, 1990).

3. K. Keyes, *The Power of Unconditional Love* (Coos Bay, OR: Love Line Books, 1990), 76.

4. H. L. Gravitz and J. D. Bowden, *Guide to Recovery: A Book for Adult Children of Alcoholics* (Holmes Beach, FL: Learning Publications, 1985).

5. According to a doctoral thesis by Carol Masheter (University of Connecticut), ex-spouses often enjoy a better relationship after divorce than during marriage. See Susan Campbell, "Divorces Can Lead to Friendship," *San Francisco Chronicle*, 15 June 1988. Scott Nelson's helpful book also addresses this theme. *Lost Lovers, Found Friends: Maintaining Friendship after the Breakup* (New York: Simon & Schuster, 1991).

6. Ralph Waldo Emerson said: "To be great is to be misunderstood."

Guide to Resources

Overcoming betrayal and building trusting, intimate relationships are not easy to do alone. Our growth is often aided by compassionate, insightful people who can provide guidance, support, and caring. Such individuals may not be easy to locate. I maintain an informal list of counselors, therapists, and educators whose orientation is compatible with the perspectives presented in this book. I may be able to provide a referral to someone in your area if you send a self-addressed, stamped envelope to:

John Amodeo
P.O. Box 564
Graton, CA 95444
(707)829-8948

You may write to the above address for information on training and workshops, as well as intensive work for individuals and couples offered by the author in San Francisco and the North Bay Area, as well as workshops offered in Portland, Oregon; Seattle, Washington; and other locations.

INSTITUTE FOR BIO-SPIRITUAL RESEARCH

This non-profit, non-denominational organization explores the intrinsic spirituality of the Focusing process. Their approach is harmonious with the perspective presented in this book. For a free current newsletter describing Focusing resources developed for the Bio-Spiritual network (booklets, audiotapes, videotapes) contact Sheed & Ward at 1-800-333-7373.

Resource persons associated with this group are educators who teach the Focusing process. They also train interested persons to guide others in Focusing, and help them form small, on-going support groups. These services are not intended as substitutes for professional counseling or psychotherapy for those who need it. These resource persons may be able to make referrals for those wanting individual therapy or couples counseling.

Contacts for Local Programs:

PACIFIC NORTHWEST: Jacqueline Dickson, 1014 N. Pines #203, Spokane, WA 99206-4935, Tel: 509-921-7693. Dave Parker, P.O. Box 499, Kirkwood, WA 98083, Tel: 206-820-2016

CALIFORNIA: Monica Kaufer, CMT, 1717 Oxford St., #308, Berkeley, CA 94709, Tel: 510-549-1844; Fran Kopp, 27101 Paseo Activo, San Juan Capistrano, CA 92675, Tel: 714-496-4838; Marletta McGannon, 2300 Adeline Drive, Burlingame, CA 94010, Tel: 415-340-7474; Ann McGlone, 604 Island View Drive, Seal Beach, CA 90740, Tel: 310-598-4984; Rose Ramsay, 252 Rocky Point Rd., Palos Verdes Estates, CA 90274, Tel: 310-541-9425; Jon & Theresa Sapunar, 1239 Pine Tree Lane, Sebastopol, CA 95472, Tel: 707-823-4264; Bill Stobbe, 12 Tiempo Court, Folsom, CA 95630, Tel: 916-985-4933

ROCKY MOUNTAIN: Loretta Flom, 5913 West 92nd Place, Westminster, CO 80030, Tel: 303-429-1060

SOUTHWEST: Joanne Knowles, 12423 Pine Rock, Houston, TX 77024, Tel: 713-465-3639

MIDWEST: Martha Bartholomew, 18 N. 600 West Hill Rd., Dundee, IL 60118, Tel: 708-428-6949; Mary Lou Heffernan, Cenacle, 1221 Wayzata Blvd., Wayzata, MN 55391-1942, Tel: 612-473-7308; Elene Loecher, 1360 Arden View Drive, Arden Hills, MN 55112, Tel: 612-635-9259; Marianne McGriffin, 115 W. Cleveland Ave., Elkhart, IN 46516, Tel: 219-522-5350; Marie Louise Seckar, Dominican Motherhouse, Sinsinawa, WI 53824-9999, Tel: 608-748-4411; **Marilyn Wussler**, 1244 Bluegrass Drive, St. Louis, MO 63137, Tel: 314-631-0555

MID-ATLANTIC: **Janet Abels**, 120 Washington Place, New York, NY 10014, Tel: 212-691-2972; **Helen Beairsto**, 154-25 Horace Harding Expwy, Flushing, NY 11367, Tel: 718-463-2073; **Jeanne Brennan**, 39 Willow Drive, New Rochelle, NY 10805, Tel: 914-632-9590; **Yvette Dargy**, P.O. Box 6, Franklin, WV 26807, Tel: 304-358-7012; **Maureen Conroy**, P. O. Box 1104, Neptune, NJ 07554, Tel: 908-922-0550; **Martha Karchner**, 202 Skytop Manor, Scranton, PA 18505, Tel: 717-342-0912; **Carol Parowski**, 6949 Spaniel Rd., Springfield, VA 22153, Tel: 703-644-3962; **Marcy Springer, SSJ**, P.O. Box 392, Rancocas, NJ 08073, Tel: 609-877-0509; **Martha Starrett**, 1525 Marriottsville Rd., Marriottsville, MD 21104, Tel: 410-442-1320; **Barbara Whittemore**, 411 River Rd., Highland Park, NJ 08904, Tel: 908-249-8100

NORTHEAST: **Betsy Boomer**, 1 Cleveland Ave., Canton, NY 13617, Tel: 315-386-4972; **Roberta J. Cote**, 71 Wedgewood Rd., Southington, CT 06489, Tel: 203-276-0158; **Justine Lyons**, 333 Ocean Rd., P.O. Box 507, Narragansett, RI 02882, Tel: 401-783-2871; **Elaine V. Shaw**, 58 Campbell Terrace, #2, Pawtucket, RI 02860, Tel: 401-725-5241; **Frank Showers**, 1123 Towncrest Rd., Williamsport, PA 17701; **Gene Waller**, 362 Granville Rd. #205, Westfield, MA 01085, Tel: 413-568-5513

CANADA: **Lea Boutin**, 525 Langevin St., Winnepeg, MB R2H 2V9; **Lucy Bowers**, 94 Birchmont Rd., Scarborough, ONT L9T 2X7, Tel: 416-690-4862; **Bill & Gloria Bruinix**, 180 Dufferin Ave., Trenton, ONT K8V 5E6, Tel: 613-392-6047; **Marie Cahill**, P.O. Box 1147, 141 Mt. Edward Rd., Charlottetown, PEI, C1A 7M8, Tel: 902-676-2942; **Paul R. Curtiss**, 499 10th Ave. E., Prince Albert, SK, S6V 2M3, Tel: 306-922-8369; **Robert Howell**, 2345 University Ave. W. #401, Windsor, ONT, N9B 1E8, Tel: 519-258-6269; **Nada Lou**, 908 Lake St. Louis Rd., Ville de Lery, PQ, J6N 1A7, Tel: 514-692-9339; **Anastasia Moore**, 50 Bonaventure Ave., St. Johns, NFLD, A1C 3Z5, Tel: 709-754-1714; **Larry & Rita Novakowski**, 601 Taylor St. West., Saskatoon, SK, S7M 0C9, Tel: 306-242-1916; **Anne Olekszyk**, 2165 Mississauga Rd., Mississauga, ONT L5H 2K8, Tel: 905-278-5452; **Anne Rozicki**, 2090 Mississauga Rd., Mississauga, ONT, L5H 2K6;

Tel: 905-278-0647; Justina Slocombe, 29 Oak St., Guelph, ONT, N1G 2N1, Tel: 519-821-7222

RECOVERY PROGRAMS

Many people have found helpful guidance and support through various twelve step programs. While there are bound to be some variations in our perspectives, there is much that is compatible in our approaches to personal growth. One such program is Emotions Anonymous, whose stated purpose is "to help people of all faiths or of no recognized faith to live a better emotional life. . . . By sharing their experiences and relationships, members find they are not alone or unique in their feelings."

> Emotions Anonymous
> International Services
> P.O. Box 4245
> St. Paul, MN 55104
> (612) 647-9712

Another twelve step program for those who feel they have issues regarding codependency is

> Co-Dependents Anonymous, Inc.
> P.O. Box 33577
> Phoenix, AZ 85067-3577
> (602) 277-7991

The above services provide referrals to local groups.

Other twelve step programs that address specific issues include Adult Children of Alcoholics, Adult Children of Dysfunctional Families, and Overeaters Anonymous. These may be located through the phone book.

Group meetings offer an opportunity to explore and share feelings in a spirit of fellowship. As always, I suggest that you take responsibility for listening to and trusting your own experience if you contact any of these programs. They may or may not be helpful and appropriate for *you*.

FURTHER RESOURCES

On Focusing and Spirituality

Institute for Bio-Spiritual Research
P.O. Box 1246
Coulterville, CA 95311-1246

(Membership information, resources, workshops on Focusing and spirituality in various locations)

On Focusing

The Focusing Institute
731 S. Plymouth Court, Suite 801
Chicago, IL 60605
(312) 922-9277

(Membership information, workshops, publication)

The Focusing Connection
2625 Alcatraz Avenue #202
Berkeley, CA 94705

(Newsletter on Focusing)

On Meditation

Insight Meditation West
P.O. Box 909
Woodacre, CA 94973

(Meditation retreats held in California and throughout the country. If you're new to meditation, I suggest you begin with a one-day or weekend course)

RECOMMENDED AUDIOTAPES

There are many helpful educational tapes that are compatible with the ideas in this book. Among them are the following. You can write to these addresses for ordering information.

John Amodeo
P.O. Box 564
Graton, CA 95444

Linda and Charlie Bloom
Empowerment Network P.O. Box 2187
Sonoma, CA 95476

(Tapes on relationships and intimacy. All are recommended)

John Bradshaw
Bradshaw Cassettes P.O. Box 980547
Houston, TX 77098

(Especially recommend series on "Building Personal Boundaries," plus all tapes on shame. Helpful descriptions of boundaries and shame)

Francis Weller
Healing Arts Media, P.O. Box 840
Occidental, CA 95465

(Especially recommend series on "Healing Shame," an excellent description of shame and how to deal with it)

RECOMMENDED PERIODICALS

The Common Boundary: Between Spirituality and Psychotherapy
7005 Florida Street
Chevy Chase, MD 20815

Journal of Humanistic Psychology
1772 Vallejo Street #3
San Francisco, CA 94123

The Journal of Transpersonal Psychology
P.O. Box 4437
Stanford, CA 94309

New Age Journal
42 Pleasant Street
Watertown, MA 02172

New Dimensions Newsletter
P.O. Box 410510
San Francisco, CA 94141

Utne Reader
1624 Harmon Place Suite 330
Minneapolis, MN 55403

Yoga Journal
P.O. Box 469018
Escondido, CA 92046-9018

Recommended Reading

Almaas, A.H. *The Elixir of Enlightenment.* York Beach, ME: Samuel Weiser, 1984.

Amodeo, John, and Kris Wentworth. *Being Intimate—A Guide to Successful Relationships.* London: Penguin Group, 1986.

Andrews, Lewis, M. *To Thine Own Self Be True: The Relationship between Spiritual Values and Emotional Health.* New York: Doubleday, 1987.

Bugental, James F. T. *Intimate Journeys: Stories from Life-Changing Therapy.* San Francisco: Jossey-Bass, 1990.

Camhi, Betty, and Elliott Isenberg, eds. *Sunyata: The Life and Sayings of a Rare Born Mystic.* Berkeley, CA: North Atlantic Books, 1990.

Campbell, Peter A., and Edwin M. McMahon. *Bio-Spirituality: Focusing as a Way to Grow.* Chicago: Loyola University Press, 1985.

Cambell, Susan M. *The Couples Journey.* San Luis Obispo, CA: Impact Publishers, 1980.

———. *Beyond the Power Struggle.* San Luis Obispo, CA: Impact Publishers, 1984.

Faber, Adele, and Elaine Mazlish. *How to Talk So Kids Will Listen and Listen So Kids Will Talk.* New York: Avon Books, 1982.

Friedman, Neil. *Experiential Therapy and Focusing.* New York: Half Court Press, 1982.

Gendlin, Eugene T. *Focusing.* New York: Bantam Books, 1981.

Goldstein, Joseph, and Jack Kornfield. *Seeking the Heart of Wisdom.* Boston: Shambhala, 1987.

Gruen, Arno. *The Betrayal of the Self.* New York: Grove Weidenfeld, 1986.

281

Guggenbuhl-Craig, Adolf. *Power in the Helping Professions.* Dallas: Spring Books, 1971.

Keen, Sam. *Fire in the Belly.* New York: Bantam Books, 1991.

Kennedy, Eugene. *The Heart of Loving.* Niles, IL: Argus Communications, 1973.

Kipnis, Aaron. *Knight Without Armor: A Practical Guide For Men in Quest of the Masculine Soul.* Los Angeles: J. P. Tarcher, 1991.

Kritsberg, Wayne. *Gifts for Personal Growth and Recovery.* Pompano Beach, FL: Health Communications, 1988.

Liedloff, Jean. *The Continuum Concept.* Reading, MA: Addison-Wesley, 1985.

Maslow, Abraham. *The Farther Reaches of Human Nature.* New York: Viking Press, 1971.

Mayeroff, Milton. *On Caring.* New York: Harper & Row, 1971.

McMahon, Edwin M. *Beyond the Myth of Dominance: An Alternative to a Violent Society.* Kansas City: Sheed and Ward, 1993.

Miller, Alice. *The Drama of the Gifted Child.* New York: Basic Books, 1981.

Mindell, Arnold. *Working with the Dreaming Body.* London: Penguin Group, 1985.

Muller, Wayne. *Legacy of the Heart: The Spiritual Advantages of a Painful Childhood.* New York: Simon & Schuster, 1992.

Nelson, Scott. *Lost Lovers, Found Friends: Maintaining Friendship after the Breakup.* New York: Simon & Schuster, 1991.

Paul, Jordan, and Margaret Paul. *Do I Have to Give Up Me to Be Loved by You?* Minneapolis: CompCare Publishers, 1983.

Rico, Gabriele. *Pain and Possibility: Writing Your Way through Personal Crisis.* Los Angeles: Tarcher, 1991.

Rogers, Carl. *On Becoming a Person.* Boston: Houghton-Mifflin, 1961.

Rosenberg, Marshall B. *A Model for Non-Violent Communication.* Philadelphia: New Society Publishers, 1983.

Roth, Geneen. *When Food Is Love.* New York: Dutton, 1991.

Small, Jacquelyn. *Awakening in Time: The Journey from Codependence to Co-Creation.* New York: Bantam, 1991.

Viorst, Judith. *Necessary Losses.* New York: Ballantine Books, 1987.

Welwood, John. *Journey of the Heart: Intimate Relationship and the Path of Love.* New York: HarperCollins, 1990.

Whitfield, Charles. *Healing the Child Within.* Deerfield, FL: Health Communications, 1987.

———. *A Gift to Myself: A Personal Workbook and Guide to Healing My Child Within.* Deerfield, FL: Health Communications, 1990.

———. *Co-Dependency: Healing the Human Condition.* Deerfield, FL: Health Communications, 1991.

————. *Boundaries and Relationships*. Deerfield, FL: Health Communications, 1993.

Wile, Daniel B. *After the Honeymoon: How Conflict Can Improve Your Relationship*. New York: Wiley, 1988.

Index